The Freedom to Choose Life

The Freedom to Choose Life

Fyodor Dostoevsky's Guide to the Theology and Practice of the Art of Ministry

Scott W. Gustafson

WIPF & STOCK · Eugene, Oregon

THE FREEDOM TO CHOOSE LIFE
Fyodor Dostoevsky's Guide to the Theology and Practice of the Art of Ministry

Copyright © 2024 Scott W. Gustafson. All rights reserved. Except for brief quotations in critical publications or reviews, no part of this book may be reproduced in any manner without prior written permission from the publisher. Write: Permissions, Wipf and Stock Publishers, 199 W. 8th Ave., Suite 3, Eugene, OR 97401.

Wipf & Stock
An Imprint of Wipf and Stock Publishers
199 W. 8th Ave., Suite 3
Eugene, OR 97401

www.wipfandstock.com

PAPERBACK ISBN: 979-8-3852-1318-4
HARDCOVER ISBN: 979-8-3852-1319-1
EBOOK ISBN: 979-8-3852-1320-7

VERSION NUMBER 05/17/24

Unless indicated otherwise, Scripture quotations are from New Revised Standard Version Bible, copyright © 1989, National Council of Churches of Christ in the United States of America. Used by permission. All rights reserved worldwide.

CREDIT LINE: From THE BROTHERS KARAMAZOV, A NORTON CRITICAL EDITION, SECOND EDITION by Fyodor Dostoevsky, edited by Susan McReynolds Oddo, translated by Constance Garnett, revised by Ralph Matlaw. Copyright © 2011, 1976 by W. W. Norton & Company, Inc. Used by permission of W.W. Norton & Company, Inc.

In Thanksgiving for the congregations with which I have ministered

Lutheran Church of the Redeemer
Bethel Lutheran Church
Christ the Servant Lutheran Church
Holy Trinity Lutheran Church
St. John's Lutheran Church.

Contents

Introduction | ix

1 Opposing Evil: The Beginning of Ministry | 1
2 The Many Sources of Evil | 14
3 Christian Freedom Is Ministry | 40
4 The Elder Zosima's Mastery of the Art of Ministry | 62
5 Other Ministers Emerge | 77
6 Alyosha and Dmitri's Transgressions | 105
7 The Church of Active Love | 116
8 The Death-Dealing Power of Unconfessed Sin | 132
9 Dostoevsky's Unabashed Antisemitism | 158

A Concluding Literary and Biblical Postscript | 175
Acknowledgments | 199
Bibliography | 203
Index | 207

"What is the hardest thing you can possibly do?" she said when I went to her for advice on the darkest day of the first half of my life.

I squirmed. How easily Matron probed the gap between ambition and expediency. "Why must I do what is hardest?"

"Because, Marion, you are an instrument of God. Don't leave the instrument sitting in its case my son. Play! Leave no part of your instrument unexplored. Why settle for 'Three Blind Mice' when you can play the 'Gloria'?"

—ABRAHAM VERGHESE, CUTTING FOR STONE

Introduction

"I have set before you life and death, blessings, and curses. Choose life so that you and your descendants may live."

—(DEUT 30:19)

NOT VERY LONG AGO I reached the age when writing a memoir about my life in ministry seemed like a good thing to do. I thought I could string together a few humorous or pithy anecdotes and interpret them theologically, but I soon realized that the only thing of universal interest might be that the address of my first church was 9664 O'possumtown Pike. (You are unlikely to get delusions of grandeur if this is ever your address). But the rest of my stories were of the "you had to be there" variety.

While I was thinking about this project, however, I realized that the Russian author Fyodor Dostoevsky (1820–881) has been my guide in my practice of the art of ministry. I became conscious of his guidance during a seminar on evil in graduate school where we read a famous episode from *The Brothers Karamazov* called "The Rebellion." Here, in the opinion of the many members of seminar and many scholars as well, Ivan Karamazov thoroughly demolishes all rational attempts to account for evil and suffering in a world created by a loving God. Since we only read "The Rebellion," we believed that Ivan's argument was Dostoevsky's. No one ever discussed the fact that Dostoevsky himself disagreed with Ivan's argument. No one knew that Dostoevsky's characters always expressed the best possible arguments that he could imagine even if he wholeheartedly disagreed with the argument, and no one knew that Ivan

Karamazov's argument is a supreme example of Dostoevsky's ability to present the best possible alternative to what he in fact thinks.

My first serious exposure led me to read Dostoevsky's works beginning with *The Brothers Karamazov* and then, over time, explore many of his creations, but I am sure my understanding has been seriously limited by the fact that I neither read nor understand Russian. Since I am not a true scholar of Dostoevsky, I rely on the translations and interpretations of some fabulous scholars. I do, however, understand the art of ministry. This means that even though I am limited in my understanding of Dostoevsky's work and will probably make some errors, it is possible that a truth about the art of ministry can be revealed even through my ignorance.

Eventually exploring the relationship between Dostoevsky and the art of ministry led me to writing an article "From Theodicy to Discipleship: Dostoevsky's Contribution to the Pastoral Task in *The Brothers Karamazov*."[1] It was around the time that this article was published that I left seminary teaching and returned to the parish ministry. In the parish ministry I further reflected and acted upon lessons I was learning about ministry from Dostoevsky—particularly from his masterpiece *The Brothers Karamazov*. So, instead of writing a memoir I have written a book about the theology and practice of the art of ministry using Fyodor Dostoevsky as one of my guides.

Ministry Is the Responsibility of All Christians

Ministry is the responsibility of all Christians. Saying this, borders on a cliché that might remind some of Martin Luther's (1483–1546) phrase "the priesthood of all believers." Luther employed this phrase to disrupt the commonly held medieval Christian belief that the ordained were somehow better in the eyes of God than the "less committed" or "less spiritual" laity. Luther thought that baptism made each Christian priest, bishop, and pope, and he used the phrase "priesthood of all believers" to promote the equality between the clergy and the laity when it comes to their respective ministerial tasks.

However, what most people do *not* understand is that ministry is usually more difficult and more dangerous for the laity than the ordained. This is because ministry always involves some version of being called to a place you do not wish to go. I resonate with Jesus' words to His disciple

---

1. Gustafson, "From Theodicy to Discipleship," 209–22.

Peter at the end of the Gospel of John. After calling him to "feed my sheep," Jesus says this to describe Peter's future ministry. "Very truly, I tell you, when you were younger, you used to fasten your own belt and go wherever you wished. But when you grow old, you stretch out your hands, and someone else will fasten a belt around you and *take you where you do not wish to go.*" (John: 21:18, emphasis mine).

As a pastor, it is my experience that I rarely desired to visit the sick, counsel the confused, help the needy (I helped those in need, but normally I did not seek them out, for example), present myself in times of crisis, witness to Jesus, pray when called upon to do so, heal the sick, speak truth to power, comfort those who mourn, preach at a funeral, or watch someone die. I do not remember ever *wanting* to do such things. Nonetheless, I often found myself in these situations precisely because the congregation *expected* me to be there. Void of such expectations, I probably would not have presented myself in many of these contexts where, like most people, I would sit around quite confused about what to do and what to say. It is incumbent upon me to add, however, that if I had not presented myself in these difficult and complex venues, I never would have witnessed an occasional miracle. I never would have understood that the power of life can flow through me in such situations. I never would have experienced many, many affirmations of life that happen in the midst of suffering and death. I never would have experienced people overcoming their poverty because of the meagre material gifts I was able to bestow at their moments of crisis. I experienced these things and more because my congregations *expected* me to go to places where otherwise I would not have gone.[2]

Ministry is usually more difficult for lay people precisely because they normally lack the institutional expectations as well as the institutional support that ordained ministers take for granted. In fact, a person's job, business, acquaintances, friends and even family can pressure a person to abandon her efforts to practice the art of ministry. It is never easy to speak truth to power, for example, but a pastor is less likely to lose her job if she does. If a lay person speaks truth to power on the job, he could lose his job immediately. If pastors do, it usually takes much longer to fire them, if they are fired at all.

There is always risk when we are called to minister. There is often danger in saying the right thing at the right time. This is where the

---

2. Nouwen, *Jesus*, 61–64.

writings of Fyodor Dostoevsky can be a guide. Particularly in *The Brothers Karamazov*, Dostoevsky's insights into the practice of the art of ministry are extraordinary. Alyosha Karamazov and his mentor The Elder Zosima distribute much of Dostoevsky's wisdom. Alyosha is a person who "shows up" in places he does not want to go. Like anyone who practices an art, he gets better with practice. Moreover, Alyosha has a mentor, and the mentor/apprentice relationship between Zosima and Alyosha demonstrates how all arts, including ministry, are communicated from one generation to the next.

Remember this

Ministry is the responsibility of all Christians. It is very difficult to distinguish ministry from Christian ethics, and ministry is often more difficult and dangerous for laypersons to perform than it is for the ordained.

The Freedom to Choose Life

This book's title, *The Freedom to Choose Life*, indicates that freedom is essential to the art of ministry. Christian freedom, however, is not the ability to choose to do whatever one pleases. It is not the same as autonomy. Christian freedom is more specific. It is a particular sort of choice. It is choosing life as opposed to death. Nonetheless, Christian freedom presupposes autonomy because Christian freedom cannot be forced or coerced. Christian freedom recognizes that we always can choose to reject life and submit once again to the bondage of slavery and death. (Gal 5:1).

Jesus' crucifixion and resurrection makes freedom possible, but it is never easy to choose life from other possibilities available to us. We strongly feel that our choices are limited by the social, political, biological, technological, intellectual, natural, and historical necessities that seem to determine our lives. Those who practice the art of ministry discern life-giving choices for themselves and for others as they live amid these necessities. The ones who practice the art of ministry listen to others and often can discern new life-giving possibilities that their interlocutors did not see until that moment. From time to time a person who has practiced and mastered the art of ministry can discover the appropriate word or action that can, in the name of Jesus, open someone's future when their future appeared to be closed, determined, and leading toward death.

Of all our available choices, some may be neutral, many are death-dealing, and a few are life-affirming. Death-dealing choices close our future. They curtail or eliminate future possibilities. They speak the last word about a job, choice of mate, place to live, education, one's value as a person, one's abilities, life's meaning, *et cetera*. Life-affirming choices, on the other hand, open the future to new, perhaps undreamed-of possibilities. It takes much discernment and creativity to identify words and actions that open the future. These choices are rarely obvious and often require an "artist's touch." Once discerned and identified, however, these life-giving words and actions "create a way where there was no way" to use a phrase from African American womanist theologian Delores Williams (1937–2022).[3] Speaking the word or performing the act that opens the future is not easy, but these acts of freedom and love are vital to ministry's performance. Ministry is an art, and the freedom to choose life is the content of this art. This book tries to demonstrate the relationship between freedom and the art of ministry using the writings of Fyodor Dostoevsky, particularly *The Brothers Karamazov*. But it should be said from the start, Dostoevsky's understanding of ministry takes us only so far. There is one thing that he needs. There is one thing he left undone.

An Insight on the Art of Ministry

Ministry enacts Christian freedom, but Christian freedom is much more specific than mere autonomy. It is a particular sort of choice that involves selecting from among all available choices the one that, in Jesus' name, opens the future heretofore thought to be closed and thereby ministry chooses freedom and life rather than bondage and death.

The Book's Outline

Viewed as a source for Dostoevsky's understanding of ministry, *The Brothers Karamazov* can be understood as having two plotlines. I will call them the active plot and the ministry plot. The active plot centers on the events surrounding the murder of Fyodor Karamazov, the acknowledged father of Dmitri, Ivan and Alyosha Karamazov as well as a possible illegitimate son Pavel Fyodorovich Smerdyakov, a servant in the Karamazov household. All events in the active plot lead one to the rational conclusion

3. D. Williams, *Sisters*, 15–31.

that Dmitri has murdered his father. All the evidence suggests he is guilty. A jury convicts him of the crime. Dmitri is eventually sentenced to years of hard labor in the mines of Siberia. Yet, all readers know that Dmitri is not guilty of the crime.

It is on the scaffold of the action plot that the ministry plot unfolds, and this book's first 7 chapters concern the ministry plotline. Chapter 1 begins where my interest in Dostoevsky began, namely, with Ivan's Rebellion. Through Ivan Karamazov, Dostoevsky introduces theodicy—rational attempts to account for evil in a world created by an all-powerful, all-knowing, benevolent God. Many modern philosophers and theologians credit Ivan for rendering all theodicies futile. Ivan is the first to argue that it is impossible to justify God if innocent children are being murdered and tortured (as they still are in modern warfare, modern civilizations, and modern cultures). This irrefutable fact leads Ivan to refrain from all rational attempts to justify God and what God plans for creation. He "returns his ticket" to God and refuses to participate in a world created by such a God. (He plans to commit suicide when he turns is 30).

When Ivan rejects participation in "God's" world because nothing can justify the slaughter of one innocent child, he does something new. In the past, Christians developed theodicies in two ways. They either appeal to "the big picture" which argued that if we only knew the whole of reality as God knows it, there would be no logical contradiction between evil and a benevolent God. Or they appealed to a future paradise that God is in the process of creating. This view accounted for evil by postulating that God needs to temporarily use evil to bring paradise to fruition and will jettison evil when paradise is complete (the end justifies the means).[4] These two sorts of theodicy enable us to redefine the terms of the debate so that a benevolent, all-powerful God is not thoroughly inconsistent with evil. In "returning his ticket," however, Ivan could not justify even engaging in such ridiculous discussions. The suffering of innocent children was already too high a price to be paid for a future paradise. For Ivan, the suffering of innocent children was "the last word." The theodicy debate was closed, and Ivan rejected God's world.

Today, many agree that Ivan's argument is, in fact, "the last word." What they fail to realize, however, is that Ivan's success and perceived independence obscures the fact that *Dostoevsky wrote The Brothers*

---

4. Hick, *Evil and the God of Love*, 33–36.

Karamazov to refute Ivan's cogent argument.[5] Here, Dostoevsky rejects the belief that Ivan speaks the final word on evil and suffering; for, Dostoevsky offers a different way to address the world's evil that takes us all beyond the limits of human reason. Dostoevsky's "solution" (if it can be called a "solution") is so strange that many people in our secular, religionless culture can neither see it nor entertain it. Even if they can, they are inclined to reject this "solution" as superstition, magical thinking, or just ignorant. This is because *ministry is Dostoevsky's solution to the world's evil.* His literary claim in *The Brothers Karamazov* is that the ministry is the only way to address and overcome the world's evil. The audacity of this claim cannot be lost upon us. If ministry addresses and overcomes the world's evil, this means it must now address and overcome evils like the Holocaust and Hiroshima—evils even Ivan could not imagine.

In *The Brothers Karamazov* it is through the practitioners of the art of ministry as embodied in Elder Zosima, Alyosha Karamazov, and many others, that Dostoevsky comes to terms with the very real fact of evil—before which Ivan Karamazov remains speechless and impotent. Against evils that seem to encompass the globe; against evils that appear to be in control; against evils that promote perpetual poverty, racism, antisemitism, and sexism; against evils that seem to be leading to humanity's potential annihilation; Dostoevsky promotes ministry's small acts of love. As we shall see, these acts of active love (all are acts of ministry) are often quite remarkable. Some might border on the miraculous. But, as even the faithful can see, they are small and vulnerable. It appears impossible for these small acts of active love—these individual acts of ministry—to overcome the fact of evil and suffering in this troubled world.

Perhaps the perceived impotence of ministry occurs because, like Ivan, we are still imprisoned by the limited understanding of evil that all theodicy arguments assume. Theodicies all think evil has but two sources: the evil for which God is guilty, and the moral evil for which living human beings are guilty. There are no other sources of evil. The Apostle Paul, however, recognizes at least two other sources. He calls them Principalities and Powers. Chapter 2 discusses how Dostoevsky presents the Principalities and Powers in two characters he creates, namely The Devil and The Grand Inquisitor. Classical theodicies do not even recognize Principalities and Powers to be a source of evil, and therefore, cannot

---

5. Frank, *Dostoevsky*, 791.

conceive how excluding these potential sources can *increase* evil's power, and how such exclusion itself becomes another source of evil.[6]

Following a philosophical inquiry into both ministry and Christian freedom in chapter 3, chapters 4–7 introduce how Dostoevsky's characters practice the *art* of ministry. These chapters use episodes from the Elder Zosima, Alyosha Karamazov and other characters as examples of ministry in all stages of maturity. Since ministry is called an art in this presentation, chapter 3 begins with a description of some relevant features of any art. One important characteristic of any art is that art expresses the heretofore inexpressible. It is this heretofore unexpressed or unspoken knowledge that an artist of any ilk wishes to convey. To articulate such heretofore unspoken knowledge, all artistic efforts assume, either consciously or unconsciously, that there is always "more than we can tell" about any art including the art of ministry.[7] This unspoken knowledge is present in, with, and under any art. It is why a mere cook like me can follow the exact recipe of a master chef's specialty to the letter and never achieve the master chef's succulent result. People might eat what I have prepared, but no one would mistake my effort for the chef's effort. There is something missing, and that something, I submit, is present in the unspoken dimension of the chef's culinary art.

Because all art possesses this unspoken dimension, an apprentice must spend time with his mentor for her to pass on the unspoken dimension of her art to him. Only by doing so, *might* an apprentice receive the unspoken knowledge of the art he has begun to practice. This is why all arts, from medicine to music, science to painting, cooking to gardening, require apprentices who, if successful, learn to embody and perhaps articulate some of the unspoken elements involved in the practice of a given art. Ministry is an art. It too requires mentors or teachers to convey the art to their apprentices in the hope that eventually their apprentices will master the art and pass both the spoken and unspoken dimensions of the art to the next generation of apprentices.

The content of art differs from one art to the next. The content of music, medicine, science, and the visual arts are obviously not the same. The content of ministry differs from other arts as well. *Freedom is its content*. But as indicated above, freedom is not synonymous with autonomy. Neither is Christian freedom the absence of external restraints on

---

6. Tilley, *Evils of Theodicy*, 221–55.
7. Michael Polanyi, *Personal Knowledge*, 69–131.

individual behavior. In fact, *the freedom the art of ministry expresses usually occurs in the context of the numerous restraints that we all experience in life.* (These restraints are called necessities in this book). It is usually within these restraints that a practitioner of the art of ministry chooses life rather than death and helps others do so as well.

Freedom could be the entire point of the Christian life. The Apostle Paul tells us that because Jesus was crucified and is risen, we are free. Indeed, his statement to the Galatians, "For freedom Christ has set us free. Stand firm, therefore, and do not submit again to a yoke of slavery" (Gal 5: 1), indicates that freedom is central, and the Christian life involves maintaining our freedom by refusing to submit to the bondage from which we have been freed. Paul later counsels the Corinthian church, "*All things are indeed lawful,*" but not all things are beneficial. "*All things are lawful,*" but not all things build up." (1 Cor 10:23, emphasis mine). The freedom of which Paul speaks affirms that a person is free to do anything, but if we are to avoid becoming slaves once again, we must recognize that the phrase, "all things are lawful," does not mean that all things are beneficial or build up the community. As is true of every art, mistakes will be made. We may, and often do, choose in such a way that we reject freedom and submit once more to bondage, but mastering the art of ministry enables us to choose from all things that are lawful, the one thing that is beneficial to the person or the one thing that builds up the community. *Ministry, then, is the quest to discern, amid all that is lawful, the words or activities that chose life rather than death and to say those words and perform those tasks in the midst of necessities that often appear impossible to overcome.* It often takes both courage and wisdom to perform ministry.

Whatever else *The Brothers Karamazov* is, it is a story about masters of the art of ministry choosing life instead of death in very difficult contexts. When this happens anywhere, the minister displays *The Freedom to Choose Life*. In *The Brothers Karamazov* these choices and actions happen in the context of a dysfunctional family and the sentencing of a man for a crime he did not commit. To the extent that Dostoevsky accomplishes this, *The Brothers Karamazov* grants us one of the greatest literary insights into the art of ministry ever written. Chapters 4, 5, 6, and 7 focus on how both the Elder Zosima and Alyosha Karamazov embody the art of ministry and how ministry addresses and overcomes the evil that paralyses Ivan and continues to paralyze those who agree with him.

The Elder Zosima summarized the art of ministry as an attempt to do two things. He says we are called to be agents of active love, and he says we are responsible *to* all people, *for* all people and *for everything*.⁸ Zosima embodies active love for all to see, but as is the case with all who master an art, much knowledge is unspoken. Zosima conveys his unspoken knowledge to Alyosha during the last year of Zosima's life where Alyosha receives unspoken knowledge through intimate association, watching, studying, and admiring his mentor. Zosima's second adage about ministry—we are responsible to all people, for all people and for everyone—is, frankly, not conveyed as well in *The Brothers Karamazov*. Nonetheless, Zosima's second adage is as crucial to the art of ministry as acts of active love.

We are responsible for (not *necessarily* guilty of) the sins of past generations that oppose the life of the marginalized. We are responsible to the marginalized for how we address issues of marginalization within civilization, and we are responsible for everything to the extent that these unconfessed sins of our predecessors have played a role in social injustices and environmental pollution. Furthermore, we who continue to benefit from the residue of unconfessed sins that are a consequence of our social status are particularly responsible if not guilty. Only by recognizing these responsibilities can we even begin to address the global evils that may very well destroy humanity.

Alyosha wants to be a monk just like his mentor. The monastery provides Alyosha comfort not only from the cares of the world, but, of even more importance, the diabolical dysfunction of his family. Zosima realizes that Alyosha's need to escape his family is not a reason to become a monk. Consequently, he sends Alyosha into the world because that is where he believes the young Alyosha is called to minister. Alyosha reluctantly obeys, and much of chapters 5, 6, and 7 narrates Alyosha's growth toward mastery of the art of ministry in the contexts of psychological, familial, intellectual, and socio/political dysfunction—the very things Alyosha hoped to avoid by becoming a monk.

This literary fact alone indicates that ministry is not the job of the ordained alone (for Alyosha is not an ordained priest). It is something we are all called to do in the places we find ourselves or in the places to which we are sent. Both Zosima and Alyosha demonstrate that ministry is the practice of the art of freedom because both men try to determine "What act of word and/or deed is the best way to choose life over death in the *context* in which we find ourselves?" As our context changes, so will the

---

8. Dostoevsky, *Brothers*, 250.

best act or word change, but such change is made in the name of freedom which remains the goal of both ministry and the Christian life.

In *The Brothers Karamazov,* other characters also demonstrate that ministry is the art of choosing life amid the death-dealing choices that present themselves in day-to-day life. It will be argued throughout this book that the crucifixion and resurrection of Jesus bestows the possibility of freedom; that the art of freedom means choosing life from all other choices that are lawful but neither benefit nor support communal life; that ministry itself is the art of choosing life. Understanding ministry as the choice of life is not something new. It can be traced to Moses who told his people this word from God, "I have set before you life and death, blessings, and curses. *Choose life* so that you and your descendants may live." (Deut. 30:19). Dostoevsky shows us how his heroes choose between life and death in very difficult contexts. This book uses Dostoevsky's characters as examples of both ministry and the failure to minister.

Dostoevsky's Antisemitism

Unfortunately, if we only understand ministry as acts of active love, it cannot withstand the force of evil. Chapters 8 and 9 acknowledge this defect. As American racism always undermines the ministry of white Americans when we refuse to acknowledge our racism, Dostoevsky's antisemitism undermines his teaching. He never admitted. He never acknowledged. He never confessed the profound and deep seeded antisemitism that he shared with most of Europe and North America. His fiction occasionally promotes Jewish stereotypes, and, even more dangerously, antisemitic conspiracy stories that Christians have promulgated for centuries (and still do). In his journalism, he refuses to entertain for one-minute assertions from his Jewish readers that he was a "Jew Hater." Instead of listening to his Jewish critics, Dostoevsky tried to justify himself and, in the process, argued that if there is a problem, it is the Jews who are at fault.

It is because of Dostoevsky's incredible creativity and his influence as one of the greatest novelists in Russian history (if not all of history) that his failure to confess the sin of antisemitism may have played some role in the sad history of Russian, American, European, and Christian antisemitism. His refusal (or inability) to acknowledge and confess his antisemitism made it easier for Russia and perhaps Europe to uncritically accepted the antisemitic backdrop against which Europeans lived their lives. This context provided the Holocaust with the fertile ground it needed to develop and manifest its demonic, death-dealing power. This sin is particularly tragic because Dostoevsky had the unsurpassed talent to take a contemporary idea, embody that idea in a character or group of characters, and push the idea to an extreme conclusion. In doing so, he exposed the potential death-dealing consequences of the contemporary ideas his work examined.

Had Dostoevsky ever explored the extremes of what he called, "the *idea* behind 'Yidism,'"[9] in the same way he explored the extremes of the Russian intelligentsia's *ideas* like scientific determinism, utilitarianism, atheism, radical capitalism, or materialistic socialism, Dostoevsky may have enabled thousands and perhaps millions of people to question their unconfessed hatred of the Jews. Who knows, such critical reflection of the "*idea*" of antisemitism might have been just enough to prevent the Holocaust. In any case, Dostoevsky's artistic talent could have undermined at least some of the antisemitic ground that polluted Europe and the rest of the Western world as well.

We can, however, still learn, in a negative way, something of profound importance from Dostoevsky's refusal to acknowledge and confess the sin of antisemitism. It teaches that unconfessed sin is very dangerous. Unconfessed sins have death-dealing powers that sometimes appear to be autonomous and beyond human control. Some consequences of unconfessed sins are the Holocaust, American slavery, Hiroshima, South African Apartheid and American Jim Crow. Other consequences of unconfessed sin may not be so dire, but unconfessed sin can also be the source of family dysfunction, psychological disorders, or an organization's malaise. Those who try to practice the art of ministry must recognize the death-dealing power of unconfessed sin, and our continued refusal or "inability" to confess these sins. Indeed, those who recognize their responsibility for these unconfessed sins still must determine how to confess these sins.

It is only through confession that we can even begin to gain control over the death-dealing power of unconfessed sin. Dostoevsky's negative teaching is this: When we do not acknowledge and confess our sin, we unleash the death-dealing power of unconfessed sin and our ability to practice ministry is undermined if not annulled. Significantly, confessing

---

9. Dostoevsky, *Writer's Diary*, 350.

unconfessed sins has global implications. Antisemitism is not the only unconfessed sin that has global, death-dealing consequences. Racism, institutional poverty, climate collapse, and sexism also have global consequences, and these consequences originate in our refusal to confess human sin. The history of some of these death-dealing consequences will be explored in chapter 8. Chapter 9 gives a brief account of the path to confession that Dostoevsky once took with respect to Russian peasants. Had he done the same with the Jews, his ministry might have had a far greater effect on the world.

An Insight on the Art of Ministry

Whenever a sin is not confessed, these unconfessed sins unleash a death-dealing force that remains in effect until we acknowledge and confess the sin that began this death-dealing process.

1

Opposing Evil
The Beginning of Ministry

The Knowledge of Good and Evil seems to be the aim of all ethical reflection. The first task of Christian Ethics is to invalidate that knowledge.

—Dietrich Bonhoeffer, *Ethics*.[1]

I HAVE DECIDED TO introduce this exploration of Fyodor Dostoevsky's (1820–881) understanding of the theology and practice of the art of ministry with his character Ivan Karamazov. I do so because Ivan introduced me to Dostoevsky when I participated in a seminar on Evil led by Dr. Charles Courtney at Drew University. The seminar did not begin with Ivan. Instead, it first explored the many ways that philosophers and theologians had tried to address the problem of evil in a world created by a loving, omnipotent, and all-knowing God. The discussion was not limited to Christian thinkers. Jews, Moslems, Hindus, and Buddhists were also considered, but, as the seminar proceeded, Christians and Western philosophers came to be our primary focus.

Theodicy is the name academics give to the problem of evil. It is comprised of four propositions: God is loving and benevolent. God is omnipotent (all-powerful). God is omniscient (all-knowing). The fourth proposition is "evil exists in this world." These four propositions create

---

1. Bonhoeffer, *Ethics*, 21.

the confusion articulated by all theodicies, namely, how is evil possible in a world created by a loving, all-powerful, and all-knowing God? Reason demands that all four propositions cannot all be true, and thereby, theodicy undermines the existence of the Biblical God.

Clearly, a contradiction can be avoided if we deny the validity of one of the four propositions that compose the theodicy dilemma. If we deny that evil exists, there is no contradiction, but our denial of evil might simply mean we are delusional. If we deny God's goodness, there is no contradiction between an omnipotent and omniscient God and the fact of evil because a God who is not good is, in fact, quite likely to create a world with evil in it. If God is not omnipotent, the fact of evil poses no logical contradiction because a loving, benevolent God may not have the power to prevent the existence of evil. Finally, if God is not all-knowing, then evil is simply a consequence of God's ignorance. (Woody Allen may have in fact been right when he said he thinks God loves us and everything, but he suspects God is an underachiever).

Christians, however, do not have the luxury of rejecting any of the propositions that compose the intellectual dilemma we now call "theodicy" because each proposition composing this dilemma is a part of the Church's preaching and teaching. The Church preaches about sin and evil in the world. It proclaims God's omnipotence, love, and omniscience as core concepts. Since Christians cannot deny any one of these propositions without rejecting their own doctrines, Christians must take a different approach. Historically this approach has been to define or describe God's omnipotence, omniscience, benevolence, or even evil itself in a way that avoids these obvious contradictions.

Christian Attempts to Explain Evil

In his book *Evil and the God of Love* John Hick outlines two basic Christian approaches to the theodicy question. He calls them Augustinian and Irenaean after two bishops of the early Church.[2] The Augustinian

---

2. While the theodicies that Hick calls Augustinian and Irenaean adequately describe two important ways we *now* try to resolve the theodicy issue, both St. Augustine and St. Irenaeus cannot be included in the descriptions that bear their names. Tilley, *The Evils of Theodicy*, 113–40 recognizes that our efforts at theodicy came into being after the Enlightenment when reason was presumed to be the final arbitrator of truth. As the final arbitrator of truth a rational ironclad solution to the theodicy question was demanded. However, both Augustine and Irenaeus were only addressing the questions of their fellow believers who only wanted a plausible not an ironclad rationalization

approach addresses the problem is aesthetically. Here, evil is not the opposite of good, *per se*. Evil is experienced as one might experience the dark shadows of a painting that an artist uses to illuminate, enhance, and increase the beauty and vividness of the entire painting. Without such shading, the painting would have less light and beauty than it has with such shading. Analogously, the Augustinian approach contends that God uses evil, sin and suffering to contribute more overall goodness and beauty to the world as there would be without so-called evil. In other words, Augustinian theodicies contend that God allows some evil so that creation might contain even more "good" or more "beauty" than it would contain without some evil. This way of addressing the theodicy issue has been called an aesthetic understanding of evil.

Augustine also notes that instead of being a defect in God, what we call evil may be a consequence of our own ignorance of "the big picture."

> And to Thee is there nothing at all evil, and not only to Thee, but to Thy whole creation, because there is nothing without which can break and mar that order which Thou has appointed it. But in parts thereof, some things, because they harmonize not with others, are considered evil whereas those very things harmonize with others and are good and in themselves good.[3]

Here evil is a consequence of our perceptions. We perceive certain things to be in disharmony with ourselves and others, and so we call these things evil. But to God, there is nothing that is evil because, unlike our limited perspectives, God sees "the big picture" or the grand design. What appears evil to us—because of the disharmony we perceive due to our limited perspective—is harmonious to God, and, therefore, is not evil. God has created an aesthetically pleasing creation. The evil we perceive only resides in our inability to comprehend the vastness and beauty of God's creation. Evil does not reside in creation itself. "For my thoughts are not your thoughts, nor are your ways my ways, says the Lord." (Isa 55:8).

Over two centuries before St. Augustine (357–430), St. Irenaeus (130–202) proposed a different approach. He suggested that evil, sin, and suffering are an intelligible, perhaps even necessary, byproduct of the end God wills for creation. Creation, according to Irenaeus, does not happen in an instant. Creation is an on-going process that has not yet reached its goal. Creation takes time, and evil, sin, and suffering are a consequence of

---

to the problem of evil and this is what Iranaeus and Augustine gave their questioners.

3. Augustine, *Confessions*, 110.

the temporal distance between the future perfection of God's completed creation and the current state of God's unfinished project. Human beings are sinners because we are immature, and small defects like sin are necessary to achieve God's goal for creation. St. Irenaeus writes,

> If (. . .) anyone say "What then? Could not God have exhibited (humanity) as perfect from the beginning? Let (it be known) that, inasmuch as God is indeed always the same and unbegotten as respects himself all things are possible. (. . .) But created things must be inferior to Him who created them from the very fact that they are of later origin. (. . .) Because as these things are of later date, so are they infantile; so are they unaccustomed to and unexercised in perfect discipline. For as it certainly is in the power of a mother to give strong food to her infant, but she does not do so as the child is not yet able to receive more substantial nourishment, so also it was possible for God (. . .) to have made (humanity) perfect from the first, but (humanity) could not receive this (. . .) being yet an infant.[4]

Himself an advocate of the Irenaean approach, John Hick asserts that it is God's will to bring as many souls to God as possible, and it is this aim that explains at least a portion of the suffering in the world.

> For if our general conception of God's purpose is correct, the world is not intended to be a paradise, but rather the scene of history in which human personality may be formed toward the pattern of Christ, (Human beings) are not to be thought of on analogy of animal pets whose life is to be made as agreeable as possible, but rather on analogy to human children who are to grow to adulthood in an environment whose primary and overriding purpose is not immediate pleasure, but the realization of the most valuable potentialities of the human personality.[5]

The Irenaean theology of creation determines this understanding of evil. If creation is not yet complete, and if creation has a goal that takes time to achieve, then sin, evil, and suffering might, in some way, be employed by God to achieve creation's goal. Thus, sin, evil, and suffering are not necessarily in contradiction to God's omnipotence, omniscience, and benevolence because they serve creation's goal. When God's goal for creation is finally achieved, evil will be discarded. Until then, evil is a tool God uses to achieve God's future goal for creation.

---

4. Irenaeus, *Against Heresies*, 521.
5. Hick, *Evil and the God of Love*, 258.

Both Irenaean and Augustinian theodicies are doctrinally sound. Augustinian views focus on the biblical belief that God's creation is good. If creation appears otherwise, this is because of our limited ability to see how God employs what we mistakenly call "evil" to achieve the "most good" possible in creation. Irenaean theodicies focus on another standard belief of Christianity, namely, that God will, in the end, establish his perfect rule which will wipe all our tears away because of its beauty, glory and perfection. Ivan Karamazov, however, rebels, and demolishes both theodicies.

The Purpose of Theodicies

Christian theodicies try to resolve the logical difficulties created by a loving, omnipotent, and omniscient God creating a world in which evil exists. They do so in two ways that John Hick describes as Augustinian and Irenaean. Both try to re-define the terms creating the dilemma to avoid logical contradiction between evil and a loving, all-powerful, and all-knowing God.

Ivan's Rebellion

Ivan's subversion of all previous theodicies begins with descriptions of instances of evil and suffering of innocent children, that, once read, remain engraved on one's mind forever.[6] Images of barbarian hordes throwing infants into the air and catching them on their sabers, or these same animals encouraging a two year old boy to play with a pistol—even smile into its barrel—only to have an explosion of death rip through his smiling, innocent face are but a small portion of the existential content that Ivan gives to the mere proposition, "there is evil in the world." Atrocity after atrocity force Ivan to regard theodicy from a perspective that is completely incompatible with Augustinian and Irenaean theodicies. It is Ivan's profound contention that no knowledge of the Augustinian "big picture" can compensate the mother who witnessed her son's smiling face explode. No Irenaean grand design can justify the need for such "necessary instruments" as these. Even before a "rational" theodicy can be argued, Ivan recognizes that too high a price has already been paid for the harmony that traditional theodicies promise. So, Ivan "refuses his

---

6. Dostoevsky, *Brothers*, 210–13.

ticket." He cannot live in a future world built on the suffering of even one innocent child.

> Listen, if everyone must suffer in order to buy eternal harmony with suffering, what do children have to do with it, tell me, please? It's virtually incomprehensible why should they suffer too, to buy harmony with suffering? Why should they also furnish material to enrich the soil for the harmony of the future? (...) But what pulls me up here is that I can't accept the harmony. (...) It is not worth it, because tears remain unredeemed. They must be redeemed or there is no harmony. But how do you redeem them? Is it possible? By their being avenged. But what do I care about revenge, what do I care about hell for the tormentors, what is hell going to fix here, if these children have already been tormented? (...) I want to forgive and want to embrace. I don't want anyone to suffer anymore. And if the sufferings of the children go into the replenishment of that sum of suffering that is needed for purchasing truth, then I declare *ahead of time* that all of truth is not worth such a price. I do not want, finally, the mother to embrace the tormentor who threw her son to the dogs! (...) She does not have the right to forgive the sufferings of her child who was torn to pieces, she dare not forgive him. But if that's the way it is, if they dare not forgive, then where is the harmony? Is there in the whole world a being who could forgive and have the right to forgive? I don't want harmony, for the love of humanity, I don't want it. I would rather remain with unavenged suffering and unquenched indignation, *even if I am wrong*. Besides, they have put too high a price on harmony, we can't afford to pay so much for admission. And so, I hasten to return my entrance ticket, and if I am an honest man I am obligated to return it as soon as possible. It's not God that I don't accept, Alyosha, only I most respectfully return to him the ticket.[7]

Ivan's critique subverts all theodicies. He even recognizes the possibility that the terms of the theodicy question can be defined in such a way that contradiction might be avoided. But such efforts, no matter how compelling, simply do not matter. Such solutions are pointless. Prior to any rational argument, Ivan correctly understands that what has already been destroyed is far more important and profound than any rational construct capable of resolving the existential fact of evil, sin and suffering in the world. The cost of the harmony embedded in both Augustinian

---

7. Dostoevsky, *Brothers*, 211–13.

and Irenaean constructs is just too high, so Ivan refuses to participate. No rational argument can overcome what has already been undone, and *because Ivan believes that reason is the only source of truth*, he has nothing more to say. The conversation is over. *He believes he has said the last word.*

In the character of Ivan Karamazov, Dostoevsky pushed theodicy to an entirely new level. After the story of Ivan's rebellion, it is no longer appropriate to address the theodicy dilemma using the rational methods of the past. In fact, twentieth-century realities like the Holocaust make such philosophical pursuits even more ridiculous and inhumane because a successful theodicy now means that evils like the Holocaust or dropping Atomic Bombs on random men, women and children can be justified and are, thereby, consistent with a loving, omnipotent, and omniscient God. *If reason is the only source of truth,* Ivan's argument is impeccable; for, if reason is the only source of truth, then the last word has been spoken. There is no rational justification for God or the world, and like Ivan we too must "return our ticket" and become paralyzed in the face of evil and suffering.

Ivan Karamazov's argument is so profound and fundamental that many people forget that Ivan is not a real person. Of even more importance is that *Dostoevsky's goal in writing The Brothers Karamazov was to refute Ivan's impeccable argument*. Dostoevsky notes this when he sent the first half of Book V of *The Brothers Karamazov* to his publisher (the part that contained the chapters on Ivan's "Rebellion" and "The Grand Inquisitor"). Worrying that it would not be accepted by the censors, he also sent a letter of explanation that said that Ivan represents the upmost in blasphemy that is "operative in our time among the young people." He hoped to refute Ivan's blasphemy in what he was then preparing in "the last words of the dying elder Zosima."[8] He emphasized that, "*it is not I who am speaking in distressing colors, exaggerations, and hyperboles (. . .) but a character in my novel, Ivan Karamazov. This is his language, his style, his pathos not mine.*"[9]

One must at least pause to note what Dostoevsky implies in this letter to his publisher. He was saying that the best way to address the problem of evil is not through rational argument. It is through *the ministry* of an old, dying monk named Zosima. In other words, *evil is combatted through ministry*. Dostoevsky's assertion that ministry is the way to

---

8. Frank, *Dostoevsky*, 788.
9. Frank, *Dostoevsky*, 791.

confront and oppose evil sets forth the dubious notion that ministry can somehow overcome evils as great as the Holocaust and Hiroshima. Nonetheless, if *The Brothers Karamazov* was written to refute Ivan, it follows that Dostoevsky believed that ministries like the ones performed by the monk, The Elder Zosima, and his apprentice, Alyosha Karamazov, can address and overcome the world's evil if performed by enough people. He proposed that ministry, properly conceived and done, was ample in the face of sin, evil and suffering! To achieve his purpose Dostoevsky does not attack Ivan with a rational argument. He does not use his status as author to abolish Ivan or his argument. He opposes Ivan through acts of love carried out by other characters and, more subtly, by the way he orders and constructs the fictional world he creates.

Evil Is the Beginning of Ministry

Ivan Karamazov destroys all rational attempts to resolve the theodicy issue because the suffering of one innocent child is too high a price to pay for the harmony Augustinian theodicies propose. Consequently, the fact of evil in the world paralyzes both Ivan and many people living today, but Dostoevsky's heroes are not paralyzed by the fact of evil in the world. In fact, through these characters, Dostoevsky will repeatedly assert that ministry, not reason, is the way to oppose, resist and overcome the world's evil.

The Limits of Reason

In many and various ways Dostoevsky denies that human reason is the only path to truth and wisdom. Furthermore, he recognizes that those who, like Ivan, believe that reason is the only path to truth are dumbfounded and paralyzed when confronted with Ivan's contention that God cannot be rationally justified because of the suffering of one innocent child. Their belief that reason is the only path to truth means that the last word has been spoken regarding evil. Nothing more can be said. Their paralysis is quite "reasonable" if reason is the only path to the truth.

One way Dostoevsky expresses the inability of reason to be the only path to truth is through the plot structure of *The Brothers Karamazov*. Dmitri Karamazov is accused of murdering his father, Fyodor Karamazov. All evidence points toward his guilt. Dmitri believed his father has cheated him out of his inheritance. Both Dmitri and his father professed "love" for the same woman, Grushenka, who encouraged this love triangle. Enraged, Dmitri goes to his father's home *intending to murder his father*. Witnesses placed him at the scene. Immediately after the murder, people saw him running through town covered in blood. He owned the murder weapon that was found at the scene, and, when questioned, he does not deny any of these facts. Any "reasonable" jurist, any "reasonable" person for that matter, would convict Dmitri of patricide. Yet, the reader *knows* that Dmitri is not guilty of this crime. The novel therefore confronts those of us who, like Ivan, think that reason is the only path to truth with the literary fact that

> the central plot is carefully constructed so as to lead, with irresistible logic, to the conclusion of Dmitri's guilt, the accumulated mass of circumstantial evidence pointing to him as the murderer is literally overwhelming. The fact remains, however, that he is innocent of the crime (though implicated in it by his parricidal impulses), and the reader is thus constantly confronted with the discrepancy between what reason might conclude and the intangible mystery of human personality, capable even at the very last moment of conquering the drives of hatred and loathing. *The entire arrangement of plot action thus compels the reader to participate in the experience of discovering the limitations of reason.* Only those among the characters who are willing to believe against all evidence—the concatenation of facts—only they are able to pierce through to the reality of moral-spiritual, as well as legal truth in its most literal sense.[10]

The book's action plot structure undermines the contention that reason is the only path to the truth and wisdom. The plot itself forces characters and readers alike to face issues of fundamental importance to human life itself. We are confronted not with an argument, but with a plot that requires that we examine fundamental philosophical issues like the limits of reason, the existence of God, the consequences of life without God, or the meaning of life. The plot itself compels each reader and each character to decide if they live in a "rational" world without God or take an "irrational" "leap of faith" into a world where acts of love can transform lives; where grace is possible; where freedom and autonomy are real; and where God is a subtle actor who orders creation in a way in which unforeseen possibilities can happen.

---

10. Frank, *Dostoevsky*, 851, my emphasis.

As the characters in *The Brothers Karamazov* will demonstrate, only those who take a "leap of faith" can understand life and living differently. They recognize the limits of all human endeavors including human reason. They see through the mundane events that life presents to the realities that reside beyond appearances. They discover alternatives that have yet to be discerned. These insights compel actions that, if experienced and remembered, often transform the mundane facts of life into windows through which God can be glimpsed and God's power becomes available.

As a member of the seminar on evil I too was somewhat paralyzed by Ivan's argument, but at the time I was also serving as a pastor at my church at 9664 O'Possumtown Pike, and because of this I intuitively suspected that even though Ivan's argument may lead me to similar paralysis and despair, the expectations of my congregation demanded that I present myself in places where people were sick, suffering, or in some cases victims of evil. I did not need a rational argument to be engaged. My vocation demanded it! I just had to show up even though my "reason" advised me that my presence was often quite useless.

Eventually my mere presence in these irrational and uncomfortable places taught me that when confronted with the absurdity of suffering, sin, or evil, no one needs a rational theodicy to engage these death-dealing powers. Theodicies can, in fact, be detrimental to ministry. At best their rational "solutions" are innocuous. At worst, they can contribute even more to a person's suffering. Sometimes suggesting that the one who suffers might benefit if she reflects on "the big picture" or "paradise" can create even more distress. Sometimes, upon hearing such rationalizations, the person who suffers experiences guilt along with her suffering because these statements of faith do not help. *My own indoctrination to the limits of reason with respect to evil and suffering began when I realized that those who suffer do not need a lesson in theology. They need something more fundamental and profound. They need presence, and in my feeble attempts to provide such presence I came to understand that Jesus did not come to bestow a doctrinally sound theology upon us. He came to offer His presence in the face of sin, evil, and suffering. Presence, not answers, are required at times of crisis. Through presence, we minister to the person. We do not minister to the person's theology.*

A Lesson from Job

One of the lessons the book of Job offers is that religious teachings and doctrines, if applied in uncompromising ways, can isolate those who suffer and add to the misery of the ones in crisis. When taken to be the last word on any subject, our religious doctrines, no matter how profound, can leave someone for dead. In the book of Job, Job is ruined financially; his children are killed; and he sits on a dung heap with open sours all over his body. This happens because God and Satan have made a bet designed to determine if Job is truly righteous. Together they inflict suffering on Job to determine if Job is intrinsically righteous or if he is righteous only because he has received so much from God in riches, children, and health. (Job 1:6–12). To their credit, Job's friends come to minister to him. Much to their credit, they sit with him *for a week* without saying anything (they must be commended for their tenacity), but they eventually speak.

Before they speak and before hearing anything from Job, however, Job's friends already "know" the reason for Job's suffering. They also "know" the remedy. Their religious doctrines said that all suffering is a consequence of sins committed by one who suffers, and their religious doctrines said that the solution to Job's suffering was for him to examine himself, discover his sin, and repent of his sin. If he did this, their doctrine promised that Job's suffering would cease. The flipside to the contention is that if suffering continues it is the consequence of the sufferer's failure to adequately discern and repent of the sin that created the suffering in the first place.

For Job, however, the remedy his friends proposed had another flaw. Job *knew* he had not sinned. He *knew* he was blameless. Now, be advised that our own doctrinal beliefs might get in the way here; for, most if not all Christians believe that Job must be wrong about his innocence because we all "know" that everyone sins. But, based on the biblical story itself, Job is correct. He did not sin. In fact, Job is introduced as "blameless and upright, one who feared God and turned away from evil." (Job 1:1). So, despite the doctrine that "Suffering is *always* a consequence of a person's sin," and despite some of our own doctrinal pre-judgments about the universality of sin, the Book of Job is a story about a blameless and upright man who unjustly suffers.

Because of the conventional wisdom of his day, however, Job's friends "know" it is impossible for a righteous man to suffer. They "know" that suffering is always a consequence of a person's sin, and they "know" there are no exceptions to this universal law. Job, however, refuses to accept their diagnosis because, as the story says, Job is in fact blameless. When Job refuses to accept their diagnosis and remedy, his friends accuse him of sinning all the more, and they gradually remove themselves from his presence. They abandon Job. They do so because their doctrines and their theological propositions led them to believe that "the last word" concerning Job's suffering has been spoken. They abandon Job because "reason" has spoken, and "reason" determines that Job suffers because he is a sinner (which he is not). Job's friends cannot even entertain the notion that there might be a different reason Job suffers because they already "know" why he suffers. They already "know" what he needs to do to alleviate his suffering. They have nothing left to say when Job rejects their doctrinal diagnosis and remedy. They firmly believe that the last word about Job's plight was spoken long ago. With nothing more to say, they abandon their friend. They leave him for dead.[11]

The story of Job reveals the limits of rational answers to questions of existential importance like death, evil, sin, and suffering. When our theological teachings give us our answers before we even begin to minister, these teachings become all that can be said. This closes the conversation and makes ministry much less likely. This fact highlights how important it is for a minister to discern if a person's difficulty is a problem or a crisis.

A problem is a difficulty that can be resolved given the resources already at our disposal. For me, but not for everyone, I have a problem if my car breaks down. It is not a crisis because I have the resources to resolve the problem. I have a cellphone to call for help. I have a credit card to pay for that help. I even have Triple A membership! My car's breakdown is troubling. It is time consuming, and it is a nuisance, but it remains a problem because I have the resources to solve the problem.

A crisis is quite different. A crisis undermines or destroys resources we normally use to solve our problems. A car breakdown is a major crisis for many people because a functioning car is a resource that they use to solve the problem of getting to work. If they live paycheck to paycheck, a car's breakdown can lead to disaster. Not getting to work might lead to getting fired. Getting fired means denial of income. Denial of income means the rent cannot be paid, and food cannot be purchased. If they have no credit or friends to help them fix their car or drive them to work,

---

11. R. Williams, *Dostoevsky*, recognizes that a dominant, recurring theme in much of Dostoevsky's fiction is the struggle between the death-dealing power of "last word," and the infusion of love and life that comes with the refusal to utter the "last word."

a cascade effect toward homelessness, hopelessness, isolation, and despair can begin. The same can happen with even more devastation during a health crisis.

The devastation wrought on Job was such a crisis. He lost his wealth, his children, his home, and his health. Each one is a resource Job used to solve certain problems. Losing them all at once created a mega-crisis. Crises like Job's have no ready-made answers, and they are not unusual. When they hit, they even undermine all the rational answers the one(s) in crisis used to solve their everyday problems. Crises require presence in order to be addressed. Answers accomplish nothing, and they often make things worse. Job's friends could not minister to Job because they thought that Job's difficulties were merely a problem that could be resolved by answers provided by a well-grounded theology. But Job was experiencing a crisis. Presence, not answers, were required if Job's friends were to minister to him. Since evil and suffering are crises and not problems, they are addressed by presence and not answers. Reason is a distant second to presence in such instances.

In future chapters the complex nature of what constitutes the sort of presence necessary to minister in crisis will often be described by recounting the words and deeds of Dostoevsky's characters. It is important here to note that listening is fundamental to presence. Listening is an important, learnable skill that will often be discussed. It is through listening that we are more likely to make proper adjustments required in a crisis. Presence also involves a conscious attempt to keep the conversation going and refrain from saying the last word. Most commonly this means refusing to moralize. Patience is also a virtue needed in the sort of presence necessary to minister in crisis. Patience is important because we need time to discover the right word or action that opens the future of the suffering one to possibilities that he or she has not yet envisioned.

Our Doctrines and Theology Can Undermine Ministry

The Book of Job demonstrates how ministry can become impossible if doctrinal or theological certainties prevent a would-be minister from ministering to someone who will not be converted to the minister's theological presuppositions.

2

The Many Sources of Evil

For we are not contending against flesh and blood, but against the principalities, against the powers, against the world rulers of this present darkness, against the spiritual hosts of wickedness in heavenly places.

—(Eph 6:12. Revised Standard Version)

All theodicies treat evil *as if evil is a mere problem*. They assume that evil can be resolved by a rational solution. This unquestioned assumption often leads to more suffering as it did in the case of Job when his friends abandoned him because he did not accept the "answer" that their reason provided to his plight. A failure of ministry like this one happens because theodicies describe evil abstractly. These abstractions eliminate the dire existential threat that *actual* evil, *actual* sin, and *actual* suffering impose.

This abstract focus has led some who construct theodicies to absolutely ridiculous conclusions like the one drawn by Charles Journet. Using an Augustinian contention that the presence of evil somehow adds to the total amount of "good" in creation, Journet concluded his book on evil with this bit of "good news." "If ever evil, at any time in history, should threaten to surpass the good, *God would annihilate the world in all its workings.*"[1] Journet's level of abstraction is so high here that he appears

---

1. Journet, *The Meaning of Evil*, 289.

to take solace in the belief that God will destroy the planet if the amount of its evil surpasses the amount of good! (Whoopee!) His assertion is a consequence of the refusal to consider evil and suffering in their concrete, existential form, and then maybe try to *do something* about the fact of evil.[2]

Terrence Tilley thinks evil lurks behind all rational efforts to defend a benevolent, omniscient, and omnipotent God in the face of evil. It is he that brought to my attention the insanity of Journet's rather buoyant contention that if the amount of evil in the world exceeds the good, God would destroy that world.[3] Like Journet, everyone who rationally constructs a theodicy does so by defining evil abstractly rather than existentially. They reduce evil to a mere idea that takes a propositional form. Limited to a mere proposition, the real, existential evils that afflict individuals, human society, and the earth itself are ignored.

But if evil is a concrete, existential reality, it is more fundamental than a mere logical inconsistency. Evil is a threat to life itself. It is not too farfetched to imagine a leader of a nation state being convinced that the amount of evil in the world exceeds the amount of good and, in his arrogance (few leaders are devoid of arrogance), concludes that God has chosen him to be the means to destroy the world. Ministry, however, must reject ready-made answers provided by such dogmatic solutions.

Ministry involves presence, patience and listening. If presence, patience, and listening are somehow accomplished, the conversation will move beyond mere reason and logic, and address the *fact* of evil, the *fact* of sin, and the *fact* of suffering in the world. This is the rationale for Dostoevsky's movement from the fact of evil to ministry in his last, great novel, *The Brothers Karamazov*. Ivan Karamazov himself begins this movement with his demolition of all theodicies. In the wake of his own argument Ivan Karamazov asks his brother Alyosha to

> (. . .)imagine that you yourself are building an edifice of human destiny with the goal of making people happy in the end, giving them peace and rest at last, but for that it was necessary and unavoidable to torture just one tiny little creature, that same little child who was beating herself on the chest with her little fist, and found this edifice on her unavenged tears, would you agree to be the architect under such conditions, Tell me and don't lie.
> No, I would not agree, said Alyosha softly.

2. Tilley, *The Evils of Theodicy*, 229–30.
3. Tilley, *The Evils of Theodicy*, 229–30.

And can you admit that the idea that the people for whom you are building it would agree to accept their happiness on the unjustified blood of a tortured little one, and, having accepted it, would remain happy forever?

No, I can't admit it, Brother.[4]

Alyosha agrees with Ivan's argument! Along with many contemporary philosophers and theologians, Alyosha thinks Ivan's argument is impeccable. But Alyosha's response is much more imaginative than his brother's. Instead of being paralyzed by the argument; instead of being immobile in the face of evil; instead of allowing the existence of evil to drive him insane, Alyosha takes the existence of evil as the starting point for ministry itself.

Principalities and Powers

All theodicies try to "justify the ways of God to Man,"[5] but they only present two ways to understand the source of evil. Evil either originates in the actions of contemporary human beings, or evil originates in God or nature. The first is often called moral evil. The second may be called metaphysical evil. Theodicies generally assign the evil that cannot be explained by human immorality to God or God's creation (nature). When they make this assignment, many also conclude that if any evil originates in God, we should reject God and God's world as Ivan suggests. But evil's origin is much more complicated.

Restricting evil's origin to living human beings or God precludes us from thinking about other possible sources. Neither God nor immoral human beings seem to be to blame for some of the world's relatively obvious evils. "When the industrial system produces undesirable consequences, who or what is responsible? How can we locate the culprit. Is a particular someone responsible for pollution, urban noise, traffic jams, birth defects, unemployment? Who? The bosses, the workers, the government, the engineers, cooks?"[6]

A similar question can be asked of Jesus' crucifixion. Who is responsible? Are the Romans, the Jews, the religious officials, the crowds, His unfaithful disciples, Judas, or supernatural powers like the Devil and

---

4. Dostoevsky, *Brothers*, 213.
5. Milton, *Paradise Lost*, 19.
6. Tiger, *The Manufacture of Evil*, 71.

his minions? The source of this evil is ambiguous to say the least. Some evils like the crucifixion, environmental pollution, or institutionalized poverty do not fit into the two categories that theodicies assume. These evils might have a source other than God, or the evil acts performed by identifiable, immoral, living human beings. Traditional theodicies do not discuss these apparent evils. In fact, if such evils exist, theodicies, in not even looking for them, hide the depth and scope of evil in the world. This allows evil to operate unobserved and unacknowledged, and its clandestine status only increases its death-dealing power.

> In the past, theodicists have declared what the evil in the world is. The point now, however, is to change the world by learning anew how to recognize the many forms and forces of evil and to counteract them, especially to counteract those discourse practices which perpetuate the power of evil practices by declaring them part of the natural process of the world or the divine plan for the world and thus efface them as actual evils in the real world.[7]

The Apostle Paul (or someone writing in Paul's Spirit) believed that Principalities and Powers are another source of evil—a source ignored by our theodicies. (Eph 6:12).[8] Powers are cosmic forces like Satan, his angels, and demons. The Powers reside in the spiritual realm where they oppose God. These powers inspire the Principalities. Principalities are embedded in government, religion, businesses, schools, family life, and other human institutions. Every human being comes under their dominion at birth, but unlike Cosmic Powers, Principalities are not eternal. Nonetheless, they are much longer-lived than human beings. Accordingly, individual Principalities are present within civilization long before our lives began, and probably will continue after we are dead and gone. This means that we normally take their worldviews for granted. The apparent "givenness" of their worldviews is an important source of their power and influence. Living human beings must repent to even begin to understand that alternative worldviews to the ones the Principalities present are even remotely possible.

Our everyday language is an example of the Principalities' clandestine operations. Americans, for example, are beginning to understand

---

7. Tilley, *The Evils of Theodicy*, 251.

8. Walter Wink's trilogy, *Naming the Powers, Unmasking the Powers,* and *Engaging the Powers* are seminal works that describe the scope of the evils perpetuated by Principalities and Powers. The following descriptions of Principalities and Powers owes much to Wink's groundbreaking work.

this through our emerging consciousness of how our sexist speech has played an important role in the marginalization of women. (For millennia we have believed that the marginalization of women to be an act of creation or God). As is always the case when it comes to the Principalities, we cannot blame one person, book, or organization for our sexist language. In fact, the use of such language implicates almost everyone in some way. Even now, we still need to repent of our sexist speech.

Words influence how we think. How we think influences how we act. How we think and act influences how we organize ourselves. How we organize ourselves determines our worldview. We are often unconscious of our worldview, and our predetermined worldviews provide the intellectual path of least resistance for all we think and all we do. For example, around 60 years ago we began to realize that when the pronoun "he" is indiscriminately employed in reference to our political leaders, priests, doctors, and bosses, the idea that a woman might actually become our boss, pastor, doctor or President hardly crossed our minds (except to be ridiculed). So long as this was so, the power to marginalize women is built into our use of language. Consequently, "decent human beings" unknowingly assist in the marginalization and oppression of half of the world's population simply by the way we speak. In short, our language itself allows Principalities to perpetuate the world's evil and unnecessary suffering. Since our sexist language has now been exposed to some degree, however, we dimly see how it infects us with the death-dealing power of evil.

A not so minor example from the life of a seventy-three-year-old man (that would be me) is illustrative. When I was a child, teenager and young adult, the use of sexist language dominated. Everyone said, "he" when referring to any random, but unknown professional like a doctor or boss. (We may have used "she" when referring to a nurse or secretary which also led to social marginalization of women as well). Everyone used the word "man" when referring to any random human being. My college, for example, had a required, capstone course titled "The Nature of Man." Growing up I rarely heard of a female medical doctor or dentist, and, on the rare occasions when I did, I remember thinking that I would never have a woman doctor. I just didn't think they would be as good as a man.

It is no coincidence that when I thought such thoughts, I had not yet begun to use the two pronouns "he or she" when referring to doctors, dentists, or other professionals. But during college, many people influenced me to speak in ways that were less sexist. In other words, we tried to repent. Today I am, as I said, a seventy-three years old man and, like many old men, I have a lot of doctors. Every one of them is a woman. I think this has much to do with the fact that for the last 50 years more and more people have been trying to repent of their sexist language. As a result of using both pronouns "he and she" to refer to doctors, dentists and scientists, our minds are primed to recognize that doctors can be both men and women. *The many women doctors, lawyers, pastors, rabbis, politicians and scientists that now are in existence are evidence that Principalities can be resisted!* Women are still marginalized. There is much more repentance to be done, but women are less marginalized in our culture than was once the case. In my opinion, this has much to do with the way we speak.

The evils perpetuated by Principalities also operate in racism, anti-semitism, nationalism, institutional poverty, and religion. Here Principalities and Powers subtly but forcefully direct us to uncritically accept these evils and understand these evils to be "just the way things are." Some of us truly believe these perennial sources of evil are established "by nature" or divine ordinance. Falsely established as a permanent fixture of reality, we become blind to the fact that many people are killed, incarcerated, impoverished, homeless, or denied the essentials of life because Principalities use our social structures and cultural norms to marginalize people. Instead of identifying Principalities as the source of such calamities, we attribute these social evils to the way God ordained things to be, or to the moral character flaws of individual human beings. But as our growing consciousness of the sexist implications of our language indicates, the evils Principalities perpetuate are not "just the way things are." Things do not have to be this way! As our slow, continuing and still far from complete progress in the elimination of sexism attests, the evils perpetuated by these Principalities can be resisted.

Principalities and Powers have been mentioned here to plant two seeds in the mind of the reader. The first is that the evil perpetuated by Principalities and Powers can be resisted by deliberate action *in the world*. Rational arguments are still important, but repentance is even more important. In the case of sexist language, for example, repentance at the very least means disciplining oneself to stop marginalizing women by using sexist language. The second seed I wish to plant is that unless such repentance is begun, people will seldom if ever recognize that the evils perpetuated by the Principalities and Powers are far greater than we first believed. Without repentance, we will continue to firmly believe that these evils are not even evil, but "just the way things are."

Such blindness is in fact what is on display in Ivan Karamazov's penetrating argument against God and God's world; for, Ivan's outrage was misdirected. Most of his rage should have been directed against the Principalities. Ivan's indignation could have exposed the socio/political structure of Mother Russia around the time serfs were emancipated from their "masters." Ivan's indignation could have also been directed against the atrocities of war. Had Ivan recognized that the governments of Russia and Turkey embodied Principalities that produced the war that produced the hordes that produced the senseless suffering, Ivan might have asked, "At whose orders were the Turks laying waste to the countryside and killing innocent children?"

Wars and the propaganda designed to convince the public of the necessity of war manifest the evil perpetuated by the Principalities embedded in all nation states (that I know). Now there is no literary evidence that Ivan even contemplated the notion that the evils he used to justify "returning his entrance ticket" have their source in the Principalities that rule the earth. Like everyone who engages *only* in the rational attempt to justify God in a world containing evil, Ivan had accepted the limited view of evil implicit in all theodicies and assumed that God and the individual Turks were responsible for the suffering of the innocent children.

Had Ivan understood that Principalities oppose God and are very, very often the source of the concrete, everyday evil against which we must contend, he might have seen evil as something to *struggle* against rather than *argue* against or rationalize. He might have understood that the way to address and overcome such evil is primarily political and, dare I say, pastoral instead of theological or philosophical. As will be seen when we discuss the practice of ministry performed by some of Dostoevsky's characters in *Brothers Karamazov*, this struggle against evil is not fought using the conventional and acceptable means employed by the Principalities, namely, armaments, propaganda, famine, pestilence, unjust laws, and deprivation. We fight by alternative means called "the Armor of Christ." This armor includes the belt of truth, the breastplate of righteousness, the Gospel of peace, the shield of faith, the sword of the Spirit (which is the Word of God) and prayer. (Eph 6:14–18). Ivan can do none of this because the source of these spiritual weapons is a God in whom he cannot believe. Lacking such a God, his only "remedy" for the evil and suffering is the dystopian world of The Grand Inquisitor and the Devil.

Other Sources of Evil to Contemplate

Traditional Theodicies do not consider Principalities and Powers to be sources of evil. This refusal hides the depth and scope of evil in the world and allows evil to operate unobserved and unacknowledged. This grants Principalities and Powers a clandestine status that increases evil's power and death-dealing rule. Principalities, for example, may be the source of perennial evils like racism, antisemitism, institutional poverty, and sexism. The discussion of sexist language in this section demonstrates how sexism is embedded in our culture in such a way that we think that the evil of sexism is "just the way things are." This discussion also demonstrates something that might be even more important, namely, that Principalities can be resisted and often overcome.

Ivan Meets a Cosmic Power

Dostoevsky is neither a theologian nor a philosopher. He is a writer, but his fiction is always about ideas, and his characters embody every significant idea and many of their unspoken implications. Dostoevsky refines these embodied ideas through dialogue. Characters change only when they engage in dialogue with the ideas that the other characters embody. Dostoevsky never ambushes a character with an idea that has not already been embodied and expressed by one or more characters in the novel. Dostoevsky's presence as author is felt largely in the way he presents and arranges his characters' conversations.[9]

Accordingly, Dostoevsky does not mention Principalities and Powers by name, but they do make important cameos. For example, late in the book on the night before Dmitri Karamazov's trial, Ivan comes face to face with the chief Cosmic Power, the Devil. Biblically speaking, the Devil is a source of *supernatural* evil. This is important because Russian atheism (as well as our current brands of atheism) was reluctant to acknowledge the existence of the Devil because this would also acknowledge a supernatural realm, and the supernatural realm is created by God. Dostoevsky, however, introduces the existence of the supernatural realm when Ivan meets the Devil.

When Ivan confronts the Devil, Dostoevsky sets up a scenario in which both the reader and Ivan must decide if the Devil is an hallucination

---

9. Bakhtin, *Dostoevsky's Poetics*, 79.

or real. For Ivan this means that he must choose between acknowledging his insanity (because he is speaking to a Devil who does not exist), or affirming the reality of the supernatural realm and God; for, even the Devil himself admits that God created the supernatural realm. In this conversation between the Devil and Ivan, Dostoevsky subtly introduces The Apostle Paul's contention that when we engage evil, we might be engaging the Cosmic Powers that oppose God. Even more subtly, Dostoevsky introduces the reader to the notion that when we deny God's existence, we have very few choices that do not involve death or insanity—but this contention, while it can be argued, is beyond the scope of this book.

On the night before Dmitri's trial for the murder of his father, the Devil appears to Ivan. This happens immediately following Ivan's conversation with Pavel Fyodorovich Smerdyakov who confesses to Ivan that he, not Dmitri, murdered the elder Karamazov, and much to Ivan's chagrin, he convinces Ivan that he was merely following Ivan's dictates, signals and teachings when he did so.

Smerdyakov is so important that he needs to be more fully described. He *probably* is the illegitimate son of Fyodor *Pavlovich* Karamazov and his mother, "Stinking" Lizaveta, was a homeless woman who the town acknowledged to be a "Holy Fool." This designation had two implications. First, it establishes Lizaveta was a very strange, physically challenged, emotionally challenged, and mentally ill women. Second, being thought a "Holy Fool" meant that townspeople would take care of her by giving her the bare necessities—gifts she would often place on the cathedral steps if she had no immediate need of them. In any case, when Lizaveta became pregnant, Fyodor Karamazov led everyone to believe that he "might" have raped her on a lark, and she gave credence to this belief by sneaking onto Karamazov's property to give birth to Pavel. She dies giving birth, and, for a variety of reasons, Smerdyakov is adopted by two of Fyodor Karamazov's serfs, Grigory and Martha. He grew up as a servant in Fyodor Karamazov's household. His first name, Pavel, is not objected to by Fyodor *Pavlo*vich Karamazov, or is his middle name, Fyodorovich, which means son of Fyodor. His very name, then, added to the townspeople and the readers' suspicions that Pavel Fyodorovich Smerdyakov is Fyodor Karamazov's illegitimate son.

Smerdyakov himself is even more puzzling than his ambiguous ancestry. His actions never make sense at least from a point of view we might call "rational." He robs and kills his "biological" father "for his money," but he returns the money before anyone discovers it is missing.

Perhaps even more mysterious is his confession of the murder to Ivan on the night before Dmitri's trial, and even more mysteriously, he commits suicide after his confession. Perhaps his motive for all of this was to wreak havoc on the family that denied his legitimacy, and, if so, it worked, for, both murder and suicide were, to say the very least, an extremely effective way to achieve vengeance on the entire family. In any case, from a literary point of view, Pavel Smerdyakov's odd and mysterious behavior moves the novel's plot.[10]

When Ivan hears Smerdyakov's confession, he proposes to go directly to the police, tell them that Smerdyakov had confessed to the murder, implicate himself in the crime, and free his brother Dmitri. He goes to the police, but he does not confess. He decides to wait until the next day when he is scheduled to testify at Dmitri's murder trial. Still unable to decide and act, Ivan, with his conscience still in an uproar, returns home. It is here that Ivan encounters the Devil—or maybe he just hallucinates the Devil.

The Devil presents himself not with horns and a pitchfork, but as a rather down and out member of the landed gentry who, being incapable of supporting himself, sponges off his friends and relatives. He has good manners, presents himself well, is very accommodating and quite amusing. He would be a great guest at a party. He appears as Ivan broods over his guilt and responsibility for his father's murder that he had just received from Smerdyakov. The Devil ridicules Ivan because of the inconsistency between the guilt he experiences and his ideas that everything is permitted because neither God nor immortality exists. The Devil says that Ivan's guilty conscience is quite charming, but he asks Ivan, "If you want to swindle, why do you need a moral sanction for it?"

Ivan's dilemma is this. So long as he believes that the Devil is an illusion, he does not have to admit that the Devil comes from the supernatural realm. He needs to avoid this to be rationally consistent because there is good reason to believe that God exists if the supernatural realm exists. Ivan's "charming" surge of conscience means that, deep down, Ivan *does* believe that the Devil, the supernatural realm, and perhaps even God is real. The supreme irony is that the Devil himself argues just this. The Devil himself leads Ivan along the path of faith; "and Ivan (. . .) realizes

---

10. Morson, "Verbal Pollution," 238.

all the incongruity of such a situation. As the Devil remarks, 'If you come to that, does proving there is a Devil prove there is a God?'"[11]

Many of the Devil's attacks come from Ivan's own words—which the reader along with Ivan might take as evidence that this is a hallucination. One attack comes from "The Rebellion." The Devil tells Ivan a story about a philosopher who, like Ivan, "refunded his ticket" because he could not justify the suffering in God's world. Nonetheless, this guy died and found himself forgiven and living in heaven. He protested his presence in heaven and was put far outside God's kingdom. He was told that he would now have to walk a quadrillion kilometers (the supernatural realm is obviously on the metric system) before reaching the gates of heaven and being forgiven once again. Out of stubbornness, he stayed put for one thousand years, but eventually he started his long walk back to God's Kingdom.

Ivan interrupts the story saying that the guy was an idiot because it would take a billion years to reach his goal (a severe understatement). But the Devil replies that the man reached the goal millions of years ago, and, in keeping with Dostoevsky's attempt to expose the limits of human reasoning, the Devil says that Ivan's *Euclidian reasoning* only pertains to earth. The present earth itself, the Devil says, has already been repeated a billion times. This story goes on in an even more humorous direction, but what is said here is enough to demonstrate that all reasoning we might call "normal" or "common sense" is quite incomplete if there actually is a God, and if eternity is the background against which we live.

> Dostoevsky's stroke of genius was to provide this thematic topaz with a religious/philosophical dimension by transforming Ivan's doubts about reality of the devil into a question of whether or not he believes in the existence of a supernatural realm, and hence of God. (Ivan) wishes to believe in what he sees in order to convince himself, on the purely psychological level, that he is not losing his mind; but he also wishes Satan to be only an hallucination so as to preserve his conviction that God does not exist. Thus, the oscillation of "the fantastic" here receives perhaps the greatest literary expression as Dostoevsky turns its ambiguities into a probing question of religious faith.[12]

At the end of the scene, Ivan throws a glass at the Devil who, nearly rejoicing, leaps up and says, "He remembers Luther's ink stand!" The Devil

---

11. Frank, *Dostoevsky*, 901.
12. Frank, *Dostoevsky*, 844.

rejoices because he has succeeded in convincing Ivan that he, the Devil, is real. In an ironic twist, the Devil may also have convinced Ivan that God is real as well because, as Ivan realized, if there is a Devil and the supernatural realm, God is their creator. The reader, however, never knows if the Devil has converted Ivan because when Ivan testifies the next day on behalf of his brother Dmitri, Smerdyakov has already committed suicide. Ivan testifies in a deranged manner, and no one believes him when he says that Dmitri is innocent—the first unequivocal assertion that he may have uttered in the entire book.

The Limits of "Euclidian" Reasoning

Through the words of the Devil, Dostoevsky exposes the limitations of "Euclidian" reasoning. Euclidian reasoning takes its cue from Euclidian geometry. It begins by assuming the validity of a small set of intuitively appealing, "self-evident" postulates or axioms. From these axioms certain propositions called theorems are deduced. For centuries these axioms along with the theorems derived from them were deemed true and certain, and the deductive reasoning process that derived theorems from axioms was considered the essence of reason itself. By the time of Dostoevsky, other geometries were developed (Rene Descartes (1596–1650) developed analytical geometry, for example), but to the extent that these also were self-enclosed systems of thought based upon "self-evident" assumptions, these new geometries are still examples of Euclidian reason.

Euclidian reason is not limited to geometry. Job's friends also employed Euclidian reasoning. They too started from what they thought was a self-evident axiom, namely, "all suffering is the consequence of sin." From this axiom they reasoned that Job's suffering had to be a consequence of his sin. Their Euclidian deductions enabled them to "know" why Job suffered long before they even spoke to him, and when Job refused to confess sins that he correctly asserted that he did not commit, his friends, who already knew the absolute truth were forced to abandon him. What could they do? Job would not "listen to reason." In other words, their absolute certainty derived from rational deductions from their "intuitively appealing, self-evident postulates" prevented them from ministering to Job. It is precisely such a closed, rational system that the Devil called "Euclidian" when Ivan objected to the story about the man who, like Ivan, had "refused his entrance ticket." Here, the Devil notes that the supernatural realm is not subject to the Euclidian limitations on earth. This is so because neither time nor space are limitations to an immortal soul.

This is Dostoevsky's literary way of acknowledging that if Jesus has overcome death, then knowledge and truth cannot be encompassed by human reason or even by the biological necessity of death. This has many implications. Probably of the most *practical* importance for ministry is that we cannot know all we need to know regarding things of importance. "For my thoughts are not your thoughts; nor are your ways my ways, says the Lord." (Isa 55:8). Remembering that the only "certain" knowledge we have is that our knowledge is, at best, incomplete creates the virtue of humility. Euclidian reasoning, on the other hand, creates a false certainty that is the source of arrogance and many calamities. Knowing that we do not know creates the wonder that inspires the imagination.[13]

The conversation between Ivan and the Devil introduces a new sort of reality, a new sort of truth, a new sort of rationality that cannot be completely comprehended by human reason or human argument. This does not undermine human reason completely, but it does mean that no matter how impeccable and clear our reasoning process might be, there will always be something left unspoken because, if the supernatural realm exists, our earth-bound intellects will never be able to fully comprehend reality. "A leap of faith" is the only way to even begin to approach some very important truths.

Ivan's Unintentional "Leap of Faith"

Søren Kierkegaard (1813–1855) gives us the phrase "leap of faith." He and Dostoevsky were contemporaries. Both are considered the founders of existentialism, but they were not acquainted with each other and never read what the other had written. So, while Kierkegaard's "leap of faith" was mostly a conscious, irrational leap, Dostoevsky's version has a more subtle dimension. For Dostoevsky, a person could make this leap of faith without even knowing it!

Gary Saul Morson demonstrates that Ivan himself may have made such an unknown leap of faith—a leap largely unrecognized by many readers. We have discussed Ivan's "Rebellion," and we are about to

---

13. Keller, *Cloud* and Morson *Wonder* are two critiques of certainty from two different but invaluable perspectives.

discuss "The Grand Inquisitor," two very famous episodes in the pivotal conversation between Ivan and Alyosha Karamazov. But these are only two-thirds of their foundational dialogue. A less familiar chapter begins their conversation, and that chapter is an important contribution to both Dostoevsky's attempt to refute Ivan, and, much more subtly, Dostoevsky's understanding of "the leap of faith."

For many good reasons, Morson recognizes the importance of the Trinity in *Brothers Karamazov*, and the Trinity plays a pivotal role in this conversation. "The Rebellion," is about God the Father. We will see that "The Grand Inquisitor" is about God the Son, and God the Holy Spirit is the subject of "The Brothers Get Acquainted" which begins the brothers' dialogue.[14] The Holy Spirit is the sheer force of life, and Ivan recognizes the presence of this life force at the very beginning of his conversation with Alyosha. Here Ivan admits that the centripetal force of our planet gives him the longing for life.

> Though I mean not to believe in the order of the universe, *yet I love the sticky little leaves* as they open in the spring, the blue sky—that's all it is. It's not a matter of intellect or logic, it's loving with one's inside, with one's stomach. Do you understand anything of my tirade Alyosha?
>
> I understand too well Ivan. One longs to love with one's inside, with one's stomach. You said that so well, and I am grateful that you have such a longing for life, cried Alyosha. I think one should love above anything in the world.
>
> Love life more than the meaning of it?
>
> Certainly, love it, regardless of logic, as you say, it must be regardless of logic, and it's only then one will understand the meaning of it.[15]

Unbeknownst to many of us who do not have Morson's profound literary insights, Ivan may have lost his "Rebellion" argument before he started. In "The Rebellion" Ivan bases his argument on the inability of reason alone to justify God's creation; yet, here, before he even expresses his clever destruction of all previous theodicies, Ivan admits that he *irrationally* loves life. He cannot immediately return his "ticket" (commit suicide) because "centripetal force" of our planet (perhaps a secular description of the Holy Spirit's sheer force of life) gives him a longing for life. Thus, before an argument based "solely" on reason; before rejecting

---

14. Morson, "Onions," 795–800.
15. Dostoevsky, *Brothers*, 199.

all previous rational efforts at theodicy; before returning his ticket and abandoning any future harmony, Ivan states that in some non-rational way, he longs for and loves life.[16] This is Ivan's unacknowledged irrational "leap of faith!"

By arranging his narrative in this fashion, Dostoevsky cautions that one must first love life for life's sake to have any sense of life's meaning. Love of life and acts of love are impossible to rationally justify. Love is not rational. It is not something that we can conjure up on our own. It is a spiritual gift (1 Cor 13). There is no way to rationally demonstrate love's value before we perform an act of love. A person can only be convinced of love's value by "doing" love. When the actions of his characters express love, this "active love," as Alyosha's mentor Elder Zosimo calls it, convinces those who love of love's value. So, it is with Ivan. Since Ivan has loved life—"*the sticky little leaves*"—Ivan's rejection of "God's World" has already been shown to be inconsistent with the meaning Ivan has already found in the act of living and loving. The sequence of these three chapters, therefore, undermines Ivan's "impeccable" argument from the start.

Dostoevsky may employ a more subtle literary technique that stresses this very point. It is called bracketing. The Gospel writers use this technique. During the week before his crucifixion, for example, Jesus was on the road from Bethany to the Temple in Jerusalem. He was hungry. He saw a fig tree and went to see if He could find a fig on it. In finding nothing but leaves "*because it wasn't the season for figs*," He cursed the tree (Mark 11:12–14), and He and His disciples continued to Jerusalem. There He cleanses the Temple; liberates the animals being sold for sacrifice; and upsets that tables of the money changers. He interprets his act saying, "Is it not written, 'My house shall be called a house of prayer for all nations?' But you have made it a den of robbers." (Mark 11:15–19). Afterward Jesus and His disciples return to Bethany. They pass by the fig tree He had cursed, and the disciples see that it had withered away to its roots. (Mark 11:20).

If we think the fig tree story and the cleansing of the temple are unrelated, we may only have a two-part story about Jesus' rather irrational hatred of fig trees that don't produce fruit on demand. But if the fig tree narrative interprets the cleansing of the Temple story, one might say that the Temple, in becoming "a den of robbers" as Jesus declared, could no longer bear fruit. The Temple is cursed like the fig tree. This technique of

---

16. Morson, "Onions," 798.

inserting one story between the two parts of another story and using the stories to interpret each other is called bracketing.

Ivan, you see, mentions his love for "the sticky little leaves" in two places. One is at the beginning of "The Brothers Get Acquainted" when he admits his "irrational" love of life saying one reason he loves life is "the sticky little leaves" of spring. Ivan also mentions "the sticky little leaves" at the very end of their conversation saying, "If I am really able to care for *the sticky little leaves* I shall only love them, remembering you. It's enough for me that you are somewhere here, and I shan't lose my desire for life yet."[17] In using the phrase "the sticky little leaves" at the beginning and end of this three-chapter dialogue, Dostoevsky subtly reminds the reader that Ivan has already demonstrated that he too may at least subconsciously recognize that he has taken a "leap of faith." Perhaps Ivan's "Rebellion" argument is already overthrown by his irrational love of life; for, reason alone cannot account for the things that matter most in life: love, the meaning of life and the joy of living because these are more fundamental than reason. They are pre-rational "leaps of faith" that are required to experience the most important life-giving things in life. The entire action plot of *The Brothers Karamazov* reflects this limitation of reason while its ministry plot demonstrates how these limitations are addressed through acts of faith and love.

Broadening Our Understanding of Faith

If God exists, and if God preserves creation, we may take an unintentional leap of faith with each breath we take. The simple act of breathing is an involuntary act (an act upon which we do not reflect) which makes our lives possible. Indeed, we would not live very long if we had to reflect on every breath we take. Furthermore, if God provides the air we breathe, breathing is an unconscious, irrational, involuntary "leap of faith" to the God who provides the air we breathe. This is true whether we consciously "believe" in God or explicitly reject God's existence; for, the act of breathing expresses our trust and reliance on the one who provides the air we breathe.

---

17. Dostoevsky, *Brothers*, 229.

The Grand Inquisitor and the Dominion of Principalities

Dostoevsky does not engage the Principalities and Powers with philosophical arguments. He does so with characters that embody the Principalities and Powers and their ideas. Like the Devil embodies Cosmic powers, Dostoevsky uses another fictional character to embody the Principalities. This character is introduced immediately after Ivan presents his massive critique of theodicy in "The Rebellion."

After presenting his argument, Ivan asks his brother Alyosha if he would agree to construct a perfect society if it was necessary to torture and kill just one innocent child, Alyosha responded "No, I would not agree (. . .) (but) you said just now, is there a being in the whole world who has the right to forgive and could forgive? But there is a Being, and He can forgive everything, all and for all (. . .). You have forgotten Him."[18] Well, it just so happens that Ivan had not forgotten "Him." Ivan had already composed a poem about "The One without sin and His blood." His poem is famously called "The Grand Inquisitor."

The story happens in 16th century Spain, in Seville, during the height of the Spanish Inquisition. Jesus Himself visits the place where, only the night before, The Grand Inquisitor ordered one hundred heretics to be burned at the stake. Jesus comes without fanfare, yet everyone knew him. The people were drawn to Him. He blessed them. His healing power was bestowed on all who touched Him. He healed an old blind man of his blindness. He raised a seven-year-old child from death. The Grand Inquisitor sees all of this, and "(. . .) his face darkens. He knits his thick gray brows and his eyes gleam with a sinister fire. He holds out his finger and bids the guards to take Him."[19]

The Grand Inquisitor *orders Jesus to be silent* and asks Jesus if He has come to hinder *us*. He tells the still silent Jesus that tomorrow he will condemn Him to burn at the stake as the worst of the heretics. He then demonstrates the power he has over the people by telling Jesus that the very people who praised you today will, "at the faintest sign from me" rush to ignite the very fires that, tomorrow, will consume you.

Dostoevsky discloses many important characteristics of the Principalities and their agents in this encounter. First, *the principalities use*

---

18. Dostoevsky, *Brothers*, 213.
19. Dostoevsky, *Brothers*, 216–17.

the power of death to maintain their control of the people. The Grand Inquisitor used the power of death the night before when he ordered the death by fire of one hundred heretics, and he threatens Jesus with death as well. Such death-dealing power is often called unilateral power, and it is backed by the Principality's apparent monopoly on the use of the legal power to kill. The Principalities and their agents either kill directly, as The Grand Inquisitor did the previous night, or, more commonly, they use the threat of death to impose their control. They do so by drastically limiting the future possibilities of the people they seek to control. Their objective is to turn living human beings into objects that they can manipulate, move, order, and control much like domestic beasts of burden. The surprise is that most human beings voluntarily cooperate with the dictates of Principalities and their agents.

Second, The Grand Inquisitor wonders if Jesus has come to hinder *us*—he says, "us," not "me." This acknowledges the second characteristic of the Principalities. *Principalities are not embodied in one person, one group or even one institution, instead, their agents are many.* An Emperor or President might be a visible agent of a Principality, but no single leader is a Principality. One Emperor can be replaced by another without damaging the rule of the Principality that is in control. Principalities manifest themselves in the institutions, political and government officials, religious leaders, common people, soldiers, teachers, husbands, important families, businesspeople, etc. All of these and more combine to support the rule of certain Principalities within certain polities.

The Grand Inquisitor describes himself as "us" just like the Gerasene Demoniac confessed his name is Legion "for we are many" (Mark 5:9). Roman Legions were agents of the Principalities governing Rome. At the time Mark was writing his Gospel (*circa* 67–69 AD), these Legions were bivouacked around Jerusalem preparing to invade and destroy the Temple. Like all agents of the Principalities, these Legions were "many" as well. Moreover, the fact that the agents of Principalities describe themselves as "us" indicates that they cannot be fought using tactics like assassination because if one agent is eliminated or killed, another will take his or her place. If The Grand Inquisitor were killed, for example, another will rise and resume burning heretics.

Third, this "us" extends through time. One emperor is replaced by another. One Inquisitor is replaced by another. One Chief Executive Officer is replaced by another. Individual leaders change, but all people who are within the lineage of a particular Principality always serve the same principality. Principalities are not, however, eternal. They come to be, and they pass away, yet Principality's third feature is *they are much longer-lived than individual human beings*. The Principalities under which we now live were in the world long before the birth of the oldest living person, and they could persist long after the death of those just born. *Their longevity makes it extremely difficult for human beings to resist them because we all grow up falsely believing that the patterns established by the Principalities are established by nature or divine decree*. We mistakenly believe that the evils these patterns establish and perpetuate are "just the way things are" and determine what is reasonable and what is not.

Finally, in the Grand Inquisitor indicates that *the Principalities are with Satan and not Jesus*. In other words, Principalities are allies of Cosmic Powers that are aligned against God. This is the reason why Principalities and Powers, though different, are often discussed in tandem. The Grand Inquisitor acknowledges this relationship when he tells Jesus that, "they" have been working with Satan for around eight centuries, but it took several centuries for "them" to establish their position.[20]

The Grand Inquisitor—Dostoevsky's Description of the Principalities

The Grand Inquisitor exhibits all the characteristics of the Principalities and their agents in literary form. They are "many" and their agents are interchangeable. They employ the death-dealing power we call "unilateral power." They are much longer-lived than human beings so human beings are inclined to confuse their rule with the way things must be. Finally, they are with Satan and opposed to Jesus.

How Principalities Rule through Necessities

Before the dawn of civilization there were natural necessities like eating, procreation, the necessity to live in community, and death. When Jesus was tempted by Satan to turn the stones into bread, He was being tempted by the biological necessity that tells us we must eat in order to live. He refused this temptation. He did not deny that it was necessary for Him to eat to stay alive. He denied that the natural necessity to eat was universal and necessary no matter the circumstances. In saying that we do not

20. Dostoevsky, *Brothers*, 223.

live by bread alone, Jesus was saying that while it is necessary to eat, He would neither feed himself nor everyone else under the conditions that Satan imposed. Jesus was also tempted by political necessity when Satan told Him he would give Him all the kingdoms of the world if He would merely worship him, and He was tempted by religious necessity when He refused to demonstrate His divine status by throwing Himself from the Temple so that the angels would "bear Him up" as Scripture promised. (Matt 4:1–11; Luke 4:1–13).

Apart from natural and biological necessities like eating and death, most of the necessities that appear to govern our lives are social necessities which are first created by human beings and perpetuated by Principalities. In other words, human beings created social necessities long ago, but these necessities are kept alive by the Principalities that rule us today. Over time, however, necessities appear even more necessary. They appear to dominate our lives more powerfully than ever before.

The increased power of social necessities comes from their "need" to expand and universalize themselves. Since nations are all subject to political necessities, all nations must become more centralized and expand until a nation is limited by geography or another nation that is also trying to achieve global dominance. There are also economic necessities of which money is its foremost expression. Money was first invented as an accounting mechanism that recorded who owed what to whom. This facilitated both trade and religious sacrifice.[21] But money as an economic necessity also seeks universality. It expands its dominion over all aspects of human life and becomes the nearly exclusive way that human beings relate to one another. Everything now has its price. Very little can now avoid being bought and sold if the price is right. This includes country, love, religion, spirituality, God, work, or people. Even the most intimate of human relations are granted their value by money. Life as we now know it appears impossible without money. Certain people might figure out ways to live without money, but very few of us can even imagine how this might be possible.

In rejecting Satan's temptation to perform a miracle, Jesus was opposing the religious necessity that dominates all religions. Religions always develop in two directions: the intellectual and the moral. Intellectual development happens in this way. The founder's teachings tend to become dogmatic "certainties" and, in a religion's quest for universality,

---

21. Graeber, *Debt*, 43–71.

these "certain truths" expand to provide the framework for religious and non-religious modes of thought. Dogmatic certainty can be deadly if it has political power to impose these dogmatic truths. (Before Jesus appearance, The Grand Inquisitor had just burned one hundred heretics at the stake). This could be why Jesus rejected Satan's temptation to perform a miracle that would establish Jesus' divine status "for certain."

It is also necessary for a religion to develop morally. Religions determine what is "good" and what is "evil." Once established, the notion of good and evil is used to justify religious atrocities like inquisitions and murder; for, it is often deemed "good" to kill or shun those deemed "evil." Like other religions, Christianity should have done otherwise. Its founder opposed religious necessities with His ethic of love; yet Christianity developed according to religious necessities nonetheless and became, in the process, the world's premier example of the quest for moral and dogmatic universality.[22]

While technology has been around since we put fire to use, it has recently emerged as an all-encompassing necessity. Its quest for universality is expressed in the apparently self-evident truth, "If you are going to do anything, do it as efficiently as possible."[23] The universality of this "self-evident" dictum *demands* that institutions be organized according to principles of efficiency, and that people always use the most efficient means at their disposal. Technological efficiency *compels* us to develop and acquire new tools and techniques that make our actions even more efficient.

Perhaps a mind experiment will make a technological necessity's easier to understand. Suppose—this is not an unreasonable supposition—that a small device is invented which can double the intelligence of its user if surgically inserted into the brain. Further suppose that the people with whom you work and are competing for promotions undergo this procedure. While you might be able to resist for a while, eventually it will be *necessary* (a technological necessity) for you to have this device surgically inserted or risk becoming the office imbecile. This is the power of technological necessity. Like every social necessity, it can be resisted, but resistance will have consequences that can be dire.

These tools and techniques are never subject to moral judgments because there is no debate surrounding efficiency. The only debate concerns which proposed technique is the most efficient. Numbers settle this

---

22. Ellul, *Ethics of Freedom*, 38–39.
23. Ellul, *Technological Society*, 18–22.

debate. The "best" number is always the efficient one, and the need to discover the "best" number removes the human element from the decision-making process. Machines have rapidly become far more efficient in determining the one number that identifies the most efficient way to do something. Once identified, the numbers make the decision. No moral, religious, or political perspective is allowed to question technology's universal goal of efficiency. In this way technology, like all necessities, seeks universality. In most cases, a necessity is stopped only when it is confronted by another necessity that is also seeking to be universal.

Several important aspects of necessities need further emphasis. All necessities demand universality and expand their domain until they become as all-encompassing as possible. Necessities have no "self-control." They must do what they must. They are only limited when they confront another necessity which is also trying to universalize itself. Their quest for universality gives necessities a spiritual dimension. As we would a god, we invest our necessities with virtues like justice and with authority and power. We must do so because we believe—sometimes in a spoken way and sometimes in an unspoken way—that our necessities are, or should be, universal.

> The state *has to* be more than an administrative and political mechanism. It *has to* represent God on earth. Technology *has to* be more than an assembly of means to achieve utilitarian results. It *has to* be the privileged expression of (our) demiurgic vocation. Money *has to* be more than a useful instrument for measuring value. It *has to* be mammon—an idol which satisfies all human needs. We have here a development which is by no means accidental or accessory. It can be observed as a general rule, so that we are justified in speaking of a kind of internal necessity.[24]

Necessities allow us to glimpse the inner workings of the Principalities that The Grand Inquisitor introduces. They show how Principalities seek universality, have their own inner dynamic, and try to be a substitute for God. The more complex a civilization becomes the more are its necessities internalized. Resisted by some people when they emerge, necessities become much less divisive as time passes. Necessities ask for our cooperation, and they often get it without a conscious decision being made.[25] Necessities become champions of our well-being and happiness.

---

24. Ellul, *Ethics of Freedom*, 40, my emphasis.

25. Once electricity is introduced to a house, for example, an entirely new world is welcomed into the home without any additional conscious decision ever being made;

Technology, for example, becomes our only hope to solve a myriad of problems created in our modern world. The state is the only way that we can even begin to feed the poor, educate the young, and grant some form of "social security" to the elderly. In the course of time, necessities are less and less resented and more and more accepted. We grow accustomed to them. They are not perceived as a burden. They become a blessing. We grant them godlike status. We think life is impossible without them.

Finally, and almost universally overlooked, the "accomplishments" of necessities come in a package. These "accomplishments" are always both good and evil. They are always both life-giving and death-dealing. Accepting the state's social security benefits, public education, good roads, and law enforcement also means accepting war, nuclear bombs, invasions of privacy, deterioration of individual rights, and imperialism. All these activities of the state—both good and bad—are the result of the political necessity that forces the state to increase and universalize its power over all walks of life. Likewise, questioning technology's efforts to do everything as efficiently as possible also means questioning economic productivity, efficiencies in healthcare, communications, entertainment, and economic growth. These "good things" are packaged with the detrimental effects of environmental pollution, overpopulation, loss of privacy and the expansion of our jobs to the detriment of our familial lives. The positive and the negative, the good and the bad, the life-giving and death-dealing come from the package that is technological necessity. You can't have the good without the bad. Once a necessity is accepted and justified, we cannot select only the good portions of a necessity and leave aside the bad. Technological necessity, like all social necessities, is an interconnected network of entangled technological realities that cannot be easily isolated one from the other.[26]

We live amid necessities, and we unconsciously accept their rule. Consequently, our future often seems inevitable and determined. Envisioning alternatives to the ways we live seems impossible. Some despair because the economic necessities that produce climate change or the political necessities that lead to war create problems that we can do little to mitigate. But even though necessities seem to create total bondage, they

---

for, the ability to turn on a light bulb means that an unlimited assortment of electrical devices are welcomed into the home without much thought, and those who resist will be overruled by future generations (with the possible exception of the Amish who continue to demonstrate that resistance is possible).

26. Ellul, *Ethics of Freedom*, 46.

are not omnipotent. Living within necessities never absolutely entails living under their dominion. This is because necessities and the principalities that create them use the power of death to rule, and the ultimate power of death has been abolished by the crucifixion and resurrection of Jesus. This fact gives us hope even in the midst of our apparent bondage to death. Freedom is the ethical expression of this hope. We live with and within necessities, but even so all is not lost. Our imaginations, if set upon freedom, can reveal possibilities that the necessities try to prevent us from seeing. Setting one's imagination upon freedom is synonymous with the practice of the art of ministry.

On Necessities

Necessities demand universality and, unless resisted by another necessity, they will expand until they become as all-encompassing as possible. This gives them a spiritual dimension. Like gods, they are invested with authority and justice, but they always come as a package that contains both the good and the bad or the life-giving and death-dealing. These are inseparably linked within a necessity. Accepting the good always involves the acceptance of the bad.

Freedom versus Happiness

When Jesus rejected Satan's offers, He rejected being governed by the necessities that both nature and society create. The Grand Inquisitor thought His rejection was madness. He thought Jesus was crazy because the Inquisitor knew that people would obey you if you can fill their stomachs. The Grand Inquisitor also thought Jesus should have thrown Himself off the Temple as well. If Jesus had succumbed to this religious necessity and performed this miracle, He would have given them the certainty they needed for them to worship Him. Finally, Jesus may have made his biggest mistake when he refused Satan's offer of dominion over all the nations of the earth in exchange for Jesus' worship. The Grand Inquisitor believed that Jesus was foolish and inhuman when he rejected this offer because the global unity provided by Jesus' rule would have stopped all war between nations (because there would have been only one nation) and thereby initiate an era of peace.

Moreover, The Grand Inquisitor thought Jesus rejected Satan's "generous" offers for an extraordinarily stupid reason. Jesus rejected these offers for the sake of freedom! In The Inquisitor's view, this was about as stupid as you can get because freedom is the source of human anxiety, confusion, fear, unhappiness, and disorder. The Grand Inquisitor and the Principalities he represented reject freedom. They offer us happiness instead.

> Freedom, free thought and science, will lead them into such straits and will bring them face to face with such marvels and insoluble mysteries that some of them, the fierce and rebellious, will destroy themselves, others, rebellious but weak, will destroy one another, while the rest, the weak and unhappy, will crawl fawning at our feet and cry to us: "Yes, you are right, you alone possess Her mystery, and we come back to you, save us from ourselves!"(. . .) Too, too well they know the value of complete submission! And until they know that, they will be unhappy.[27]

Rejecting freedom in favor of happiness, The Grand Inquisitor tells the still silent Jesus that His insistence on freedom makes Jesus responsible for humanity's unhappiness and confusion. Instead, The Inquisitor tells Jesus that *we* will set these confused, disordered, unhappy, anxious, and fearful beings to work (we will give them jobs),[28] but the people will be given holidays and leisure hours where they will play children's games and sing children's songs. *We* will love them like children. *We* will allow them to sin and tell them every sin can be redeemed by our permission. *We* shall allow them to have (or not have) children, wives, mistresses according to their obedience or disobedience, and they will gladly submit to us. They will inform *us* of their most painful inner secrets, and they will gladly believe *our* answer because *our* answer will save them from the great anxiety and agony they endure when they make free decisions for themselves. They will die in peace. They will expire in Your name. And beyond the grave there will be nothing but death. But *we* will keep this secret (this mystery), and "for their happiness *we* shall entice them with the reward of heaven and eternity."[29]

---

27. Dostoevsky, *Brothers*, 225.

28. Since every candidate for nearly every federal or state and local office in the United States promises us more and better jobs, jobs, perhaps along with lower taxes, are still the best that the Principalities have to offer. Personally, after working many "jobs" I concluded that I never wanted a "job" in my life. I prefer a vocation. There is a difference.

29. Dostoevsky, *Brothers*, 225–26.

The Grand Inquisitor longed for Jesus to say something, anything, no matter how terrible it might be, but Jesus remains silent. Jesus was silent out of respect for The Grand Inquisitor who had requested His silence. Jesus even respects the autonomy of The Grand Inquisitor himself! He will not intervene even though the Inquisitor and the Principalities he represents make decisions that oppose life. (Decisions like slavery, consumerism, war, patriarchy, etc. All these are kept alive by the Principalities that govern). Jesus' respect for The Grand Inquisitor's autonomy is, therefore, analogous to the Biblical God's respect for the autonomy and choices of human beings even though many of us engage in ungodly, death-dealing activities.

So, instead of confronting The Grand Inquisitor with the same death-dealing power by which The Inquisitor ruled, Jesus, rejecting such power, "softly kissed him on his bloodless, aged lips." The Old Inquisitor shuddered; got up; went to the door; opened it and told Jesus to leave and never come back. Jesus went into the dark street of the city. Ivan tells Alyosha that the kiss glows in the heart of the old man, but the old man still clings to his idea. The struggle between freedom and happiness (often expressed as the struggle between life and death) plays itself out even in the cold nearly dead heart of The Grand Inquisitor.

The same struggle is, in some sense, narrated throughout *The Brothers Karamazov* in the psychological and social conflicts that grip nearly all the characters. As we will see in the chapters that follow, freedom—the choice of life in the midst of necessities themselves—is embodied in many characters. Bondage is embodied in others. When a character engages in ministry, he or she receives the power to choose life amid a world governed by Principalities and Powers. Since an understanding of Christian freedom helps us choose life, it is important to understand how unique Christian freedom is before discussing how ministry can be expressed as the art of Christian freedom.

3

Christian Freedom Is Ministry

Now the Lord is Spirit, and where the Spirit of the Lord is, there is freedom.
—(2 COR. 3:17)

WHILE THERE WERE EXCEPTIONS along the way, Western philosophy from Plato through the Middle Ages thought that the human soul had three faculties: the intellect, the appetites, and the will. Intellect was the locus of human reason, and appetites contained drives like hunger, thirst, greed, sexual desire, the desire to live, *et cetera*. In each decision, the will determines if the intellect or the appetites would govern the decision-making process. The will (we now often call it "the free will") was the locus of human freedom. If the will does not exist or if the will is not free, freedom does not exist.

This traditional view of the free will is often called the metaphysical understanding of freedom. According to this view human beings are by nature free because we all have the free will to choose one thing or another. Free will is metaphysical because free will does not physically exist in the physical world, but it accounts for our actions in the world. To this day, most philosophical debates between freedom and determinism think that freedom, if it exists, must be metaphysical freedom.

Those who think of freedom in this way probably think that Martin Luther opposed the existence of human freedom when he wrote *The*

Bondage of the Will. While maintaining the existence of the human will, Luther writes that our will is not free because our will is in constant bondage to sin. Since most still think that metaphysical freedom resides in the will, and since Luther taught that the will is in bondage to sin, many conclude that Luther believed human freedom is impossible. It might be a surprise, therefore, to note that Luther also wrote *The Freedom of the Christian*. A treatise so named is a glaring contradiction to anyone who thinks that the will's bondage negates freedom. In fact, the will's bondage clearly does contradict freedom, unless . . .

Freedom does not reside in the will at all as both Luther and St. Paul apparently believed. For both, freedom has nothing to do with the metaphysical make-up of human beings. It does not even have to do with the necessities that seem to determine our lives. Freedom may not even have to do with whether the entire cosmos is determined by natural laws. For Luther and St. Paul, freedom is a gift bestowed by the Holy Spirit. As St. Paul writes, "Now the Lord is the Spirit, and where the Spirit of the Lord is, there is freedom" (2 Cor 3:17). The Holy Spirit gives us the freedom and faith to say that Jesus, the crucified, is truly risen from the grave. Since this is so, and since death is overcome, there are no *insurmountable* obstacles to our freedom.

Christian freedom is neither natural nor metaphysical because the locus of freedom is not the human will or nature. It is the Holy Spirit. Christian freedom is not intrinsic or essential to human beings. It is something that is externally bestowed by the Holy Spirit; for, "Where the Spirit of the Lord is, there is freedom."

The Art of Christian Freedom

In Galatians 5:1 St. Paul writes, "For Freedom Christ has set you free; stand firm therefore, and do not submit again to the yoke of slavery." This succinct verse discloses Paul's understanding of freedom. It says that *freedom is an end in itself*. It says that the reason Christ sets us free is for us to be free. There is no other reason! We have not been set free to do some specific, predefined task. We have not been set free to hold some predefined dogmatic position. We have not been set free to take care of our parents or even our children. We have not been set free to be a revolutionary. We have not been set free to make more money. We are set free to be free. That's it! "For Freedom Christ has set you free."

Paul believes the crucifixion and resurrection of Jesus Christ sets us free. *This implies that instead of dying to "save individual souls," as many Christian doctrines assert, Jesus died to make us free so that we might act freely in a world dominated by necessities.* This makes sense because agents of the Principalities like Ivan's Grand Inquisitor use the power of death to enforce their rule. They seek a monopoly on violence, and when they achieve this monopoly, Principalities and their agents legitimize the violence they perpetuate and criminalize the violence used by others. The power of death the Principalities employ is further enhanced by the fact most people firmly believe that death is final and irreversible. The resurrection of Jesus, however, undermines the universality of the power of death–the only sort of power that Principalities use, and, quite often, the only sort of power we mistakenly think there is.[1]

Death, of course, *appears* to be the ultimate "No" to all future possibilities. It *appears* to be an insurmountable obstacle. It *appears* to negate all our hopes and dreams. But Jesus' victory over death means that in Jesus, God bestows a future despite the fact of death. Death is real, but it is not insurmountable. It might appear to crush us. It might appear to be the ultimate negation of all our hopes and dreams, but it is not. We often forget that all of our groundbreaking scientific discoveries have demonstrated that very little in reality is exactly as it seems! If death leads to nothingness, as many people now believe, death is may be unique. It might be the only thing in nature that is exactly as it appears![2]

So, following the Apostle Paul and this observation about science and the natural world, death may not be the ultimate negation of all our hopes and dreams. Death is real, but there is hope, and perhaps the only way we can express this hope is by "not submitting again to the yoke of slavery" and acting freely in the world. The crucifixion, death and resurrection of Jesus makes such freedom possible, and acting freely in the world of necessities is the essence of the art of ministry and perhaps the essence of the Christian life itself.

Normally, we do not express Christian freedom by escaping from necessities. We express Christian freedom while living amid the social and biological necessities that appear to govern life. These necessities often appear to have the last word. A man might live under the necessity

---

1. For a discussion of the sort of power Jesus uses and some of its implications see my *Ministry with the Power of Jesus*, 86–105.

2. Alice Fulton, *Cascade Experiment*, 1—2. Gives a far more beautiful and poetic account of the idea expressed here.

of disease and believe his life and his future are determined by his disease. A woman might feel enslaved by her family and believe her future is limited by her parents, husband, or children. Nearly everyone appears in bondage to technological necessity. We find life impossible without our cell phones or automobiles. Many live in bondage to religious necessities which, on some well-known occasions, compel us to despair or even to terrorism, and who is not in bondage to the economic necessity of money? Life itself appears to be impossible without it.

Even on a global scale, necessities appear to dominate. Entire nations and many global corporations are subject to necessities that deny them certain possibilities. Nations very often say that they have no choice in how to proceed. Whenever we go to war, for example, it is because "we were left no other option." If large Fortune 500 companies are to survive, they "have to" make and more money and grow (an economic necessity). Lack of growth, we are taught, will eventually lead to business failure or even economic collapse. Economists, for example, frequently point out that the economy will be much less robust and perhaps in jeopardy if it becomes subject to any concern other than economic growth. We are often called upon to sacrifice the environment, jobs, public health, and moral concerns to economic growth. Finally, we are all in bondage to the necessity of death which, we believe, brings to naught even our greatest accomplishments.

Ministry focuses our imagination on freedom. Ministry's purpose is to express freedom regardless of the necessity in which we find ourselves. In any context and within any necessity ministry involves asking, "What can be said in Jesus name that opens (rather than closes) the future?"[3] Answering this question requires an active imagination, and this question can be asked (and sometimes answered) in any context or under any necessity heretofore thought to totally determine our lives. In counseling, youth work, work among the poor, feeding the hungry, caring for infants, children or the elderly, in a church meeting, in preaching, in worship, at home, on the job, in sickness, to the powerful, to the nation, in times of war, in times of peace, to those in bondage to their cellphones, *et cetera*, asking and answering the question, "What can be said or done in Jesus name that will open the future?" bestows the Christian freedom which

---

3. On numerous occasions as a student and later as his colleague, I heard Robert W. Jeson (1930–2017) utter these words of wisdom. Over the years I gradually came to understand that asking and answering this question with both words and deeds is synonymous with the art of ministry itself.

is made possible by Jesus' crucifixion and resurrection. The particular act or particular word that bestows Christian freedom is almost always different because ministry happens in different arenas, is governed by different necessities, and meant for different people. But in all cases, ministry is the search for the life-giving word that allows us to envision and enact alternatives to closed futures that we mistakenly think rule our lives. Those who accept these new possibilities as worthy alternatives to the way we believe "things must be" are freed when these new possibilities are enacted and become real.

Still, the Grand Inquisitor was probably far more right than wrong when he said that people prefer bondage to freedom. He was probably more right than wrong when he said people prefer happiness to freedom. He was probably far more right than wrong when he recognized that people prefer diversion to dealing with reality, and he *was* more right than wrong when he recognized that freedom is a burden from which most of us wish to escape.

If the art of ministry is the application of the imagination to the heretofore disconnected experiences of human freedom, then ministry will never be easy or even desired by those of us who feel more secure in our bondage than we do in the insecure realm of freedom. Yet, freedom is so important to Jesus that he was crucified to set us free so we can continue His liberating work in the midst of the necessities that hold our lives in bondage. Freedom is central to the art of ministry and the Christian life. When practiced it is, for a moment or for a lifetime, life shaping, dangerous, but often quite fun. Through such acts of freedom, we often can glimpse the Rule of God in our midst.

Christian Freedom Is the Essence of Christian Ministry

In any context, amid any necessity that we mistakenly believe determines our life, asking and answering the question, "What can we say or do in Jesus' name that opens the future to new, life-giving possibilities?" is both an enactment of Christian freedom and an act of the art of ministry.

Christian Freedom Amid Necessities

First Corinthians offers one of Paul's most enlightening ways to think about how to actualize the freedom Christ bestows in a world governed by Principalities and necessities. But before he begins this discussion, he reminds the Corinthians that when he was among them, he chose to dispense with lofty words (rhetoric and philosophy is how the Hellenistic world understood wisdom) and "know nothing among you except Jesus Christ and him crucified." (1 Cor 2:2). Paul thought the cross of Christ reveals God's wisdom, and God's wisdom destroys the wisdom of the wise and undermines the power of the powerful.

Knowing nothing except Jesus Christ and Him crucified negates necessities' quests for universality. Knowing nothing except Jesus Christ and Him crucified undermines the Principalities' efforts to pre-determine all human thoughts and possibilities in the name of "the wisdom of the wise." When the cross of Christ is understood as the fundamental manifestation of God's wisdom, it is the wisdom of the wise that becomes folly. To quote Mary's Magnificat slightly out of context, the cross of Christ has "scattered the proud in the thoughts of their hearts (. . .) brought down the powerful from their thrones (. . .) lifted up the lowly (. . .) filled the hungry with good things and sent the rich away empty." (Luke 1:31–33). Like the exodus and other examples of liberation of the people of Israel, the cross of Christ frees people of faith from whatever it is that enslaves them. But how such freedom can be lived out in the world dominated by necessities is still difficult to discern. One thing it does require, however, is the mastery of the art of ministry.

In 1 Corinthians 10:23, Paul reiterates his radical doctrine of freedom when he reminds the Corinthians of what they already seem to know, namely, "*All things are lawful.*" "All things are lawful" literally means that a Christian is free to do anything. Nothing is off limits because of the crucifixion and resurrection of Christ. One person is free to do action X, and another is free to do its opposite. Even so, it is conceivable that both are acts of Christian freedom. To complicate matters even further, the same individual Christian is free, on separate occasions of course, to do both action Y and its opposite; for, as Paul says, "*All things are lawful*" without qualification–even if a Christian is inconsistent.

Both Ivan Karamazov and Pavel Smerdyakov believed that if there is no God then "all things are permitted." This obviously included the murder of their father (which, by the way, would be permitted under Paul's unqualified assertion, "All things are lawful," as well). St. Paul, however, immediately adds the word "but" to perhaps qualify such a comparison. He writes, "All things are lawful, *but* not all things are beneficial. All things are lawful, *but* not all things build up." He then councils, "Do not seek your own advantage, *but* that of another." (1 Cor 10:23–24).

The difference between Ivan and The Apostle Paul is that Ivan's assertion that all things are permitted assumes both the absence of God and, an *individualistic* understanding of freedom. For Ivan, the "fact" that there is no God means that there are now no external restraints on the behavior of an individual human being; hence, "all things are permitted." Ivan's understanding of freedom is like our modern, Western, conventional understanding which asserts that we are all isolated individuals in pursuit of whatever suits our fancy. This individualistic understanding of freedom is clearly behind what might be called radical capitalism where one's economic freedom of choice is not and should not be restrained by anything external to the individual. (This individualistic understanding of freedom is also what Paul would call licentiousness, one of the seven deadly sins).

In contrast, Paul understands freedom *communally*. For Paul the decisions of the free Christian must attempt to choose life. This means the one who acts with Christian freedom should consider the welfare of the church, its members, and perhaps potentially anyone who might become a member (which includes everyone in the world). When Paul says, "All things are lawful, but not all things are beneficial. All things are lawful but not all things build up," and "Do not seek your advantage, but that of another," Paul sets forth an understanding of freedom that demands that the community be kept in mind when considering what it means to say and do something in Jesus' name that opens the future. There are many possible actions, but what is best for the community, people within the community, and those who might one day be included in the community has to be considered if these actions are acts of Christian freedom.

Much could be said about this distinction between the Apostle Paul's communal understanding of freedom and Ivan individualistic understanding, but instead of doing what itself would require a book, it is more important to ask if Paul's communal understanding of freedom undermines Paul's contention that *all* things are lawful? By adding these qualifications, is Paul himself abandoning freedom and "submitting again to the yoke of slavery"? (Gal 5:1b). If so, Paul's qualifications become another way we exchange the freedom of the Gospel for a new set of laws.

What Paul adds here, however, are not laws. What he adds is not a legal code. When he says, "All things are lawful, but not all things are beneficial," he gives no definition of what "beneficial" might mean. What is beneficial cannot be codified because that which is beneficial in a given situation is discovered through a dialogue that helps us imagine what, out of many possibilities, would be life-giving (or beneficial) in this unique situation. Likewise, when Paul reiterates the proclamation that "all things are lawful" and adds, "but not all things build up," he rejects a written code because determining what "builds up" also depends on similar considerations. Paul *does* suggest that the way to achieve some clarity is to discern what promotes the advantage of others instead of ourselves. (1 Cor 10:23). Since our imagination and judgment rather than legal codes decide such matters, the central status of Christian freedom is not violated.

Paul proceeds to a discussion of eating meat sacrificed to idols to illustrate how we might use our imagination and judgment to the advantage of others rather than ourselves. In this concrete case, "all things are lawful" means that a Christian is free to both eat meat sacrificed to idols and refrain from doing so. Paul suggests that eating or not eating should be based upon whether eating would offend or tempt some Christians of weak or immature faith who may still be drawn to false gods. If these new Christians were likely to be offended, eating meat previously sacrificed to idols would neither benefit nor build up the community. Under these conditions, eating should be avoided even though it is permitted.

In a similar, slightly more contemporary vein, I was once asked to participate in an installation service of a good friend of mine who was starting a new ministry. About an hour before the service, I found myself sitting in a room where members of his new congregation were preparing for a party that would follow the service. I was not helping. I was just sitting at a table. Suddenly a disagreement arose over whether alcohol should be served at this gathering. I tried to make myself as inconspicuous as possible, but my efforts were of no avail. Someone noticed that a guy wearing a clerical collar (that would be me) was sitting in the corner. Silence overtook the room as all eyes turned to me. Like a well-rehearsed choir, everyone in unison said, "Well pastor, should we or should we not serve alcohol?" (As Dostoevsky often shows in *The Brothers Karamazov*, the wish for someone else to decide for you indicates the rejection of the responsibility that comes with freedom). I said that I did not know what they should do. I said that they were free to serve alcohol or not serve alcohol, but I also asked them a couple question, "Do you know if someone among those you expect at this gathering will be offended if alcohol is served, and do you think you know why they might be offended?" I told them that I sure did not know, but I thought that if they thought that serving alcohol would be offensive to certain people, serving alcohol would not build up the congregation at a very important time in its life. The group, realizing that it was free to do one or the other, made its decision.

This is one of the best illustrations of both Paul's acknowledgment that all things are lawful, but all things are neither beneficial nor build up. In retrospect, I did a couple of important things on this occasion. My refusal to make their decision for them respected the group's freedom. It also affirmed Paul's contention that Jesus was crucified and rose *for our freedom*. Finally, I would now like to think that in asking them to refrain from seeking their own advantage but the advantage of others, the group's decision was both consistent with Paul and an invitation for them to act out their freedom in such a way that was consistent with what the Elder Zosima in *The Brothers Karamazov* called "active love." Active love guides our imagination as we decide how to make difficult decisions without, at the same time, violating the fundamental status of freedom itself.

Unspoken Knowledge and the Arts

Ministry is an art, but, frankly, when we hear the word art, ministry is not the first thing that comes to mind. First, we think of obvious arts like painting, sculpting, music, drama, poetry, fiction, and film. Next, we might include cooking, athletics, medicine, science, gardening or even farming (Amish style). Because arts are of such variety, it is hardly a surprise that there are many definitions and descriptions of what constitutes an art or an artist. It is also no surprise that even when we agree that something like painting or drama is an art, people will argue that a particular painting or a particular play is an abomination and not a work of art at all.

What is or is not art is sometimes controversial. It often takes many years for a work of art to be recognized as art. In other cases, what is immediately praised as a magnificent work of art is quickly forgotten. There is even some controversy surrounding William Shakespeare (1564–1616) being an artist; for, another great literary talent, Leo Tolstoy (1828–1910), could find little if any artistic value in Shakespeare's work despite the popular consensus that Shakespeare is one of the premiere artists that ever lived.[4]

---

4. Leo Tolstoy, "Shakespeare," 207–68.

Despite their obvious diversity, all arts do have one thing in common. It is the way they are transmitted from one generation to the next. Great masters, teachers, or mentors communicate their knowledge of their art to their disciples, students, or apprentices. Their guidance is indispensable because transmitting an art involves much more than the mere conveyance of a written formula or a set of rules. A master chef, for example, may give her disciples the recipe for her specialty, but it is highly unlikely that her apprentices will immediately be able to produce the same succulent dish simply by following the recipe to the letter. Something will be missing that is blatantly obvious to our taste buds but cannot be explicitly articulated even by the master chef herself. This certain missing something is called "unspoken knowledge," and all arts have some form of "unspoken knowledge" that is passed from one generation to the next, and that is central to the particular art.[5]

Unspoken knowledge does not prevent artistic knowledge from being taught. It merely means that artistic knowledge cannot be *completely* conveyed in propositional form. No matter how thorough a master conveys her art in propositional form, there will always be more that can be said. As an apprentice becomes a master, however, it sometimes happens that he can articulate some of what the master had left unspoken, but this never exhausts the unspoken knowledge that is always present in art. In fact, if unspoken knowledge ceases to exist, then the art in question also ceases to exist as art and becomes a technique that a well-programmed machine can perform.

For an apprentice to become a master artist, he must dwell-in the art with his mentor. In doing so, the apprentice might absorb his mentor's unspoken knowledge by witnessing her body language, style, and hearing her speech. Dwelling with the master provides the apprentice with access to an unspoken dimension that the master cannot explicitly express but can convey, nonetheless. Since the transmission of artistic knowledge depends on the transmission of unspoken knowledge, apprentices must first accept certain persons as authorities before they can master the art. Here we encounter that "leap of faith" that has already been discussed with respect to fundamental questions of life like God, life's meaning, and even love. To accept the authority of a mentor/master/teacher, every new disciple/student/apprentice must, often unconsciously, make a similar

---

5. Polanyi, *Personal Knowledge*, 69–131.

leap of faith to accept the authority of their master/teacher/mentor. If he does not do so, he cannot be taught.

When a would-be student takes this "leap of faith," she also accepts the authority of the community that supports the art in question. After all, it is this community that decides who is a master and who is not, and it is the master/teacher who conveys the unspoken knowledge intrinsic to all arts. Thus, the way an art's unspoken knowledge is conveyed demands the existence of a culture that supports it, and, thereby, the community that supports a given art conserves the art's unspoken knowledge.[6] Such conservation hardly means that each succeeding generation is defined by the preceding generation. Instead, this means that previous generations bestow the foundation from which all subsequent innovations emerge. These foundations will be modified somewhat as the art is conveyed from one generation to the next.

Michael Polanyi (1891–1976) believed the sciences themselves also depend on mentors conveying their unspoken knowledge to their students. He once observed a distinguished psychiatrist ask his students to diagnose a seizure a patient was having. He gave them the choice between an epileptic seizure and a hystero-epileptic seizure. His students could not decide. The doctor responded, "You have just seen a true epileptic seizure. *I can't tell you how I recognize it.* You will learn this by more extensive experience."[7] The expert psychiatrist admitted that he could not articulate *how* he diagnosed the disease, yet he accurately diagnosed the disease. His diagnosis depended on his knowledge of the whole. His students could not make the diagnosis because they still focused on the parts of the whole and had not yet achieved the expertise to shift their focus to the whole. "More extensive experience" was required for the students' to diagnose this particular seizure, and this "more extensive experience" happens in the presence of the expert psychiatrist who conveys the unspoken knowledge necessary for them to master their field. Even the "hard" sciences depend on this process. Before being granted a PhD. in chemistry, biology, or physics, for example, students spend years in the lab of an expert where this unspoken knowledge is conveyed from the teacher to the students.

Both the sciences and the arts have unspoken dimensions that must be conveyed from a mentor to an apprentice in ways that cannot

---

6. Polanyi, "Faith and Reason," 239.
7. Polanyi, "Faith and Reason," 237.

be explicitly articulated by the mentor. Moreover, the spoken dimension depends on the unspoken dimension. The would-be artist recognizes the truth and beauty of a painting before learning to be an artist. A musician enjoys music before becoming an expert musician. Even a scientist knows or thinks that there is something specific out there to be discovered long before that something is discovered and the way to a discovery is articulated. This means that in the arts, and the sciences as well, the unspoken dimension is more fundamental than the spoken because the spoken depends on the unspoken. This also suggests the need for a mentor in all artistic and scientific endeavors because it is through the mentor that this fundamental, unspoken knowledge is conveyed.

Mentors and Unspoken Knowledge

All arts contain unspoken knowledge that cannot be conveyed in propositional form. Unspoken knowledge is, however, conveyed from teachers, mentors, and masters to students, apprentices, and disciples if these neophytes who associate with their mentors can dwell long enough with the master to obtain this unspoken knowledge through the mentor's demeanor, body language, voice, and actions. When an apprentice becomes a master of the art herself, she embodies this unspoken knowledge and can pass it on to the people she will educate.

Art and the Human Imagination

This line of inquiry leads to the conclusion that science itself is an art. All arts are works of the human imagination that combine pieces of information, once deemed separate and distinct, into a unity that was unseen or unspoken until manifested by the work of art.[8] It was imagination that combined the head of a man with the body of a lion in the sculpted metaphor known as the Egyptian Sphinx. It was the imagination of Sir Isaac Newton (1643–1727) that combined the heretofore distinct laws of planetary motion with the heretofore distinct laws of terrestrial motion. This imaginative combination allowed Newton to apply the same physics that Galileo developed to study terrestrial motion to the movements of planets and stars.

---

8. Polanyi and Prosch, *Meaning,*

Obviously, one's imagination can lead a person astray. It can make wild combinations like winged dogs or one eyed, one horned flying purple people eaters, or political conspiracy theories. These flights of imagination are checked to some degree by a community of recognized experts who, through discussions and argument concerning artistic or scientific merit, help prevent such flights of imagination from going awry. These discussions judge if a work of the imagination is scientific (in the case of a potential scientific discovery), or true poetry, or an actual example of the art of painting, or drama, or even an example of the art of ministry. In other words, the "validity" of a particular work of art depends on the ideals and objectives of the community that performs and supports a given art. These objectives slowly change over time, but they are consistent enough to guide a particular art form.

Although the arts hold some important things in common, they are obviously different from each other. Their differences are a consequence of their differing subject matter. A true scientific discovery is an act of the imagination that integrates portions of nature that have heretofore appeared unrelated. Once upon a time people thought that the motions of the planets and the everyday motion on earth had nothing in common. Newton's imagination prompted him to conceive of and test a theory of motion that integrated the motions of the celestial realm with the motions of the terrestrial realm. Newton's scientific judgment prevailed because, in the judgment of the emerging community of modern scientist, Newton's discovery appeared more plausible than the older theories of Aristotle (384–22 BCE) and Ptolemy (100–186).

The fine arts (painting, sculpture, fiction, poetry, film, etc.) also use the imagination to integrate and transmit the disjointed works of the imagination itself and present these now unified images to the external world. These once disjointed events of our imaginations are composed of "All our hopes and fears, all our memories and our very feeling of ourselves, our suppressed desire and hidden feelings of remorse, all that we in sleep and indeed in daytime perceive."[9] The fine arts frame these formless acts of the imagination into artificial patterns, and artists use their imaginations to make sense of what once appeared separate, unrelated, and disorganized. The art of ministry has all these characteristics, and, like all arts, ministry differentiates itself from the other arts by the subject

---

9. Polanyi and Prosch, *Meaning*, 101.

matter on which the imagination works. Its subject matter is the many seemingly unrelated acts of Christian Freedom.

The art of ministry is also conveyed from one generation to the next from teachers and mentors to students, disciples, and apprentices. This means that, like all arts, there is an unspoken dimension to the art of ministry. There is always more that can be told. The implications of this fact are enormous and, if remembered and focused upon, can become an indispensable guardrail to ministry itself. In other words, *consciousness of the fact that there is unspoken knowledge in ministry can act as a guardrail that keeps a minister from going off track.* A minister who remembers that there is always more that can be told is much less likely to think that there is nothing left to say, and the future is closed.

Christian Freedom—the Content of the Art of Ministry

All art forms are works of the human imagination that unite elements that were once deemed separate and distinct into a unity that was unspoken and unseen until made manifest by the work of art. In the art of ministry, the human imagination unites the separate, distinct, and sometimes conflicting acts of Christian freedom by discerning the life-giving choices that can be made in Jesus' name.

Reflections on Ministry as an Art

Believing that the last word has been spoken justifies many atrocities on the part of those who practice absolute religious beliefs.[10] Dostoevsky's Grand Inquisitor fits this category. It must be remembered that Dostoevsky can easily imagine such a "fictitious" person because there were so many people like The Grand Inquisitor in Church history. In our own non-fictional world, religious terrorism is justified by people who believe that the last word has already been spoken by their God. When there is nothing left to say, all we can do is repeat the last and final word. If people still do not agree even after our "patient" repetition of the truth, they must either be shunned, killed or left for dead—the condition in which Job's friends left Job.

---

10. Juergensmeyer, *Terror*, demonstrates how certainty in religious beliefs has led to violence in this study of many different religions.

To prevent this sadly common abuse, we must realize that Jesus Himself seldom if ever said the final word on any subject. By this I mean that he never expressed a proposition that left nothing to the imagination or closed the conversation. Now to argue this would take an entire book and is far beyond the scope of this one; however, certain examples might make this contention at least plausible and a starting point for further reflection.

In the Gospels there is something unspoken in every text, story, or passage. (This is the reason why we preach rather than merely read the Biblical text. If the Bible truly was the last word, there would be not need to interpret it). Central metaphors in the Gospel of John, for example, leave much to the imagination. When Jesus says, "I am the bread of life" (John 6:35); "I am the light of the world" (John 8:12); "I am the good shepherd" (John 10:11); "I am the resurrection and the life" (John 11:25) and "I am the true vine" (John 15:1), there is much that is left unspoken. All one needs to note to prove this point is that Christians have been saying new things about these words for almost two millennia. The final word about these metaphors has not yet been spoken.

The fact that there is *always* more that can be said demonstrates how the Word of God creates new things. It is precisely because these "I Am" sayings leave so much unspoken that Christians have found it necessary to gather and discuss parables and metaphors like these for two thousand years. In other words, just like the *Word* of God created the heavens and the earth and all that is in it (Gen 1), Jesus' "I Am" sayings create the gatherings around His *Word*. We call these gatherings the Church. In fact, the Church happens precisely because Jesus' *Words* always leave some important things unspoken.

One "I Am" metaphor was not listed above because it is an excellent example of how easy it is to make any utterance into "the last word." This verse is "I am the way, the truth and the life", and it goes on to say, "No one comes to the Father except through me" (John 14:6). This passage has often been taken as the last word on salvation; namely, that salvation is possible only through Jesus. This interpretation could be faithful, but if we unpack this metaphor, we find that if it is a faithful interpretation, it is faithful in a way that does not close the future.

This particular "I Am" saying includes three metaphors, which, if combined, create three more metaphors. "I am the way, the truth and the life" means "*Jesus* is the way," "*Jesus* is the truth," and "*Jesus* is the life." Reconfiguring these metaphors creates even more metaphors. "The way" (because it is Jesus) is also "the truth" (because it is also Jesus), and also "the life" (because it too is Jesus). "The life" is also "the way," and "the life" is also "the truth." Thinking of these metaphors in this way makes your mind run in circles. One reason for this is that Jesus identifies himself with *processes* like life (life is a process) or a way or journey (which is also a process). Moreover, when truth is associated with these two processes, it means that truth is an ongoing process as well. Indeed, much can be said about the truth, but if truth is an ongoing process, there will always be more that can be said about the truth.

Still, we try to close the conversation. We try to say the last word. In attempting to do so, people rightly recognize that Jesus goes on to say, "No one comes to the Father except by me," and conclude that salvation is impossible unless Jesus is *acknowledged to be* "The Way" to the Father. But two questions might be raised at this point. First, "Does a person have to *know* that they are on "The Way" to be on "The Way?" Apparently, Jesus' disciple Thomas did not *know* he was on "The Way" when he was, in fact, on "The Way." If he had known, he would not have asked "Lord, we do not know where you are going. How can we know The Way?" (John 14:5). Thomas' question prompted Jesus to tell His disciples that He is "The Way, The Truth and The Life". The second question is "Does a person have to know *the name* of the way, street or road that she is travelling in order to successfully reach her destination?" Apparently, Jesus' disciple Philip did not know that the Way to the Father was named "Jesus" because Philip asked Jesus to "show us the Father and we will be satisfied" (John 14:8). Philip and the rest of the disciples did not know they were on the way to the Father, and they did not know the name of the road is Jesus. Nonetheless, they were on "The Way." A question one might ask is how many people are on the way and do not know this. This conversation can take us far and wide.

As is the case with all of Jesus' "I Am" metaphors, the implications of this metaphor as well as the conversations that surround it are limitless. We could discuss this forever and never achieve closure because there will always be more that can be said. This conversation will continue unless we delude ourselves into thinking that the last word has been spoken, and only one answer is possible. The consequences of this delusion could be death-dealing if those who hold this false conviction have the power to enforce their beliefs on others. Christian and other religious fundamentalist have often done this in the past and still do so.

In the synoptic Gospels (Matthew, Mark, and Luke) Jesus also refuses to say the last word. For example, He often refuses to answer a moral question with a simple "Yes" or "No." (If He had done so, He would have closed down any conversation on the issue under discussion at least among those who consider themselves His followers). One day, in an effort to trap Him, some Pharisees (who did not believe taxes to Rome should be paid) and some Herodians (who thought taxes to Rome should be paid) asked Jesus if it is lawful to pay taxes. They wanted a "simple" yes or no. Jesus, knowing that this was a trap, asked to see a coin. He asked, "Whose head is this, and whose title?" When told it was the Emperor's, Jesus responded, "Give to the emperor the things that are the emperor's and to God the things that are God's." (Mark 12:13–17). Jesus' ironic response left those who questioned Him about taxes with the same problem that they had in the first place. He left it to their imaginations (and to ours) to determine for themselves what to render to Caesar and what to render to God.

Jesus' response also indicates that there is no absolute answer to this moral question. At certain times conditions might warrant withholding the payment of taxes, and at other times the payment of taxes is warranted. It depends on the circumstances, and to complicate matters even further, Jesus says nothing about the nature of the circumstances that warrant the payment of taxes or the circumstances under which we should refrain. Once again, our responses are left up to our imagination, and Jesus respects our autonomy, imagination, and judgment enough to let us make the decision.

He also leaves open to faithful debate the more encompassing question about the relationship between religion and politics. Jesus makes only one important caveat that always should be remembered, namely, there is a difference between God and Caesar. Regardless of whether "Caesar" is a liberal or conservative, man or woman, a monarch or a revolutionary, a dictator or a believer in democracy, "Caesar" tends to forget that he or she is not God. Jesus' followers must remind the Caesars of the world that they are not God, and this is often a very dangerous thing to do.

Jesus left many important things to be determined by our imagination and judgment. He did this out of respect for our autonomy even though our choices are often death-dealing rather than life-giving. He did so even though we are quite likely to choose bondage instead of the freedom that is bestowed by Jesus' crucifixion and resurrection. The Grand Inquisitor recognized Jesus' respect for human imagination, human judgment, human freedom, and the Inquisitor thought that such respect was an ignorant but correctable defect in Jesus' program. The Inquisitor recognized that human beings preferred happiness to freedom, and he may have been right about our preference.

What Happens If We Speak the Last Word!

Through his work as a scientist, Michael Polanyi recognized that unspoken, personal knowledge was indispensable to the scientific enterprise. Nonetheless, personal knowledge such as Polanyi proposed is generally understood to be the antithesis of scientific knowledge. Most think that the more the human element is attached to knowledge, the less scientific is the so-called knowledge. Relying on his scientific experience, however, Polanyi argued that in scientific experimentation there is no such thing as "detached, objective knowledge." He argued that scientific knowledge *requires* the passionate, personal contribution of the person trying to discover what is to be known. Moreover, this is not an imperfection in scientific knowledge. The personal component is a vital and *indispensable* component of scientific knowledge as well as the knowledge of the arts.

Polanyi does not oppose the ideal of detached, objective, de-personalized knowledge just because it does not conform to the actual process of scientific discovery. He also opposes it because, if pushed to an extreme, the ideology of detached, objective knowledge leads to absurdities. He begins his most comprehensive analysis of his alternative description of scientific knowledge with the following words,

> In the Ptolemaic system, as in the cosmogony of the Bible, (humans were) assigned a central position in the universe, from which (we were) ousted by Copernicus. Ever since, writers eager to drive the lesson home have urged us, resolutely and repeatedly, to abandon all sentimental egoism, and to see ourselves objectively in the true perspective of time and space. What precisely does this mean? In a full 'main feature' film, recapitulating faithfully the complete history of the universe, the rise of human beings from (our) first beginnings to (. . .) the achievements of the twentieth century would flash by in a single second. Alternatively, if we decided to examine the universe objectively in the sense of paying equal attention to portions of equal mass, this would result in a lifelong preoccupation with interstellar dust, relived only at brief intervals by a survey of incandescent masses of hydrogen—not in a thousand million lifetimes would

the turn come to give (human beings) even a second's notice. It goes without saying that no one—scientists included—looks at the universe this way, whatever lip-service is given to 'objectivity'. Nor should this surprise us. For, as human beings, we must inevitably see the universe from a center lying within ourselves and speak about it in terms of a human language shaped by the exigencies of human intercourse. *Any attempt rigorously to eliminate our human perspective from our picture of the world must lead to absurdity.*[11]

Nonetheless, the quest for objectivity and detachment is so prevalent that the removal of the human element has become the goal of all disciplines that seek to be scientific. Particularly in social sciences like psychology, sociology, and economics, the quest for detached and objective knowledge has nearly become ubiquitous. In fact, trying to be as objective as possible can yield dramatic results, but if detached, objective knowledge becomes an ideology, it can yield absurd or even death-dealing results.

Economics can be described as anything that has to do with the production, distribution and consumption of goods and services. If this is the case, then economics is an important branch of ethics because the production, distribution and consumption of goods and services is an ethical question that can be decided in many ways. In the past religious leaders and political authorities have made such decisions, and it must be admitted that their decisions have mostly been neither life-giving nor humane. Lately, however, we have left these economic decisions up to the Market, and in so doing we have replaced the human decision makers with the Market. This too has had death-dealing consequences.

For many Capitalist economists the word utility describes an important and often reasonable way to determine what policy among many possibilities ought to be implemented. Utility is based on a public policy and private morality that emerged in the 19th century called utilitarianism. Utilitarianism is frequently summarized by the slogan "the greatest good (or happiness) for the greatest number of people." The utilitarians think, for many good reasons, that this slogan is the most rational way to determine both individual morality and public policy. It makes intuitive sense in public policy, and it is a good way to approach the conflicts that might arise within a family or other small communities.

But finding the greatest good for the greatest number of people requires determining both what is "the good," and how to measure "the

11. Polanyi, *Personal Knowledge*, 3.

good." In a family this might involve a discussion where agreement is reached on what is good for the family and decisions are made accordingly. Public policy is more complex. Disregarding the difficulty if not the impossibility of agreement on what constitutes "the good" in a complex society, finding the greatest good for the greatest number now entails developing a methodology that assigns a number to a potential outcome. The numbers projected from each competing method will then be compared and best number (and program) will be selected. Assuming that the greatest good is determined by the highest number, the highest number will tell you the proper decision. This means that utilitarianism implies that *the best number, instead of a human being, will settle issues of policy.* The human element is eliminated because calculating machine can compare the relative value of numbers.

Capitalist economists are attracted to utilitarian thought because it appears to be the apex of detached, objective, scientific reason; for, if everyone agrees on what should be measured to achieve the greatest possible good, utilitarian decision making simply requires comparing one number to another. Difficulties arise, however, when "the greatest good" cannot be clearly defined and calculated. (A further difficulty emerges if one recognizes that human history suggests that we are incapable of knowing what the greatest good is).

If, despite such concerns, we push utilitarian to an extreme, possible death-dealing consequences of utilitarianism emerges, and we do not even need Dostoevsky to create fictional characters to embody utilitarianism's radical extremes. This has already been done! Utilitarian economists have "solved" the problem of calculating "the good." They reduced "the good" to a monetary value. The higher the monetary value, the greater is "the good." Such calculations allow them to determine the worth of human beings in terms of their earning potential. A woman "slated" to earn $100,000 in her lifetime is worth-less than a man "slated" to earn $2,000,000. It's that simple.

In 1991, this "utilitarian calculation" led Lawrence Summers, then the Chief Economist of the World Bank, to circulate a memo. Based on utilitarian calculations, Summers' memo argued that because the earning potential of people living in less developed countries (to which he supplied the acronym LDC) was much less than the earning potential of people living in developed nations, it was *incumbent upon* the World Bank to dispose of toxic waste in the less developed nations. This conclusion was based on the following calculation. Since the potential earnings of human beings in developed nations is much greater than the potential earnings of people in less developed nations, people in less developed nations were worth-less than people in developed nations. For Summers this calculation meant that toxic waste products should be stored in less developed nations. Given his assumptions, the logic was impeccable. "I think," Summers wrote, "*the economic logic* behind dumping a load of toxic waste in the lowest wage country *is impeccable* and we should face up to that." He closed his memo with this scary and all-encompassing thought about the philosophy of the World Bank and all radical utilitarian capitalists saying, "The problem with the arguments against all of these proposals for more pollution in LDCs (intrinsic rights to certain goods, moral reasons, social concerns, lack of adequate markets, etc.) *could be turned around and used more or less effectively against every Bank proposal for liberalization.*"[12]

Summers' memo became public in February of 1992 and Brazil's Secretary of the Environment José Lutzenburger (1927–2002) responded, "*Your reasoning is perfectly logical but totally insane* (. . .) Your thoughts (provide) a concrete example of the unbelievable alienation, reductionist thinking, social ruthlessness and arrogant ignorance of many conventional 'economists' concerning the nature of the world we live in (. . .) If the World Bank keeps you as vice president, it will lose all credibility. To me it would confirm what I often said (. . .) the best thing that could happen would be for the Bank to disappear."[13]

Lutzenburger exposed the death-dealing reality behind radical utilitarianism as an attempt to remove the human element from any consideration. Summers' proposal was both logical and insane. It was logical because it was what Dostoevsky's Devil might have called "Euclidian reasoning" that deduced public policy from a mathematical equation. It was insane because, in removing the human, personal knowledge from consideration, the memo "impeccably" argued for the less than human status for certain human beings who, according to monetary calculations, were worth-less than their richer fellow human beings. The danger is further augmented by the fact that the logic Summers employed is, by his own admission, the same reasoning that undergirds "every (World) bank proposal for liberalization." All such reasoning is more than just absurd. It can easily be death-dealing.[14]

12. Summers, *Memo*.
13. Summers, *Memo*.
14. Gustafson, *At the Altar*, 69–71.

Along with Lutzenburger, Michael Polanyi also opposed removal of the personal, human element, but he did so based on scientific practice. He was a world renown chemists and member of the Royal Society. He did not agree that the scientific enterprise yielded detached and objective knowledge because his personal experience of how scientists actually work demonstrates that scientists are not detached from their subject matter. He found that all scientific endeavors contained a personal element. Moreover, this is not something to be overcome as most scientists believe. The unspoken element is embodied in the person of the scientists and is vital to the scientific enterprise itself. As Lawrence Summers inadvertently demonstrates, completely overcoming the personal element leads to absurdities and even death.

4

The Elder Zosima's Mastery of the Art of Ministry

"All things are lawful," but not all things are beneficial. "All things are lawful," but not all things build up. Do not seek your own advantage, but that of the other.
—(I Cor. 10:23)

WHILE HUMAN BEINGS MAY prefer happiness and bondage to the freedom Jesus bestows, freedom is fundamental to both ministry and Christian ethics. As discussed, Paul's admonition in Galatians 5:1, "For freedom Christ has set you free; stand fast therefore, and do not submit again to the yoke of slavery" implies that Christian freedom, perhaps instead of individual salvation, is the point of Jesus' death and resurrection. We are autonomous beings. We make a myriad of decisions. Some are beneficial. Some are idiotic. Some are completely self-centered. Some are death-dealing. Others are life affirming. As scientific imagination unifies what once appeared disconnected in nature, and as the fine arts unify heretofore disconnected experiences of our imaginations, the art of ministry applies the human imagination to the seemingly disconnected experiences of Christian freedom to discern the most life-giving possibilities.

Christian freedom, after all, means "*all* things are lawful" (1 Cor 10:23), but all things are not beneficial, build up the community, or help those in need. In Christian ministry we use our imaginations to discern what to say or do in the name of Jesus that opens the future. Since "all things are lawful," this might mean that action X is appropriate in one context, and the specific rejection of the same action X is appropriate in another. Since this is so, specific acts of human freedom can appear to be diametrically opposed; yet, our imagination finds them united nonetheless.

An imagination set upon the art of ministry integrates the heretofore disconnected and unrelated acts of human freedom. An imagination set upon the art of ministry discerns which acts of human freedom from among all that is lawful are life-giving instead of selfish, or irrational, or idiotic, or death-dealing, or just plain innocuous. An imagination set on ministry even discerns which response, among many faithful responses, is the best, most life-giving and loving response. And since death is the reason our futures appear to be closed, an imagination set upon ministry attempts to discover how we can choose life in the face of the death-dealing powers that the Principalities and their necessities exert over all of us. This is hardly an easy task, but Dostoevsky gives us a fantastic example of how a master of the art of ministry performs this loving, life-giving function in the Elder Zosima.

Zosima's Adages for Ministry

The Elder Zosima has three motivations for his ministry. First, when we meet him, Zosima is motivated by the fact that he is dying and dying very soon. In my opinion, all who are engaged in the art of ministry should try to be very conscious of their mortality. The fact that each one of us is going to die should be a part of our decision-making process because consciousness of one's mortality helps prioritize the many possibilities that are presented to us each day. Consciousness of our mortality in the decision-making process sometimes demands that we say, "No" to certain requests because these requests are not a good use of our time or our talents. Those who are not conscious of their mortality are much more likely to busy themselves with the many unimportant things that divert our attention and action. Remembering you are going to die demands that you prioritize.

Without such consciousness, we are likely to assume that we can wait and avoid doing some difficult but important things because we wrongly belief that there will always be time. This selective amnesia can make us much busier than someone who makes mortality a part of the decision-making process does. Consciousness of mortality makes it more likely that difficult, but important things will get done. A person who is aware of both her own mortality and that of others, for example, is more likely to mend important relationships or even compose a last will and testament that will support her family after her death. Consciousness of his own mortality provoked a friend of mine to tell his friends and family that he loved them whenever he left their presence. Unfortunately, he died in an accident. "I love you" was the last words he spoke to many of us.

Zosima, however, is not simply conscious of his mortality. He *knows* he is dying and dying very soon. This adds even more urgency to his actions. Given the fact that he knows he is dying, everything he does will be what he thinks is the most important thing to do at the time he acts, and since he is a master of the art of ministry, it is quite likely that what he chooses to do actually is the most important and urgent thing that needs doing.

Zosima explicitly states his other motivations. He learned these from his brother Markel who he credits with planting the seeds for his conversion to Christianity. One is the belief that "everyone is really responsible to (all people), and for (all people) and for everything."[1] Unpacking this important motivation will be attempted in the future discussion of Dostoevsky's antisemitism, but it is important to say that *had* Dostoevsky himself remembered Zosima's insights, not only would Dostoevsky have avoided the antisemitism that plagues both Christianity itself and his writings, but his work might have articulated how antisemitism leads to destruction and death—something he accomplished quite well with other ideas that dominated the Russian intelligentsia in his day.

Acts of active love is the other adage Zosima inherited from his brother. Active love is difficult. It requires a great deal of patience and persistence. Moreover, if ministry attempts to discern which choice among many possibilities is the best way to choose life, active love might be described as an attempt to actively embody a word that, in the name of Jesus, opens a person's future to life-giving possibilities which have been obscured by the necessities that we think enslave us and close the future. No person is free if their future is settled or closed. When a person accepts or performs an act of active love, he or she is freed for possibilities that were once thought impossible.

---

1. Dostoevsky, *Brothers*, 250.

Principles Guiding Zosima's Ministry

Three principles that guide Zosima's ministry are his consciousness of his mortality; acts of active love, and the recognition that we are all responsible to all people, for all people and for everything. Anyone engaged in the art of ministry should consider this master's advice.

The One Thing Needed

The Elder Zosima is a master of the art of ministry. Such mastery occurs after years of practice which often allow him to quickly diagnose the situation and recognize *the one thing* that a person needs to either avoid death or be emancipated from death's bondage. Recognizing "the one thing" does not come easily, but it is important to any act of ministry. Furthermore, finding "the one thing" mimics Jesus' encounter with a rich young man who asks Jesus what he must do to receive eternal life. Jesus tells him that he should keep the commandments: you shall not kill, commit adultery, steal, bear false witness, defraud, and honor you father and mother. The young man replies, "Teacher, I have kept all these since my youth." Then "Jesus, looking at him, *loved him* and said, '*You lack one thing*; go, sell what you own, and give the money to the poor (. . .) then come, follow me.' When he heard this, he was shocked and went away grieving, for he had many possessions." (Mark 10:17–22).

This passage reveals two things that Elder Zosima incorporates into his ministry. The first is the idea of active love; for, Jesus *loved* this young man. Second, the passage demonstrates that active love can reveal the *one thing* a person needs or lacks. In all the episodes from Zosima's ministry that follow, he demonstrates the relationship between the practice of active love, the ability to listen, and the discernment of the one thing a person needs.

In an early conversation between Zosima and Fyodor Karamazov, Zosima identifies the one thing Karamazov needs. Upon encountering Zosima in his monastic cell, Fyodor begins to play the role of a buffoon. Zosima listens to him and discerns that Fyodor's actions are motivated by shame saying, "And above all, do not be so ashamed of yourself, for that is the root of it all." To which Fyodor Karamazov, most likely trying to regain the upper hand, replies, "You pierced right through me, and read me to the core with that remark. 'Teacher,' he fell suddenly on his knees, what must I do to gain eternal life (. . .)

> The elder, lifting his eyes looked at him and said with a smile: "You have known for a long time what you must do. You have sense enough: don't give way to drunkenness and incontinence of speech; don't give way to sensual lust; and above all, to the love of money. And close your taverns. If you can't close all, at least two or three. And above all—don't lie.[2]

Even when Fyodor Karamazov mockingly asks what he must do to gain eternal life, Zosima respects Karamazov's autonomy. He refrains from telling him what to do, but he asserts instead that Fyodor Karamazov *already knows* what he should do (but chooses not to do). What Karamazov needs is to resist his love of money, his sexual lust, drunkenness and lying.[3] Nonetheless, Fyodor Karamazov persists in his idiotic behavior as Zosima leaves the room. An embarrassed Alyosha Karamazov happily follows his mentor. Outside Zosima's cell they encounter five peasant women and one woman of rank. Zosima, transgressing the rules of social hierarchy, first ministers to and with the peasant women. (Perhaps Zosima's consciousness of his immanent death tells Zosima that these people are more important).

As Paul Contino recognizes, the first encounter is wordless. Zosima sees a woman who he has seen many times. She is somewhat hysterical as she usually is. Because he has seen her behavior many times before, Zosima knows the one thing she needs. He places his stole on her forehead, and she is immediately soothed and comforted. In resting his stole on her forehead, Zosima performs a familiar sacrament-like ritual that she had quite likely received many times. He discerned that it was the *one thing she needed* and, she would need this again just like people need to receive the Eucharist again and again or to confess their sins again and again. Zosima discerned this because he, like many pastors in their respective congregations, had known her for a long time. He knew the one thing she needed, and he bestowed the one thing in this act of active love.

When Zosima performs this sacramental act, we can see that, in this case, the license to administer similar acts can make ministry easier for church professionals. Here Zosima's intentional act alone was enough to comfort the troubled woman. But it is also possible for priests, pastors,

---

2. Dostoevsky, *Brothers*, 43.
3. Contino, *Dostoevsky's Incarnational Realism*, 66.

and ministers to use the sacraments to gain access into peoples' lives at very important times. Times when change or even crisis might be more likely to happen. (In identifying that sacraments might provide access to people during times of potential crisis, I may now be passing on some unspoken knowledge (to some) that is contained in certain sacraments).

If infant baptism is practiced slightly more intentionally, for example, it grants a pastor or priest access to a family that has just received a new life into their midst. Sometimes this is a time of pure joy. Sometimes it constitutes a crisis in the household. It is always an adjustment. A pastor can use baptism to help determine how the family is coping with the new life and new responsibilities. Perhaps the church can help if the pastor discovers that help is needed.

Likewise, confirmation grants access at the beginning of adolescence which, as most know, can also be a challenge to any family dynamic. These challenges might be eased somewhat if they are known through a visit by a priest or pastor. Marriage, while happy and joyous, is also a time of change and challenges. It too is a time where, through pre-marital counselling, and perhaps post-marriage visitation, certain patterns of behavior that might be detrimental to the relationship can be observed, discussed, and altered before they become insurmountable obstacles to the young relationship.

Last rites and funerals also grant access to those who mourn and grieve. Since most people in our culture try to avoid mourning, intervention in this context is crucial. Its purpose is to help the grief stricken mourn their loss because in the Beatitudes, Jesus says, "Blessed are those who mourn, for *they* will be comforted." (Matt 5:4). Comfort is promised not to those who successfully avoid mourning, but those who mourn. A practitioner of the art of ministry can guide that process, and in doing so, allow us to understand how mourning itself reveals the fundamental connections that exist in all life.[4] These examples, along with the sacraments we repeat time and time again like Holy Communion and Confession and Absolution are avenues whereby the art of ministry can be more intentionally performed. Zosima demonstrates the healing power of repeatable sacraments and sacramental-like acts in this "wordless" encounter with the first peasant woman.

---

4. Butler, *Precarious Life*, 22.

Listening and Repenting

The second woman is undergoing profound and unbearable grief and suffering. Her name is Nastasya. She and her husband Nikita have suffered the loss of all four of their children! She has come from 200 miles away and has already visited three other monasteries where she was told to visit Zosima. Zosima tries to quickly comfort her telling her a story of saint who told a woman to take comfort in the fact that her child was singing with the angels in heaven. Nastasya, however, politely suggests that Zosima's attempt to quickly comfort her—as he had quickly comforted the first woman—is both superficial and inadequate. She tells him that her husband Nikitusha tried to comfort her with the same words saying, "Why weep? Our son is no doubt singing with the angels before God (. . .) but he weeps himself. I see that he cries just like me."[5]

At this point something that is sadly unusual happens. *Zosima listens!* He makes an adjustment based on what Nastasya said. When he used the story of the saint, Zosima was being superficial. He was trying to utter the final word to Nastasya and move on to the next person. (Here, knowing that he was dying and dying soon may have *conflicted* with his ministry. Nothing "works" all the time). If he had uttered this final word, he would have closed the conversation before it even started. He would have sent the woman "empty away," but Nastasya does not allow him to do this. Her reply was a polite way of saying that Zosima had missed an opportunity to minister to her. Zosima listened. He made an adjustment. Zosima *repents* of his sin against her, and an in-depth conversation ensues.[6]

They speak of grief. They speak of how grief can become less burdensome over time. Zosima talks about her son and promises to pray for him. *Zosima recognizes that Nastasya is not grieving well because her grief has cut her off from her village, friends, and, of most importance, her husband.* He says that when her son who is now a living soul looks for her to give her comfort as he will, he may not be able to give her comfort because he cannot find her. Zosima tells her that it is a sin for her to leave her husband. Nastasya, who also listens, can now also repent. She says Zosima has touched her heart and pledges to return to her husband.[7]

Nastasya had travelled hundreds of miles and seen many priests and elders, but Zosima did what no one who else had been able to do. He

---

5. Dostoevsky, *Brothers*, 48.

6. Contino, *Dostoevsky's Incarnational Realism*, 67–68.

7. Dostoevsky, *Brothers*, 49.

identified the woman's sin. The difficulty of doing so cannot be overestimated. The reason Zosima was able to identify the woman's sin (the one thing she needed) was because Zosima's own sin had first been identified by Nastasya! Initially, he had not listened to her! Zosima's first reading of her situation was both doctrinally faithful and completely inadequate. He had closed her future.

However, the task of ministry is saying the one thing that opens a person's future and, thereby, grants that person the freedom to enact new possibilities. Nastasya did this for Zosima when she politely but firmly told him his words had failed to free her. She told Zosima the one thing that *he* needed to minister to her in this situation. Zosima needed to listen and repent of his sin before he could minister to Nastasya. This he did, and his ability to repent and listen enabled him to turn around and identify *her* sin—the sin that was keeping her in bondage to her grief. Because she knew she had been heard, Zosima's words enabled Nastasya to repent of her own sin and begin her journey home where she could grieve in a more life affirming way.

Zosima's ministry to and with Nastasya reveals that active love cannot happen without listening. Listening is indispensable to the practice of the art of ministry. As the scene indicates, listening is not accomplished by being in the same room when someone is speaking. It does not even equate to the ability to repeat what was said. No, as both Nastasya and Zosima's actions illustrate, *listening involves making an adjustment because of what was said by another.* First, Zosima made such an adjustment because of what Natasya said. Then Nastasya began to make an adjustment in the way she was grieving because of what Zosima said. If there is no listening, there is neither ministry nor active love.

Not only is listening vital to Dostoevsky understanding of ministry, but listening is also essential to the life of the church as well. Matthew's Gospel is illustrative. Indeed, listening is so important that in Matthew's church, the failure to listen is grounds for excommunication.

> If your brother sins against you, go and tell him his fault, between you and him alone. If he *listens* to you, you have gained your brother. But if he *does not listen,* take one or two others along with you, so that every word may be confirmed by the evidence of two or three witnesses. If he *refuses to listen* to them, tell it to the church; and if he *refuses to listen* even to the church, let him be to you as a Gentile and a tax collector. (Matthew 18:15–17, RSV)

In this text, there is absolutely no mention of what the brother's original sin was. This is because the most important affront is the brother's refusal to listen. This affront was not limited to the initial complainant. He listened neither to the one or two others nor to the entire congregation. He did not want to talk about it! In doing so, the brother said the last word and in saying the last word he treated the people involved as if they meant nothing to him. He refused to recognize the existence of the profound hurt the other experienced. He treated the other person as if that person did not matter. He treated the person as if he or she was dead. This death-dealing response did not end here. When he refused to listen "even to the church" he was treating the church the same way as he treated the one who reported the original sin. He treated the church as if its opinion did not matter. He treated the church as if it were dead. His excommunication merely recognized the fact that he had left the church long before his excommunication.[8]

In the encounter between Zosima and Nastasya we have an excellent example of the relationship between active love and listening. Here we find that listening often forces the sort of adjustment one might call repentance. We also find that active love is impossible without listening because love is not possible if adjustments are not made because of a conversation. Moreover, although listening is possible for everyone, it is less likely that a "social superior" will listen to a "social inferior" because those with higher social status can ignore those with lower status without social consequences. (A boss can ignore what an employee says with fewer immediate consequences than employees would incur if they did not listen to their bosses). This demonstrates that listening is often a counter cultural activity particularly if the culture is designed hierarchically (as most cultures within modern civilizations are). Since hierarchical design is often an attribute of the rule of Principalities, listening may also be a way to resist their rule as well.

---

8. One thing must be noted about this excommunication. When most people are formally excommunicated, they are shunned and treated as if they were dead by the church that excommunicated them. In Matthew's church they are to be as a Gentile or Tax collector. This is somewhat ironic in Matthew "The Tax Collector's" Gospel. Not only was this tax collector treated quite well by Jesus—particularly when he was a tax collector—but the Apostolic Commission that ends the Gospel of Matthew urges Jesus' apostles and perhaps the Christian community that grew up around Matthew, to make the Gentiles the purpose of their mission. So, the one who they excommunicated now becomes the purpose of their mission.

On the Importance of Listening

Listening, described as making an adjustment in one's life because of what is heard, is fundamental to ministry. Since love can be described as giving what is needed (not necessarily desired), active love is impossible without listening. Since it is difficult to be responsible to all people. for all people and for everything without listening, listening is a prerequisite for repentance as well. Listening's role in Zosima's ministry with and to Nastasya illustrates both contentions.

Pastoral Authority—Use Only in the Service of Life

The next woman to whom Zosima attends is from town. He knows her and has often seen her. She has neither seen nor heard from her son in a long time and confesses that she is tempted to pray for him as if he were dead. Relying on the long relationship he has had with this woman, Zosima acts more as an authority figure than as a counselor. He calls her by her name and chides her for considering such a sin—a sin which Zosima believes resembles sorcery or magic. He then uses the authority that the many years of their relationship has yielded to *give her the one thing she needs*. This one thing could even be something she can only receive from Zosima himself. He *promises* her that her son is alive and that she will hear from him soon. As the story unfolds, upon her return home she finds a letter from her son saying that he will arrive soon.

Some would question the promise Zosima made to this woman. How, after all, can he possibly promise what he cannot possibly know? By what authority does he make such a promise? We must remember, however, that there is a significant number of people who always assume what one might call "the worst-case scenario" and make the mistake of treating this hypothetical worst-case scenario as a fact. You only know if a person tends to make such an assumption if you have known him for a while. In any case, people who assume the worst-case scenario often order their lives and make decisions based upon this highly unlikely but still remotely possible worst-case. They might feel a pain and believe that this pain indicates that they have terminal cancer, or, like the woman Zosima encounters, they might worry about all the possible evils that could happen to their children.

It is normal for parents to have such worries. I have had such worries, but you can do a great deal of self-inflicted psychological, emotional, and spiritual damage if you act as though these worries are facts before you *know* them to be so. In these instances, a clear voice of authority is the one thing that may be needed if a person is being dragged down into this spiritual morass. Zosima was a person of authority in the life of this woman. He knows this, and with the voice of authority he promises her that her son is alive. In doing so he opens this mother's future by diminishing some of her obsession with her worst-case dream about the death of her son.

The use of authority can be extremely dangerous and death-dealing if it is used to close the future. Too often we use our authority to maintain the status and power of social hierarchy. The Grand Inquisitor used his authority in this way. Zosima, on the other hand, demonstrates how the one who practices the art of ministry uses authority in the service of life. Sometimes a person is saved from much agony by an authoritative word from a respected source. The woman to whom Zosima ministered in this episode is an example.

Transgressing Doctrine

Next Zosima encounters a woman who is consumed by an overwhelming sense of guilt. Three years ago, she confesses, she murdered her abusive husband. Perceiving the gravity of this situation, Zosima draws near. As Paul Contino describes this encounter,

> She has finalized her sin. Like any good confessor, Zosima (attends) to the particulars of her situation. She is an abused woman who has committed the sin of murder in self-defense. He assists in restoring her "good take of self" by recalling her to the reality of God's forgiveness. *"There is no sin, and there can be no sin on all the earth which the Lord will not forgive the truly repentant! (A human being) cannot commit a sin so great as to exhaust the infinite love of God. . . Believe that God loves you as you cannot conceive; that he loves you with your sin, in your sin."*[9]

His words quell her obsessive compulsion to confess. Silently, she accepts his blessing and gift of a little icon.

---

9. Contino, *Dosotevsky's Incarnational Realism*, 68–69.

The Elder Zosima's Mastery of the Art of Ministry

The woman's guilt is overwhelming. Confession alone does not work. Despite many confessions of her sin, the woman still felt the need for forgiveness. In fact, confession made her plight even more dire. Zosima recognized the one thing she needed was to be convinced that forgiveness was possible for her. Her plight, reminiscent of Luther, was to find a Word from God that would open her future and free her from her bondage to the overwhelming guilt that closed her future. The word that Zosima utters was a word that could confer freedom from this sort of bondage.

Additionally, some still think that Zosima's statement, "There is no sin, and there can be no sin on all the earth which the Lord will not forgive the truly repentant," boarders on heresy because it suggests universal salvation which, for reasons I do not understand, is deemed heretical by some. Zosima, however, is engaged in the art of ministry. He knows that our orthodox doctrines are often interpreted to be words that close the future rather than open our future to freedom and life. Zosima here demonstrates that we do not minister to the integrity of our doctrines. Since "all things are lawful," a minister must find some faithful word that, in the name of Jesus, will open the future even if these words appear to contradict an established doctrine. Zosima's word of forgiveness opens the door to her future. She leaves with the notion that she may have a God that does forgive her for what she once thought was unforgivable. Furthermore, this is a case where Zosima subtly teaches that our doctrines are supposed to support our ministries. They are not supposed to be a barrier to ministry. Using our imagination to discover the word or action that in Jesus' name opens rather than closes our future sometimes makes it necessary to violate certain teachings.

Giving Thanks!

The next encounter is brief, but also of vital importance to the articulation of the unspoken knowledge Zosima embodies. A woman who Zosima also knows has heard that he is ill. She has travelled to see how he is doing and to extend him good wishes. She then gives him sixty kopecks for someone poorer than she is. Gladdened by this gift Zosima says,

> Thanks, my dear, thanks. You are a good woman. I will do so certainly. Is that your little girl in your arms?
> My little girl, Father, Lizaveta.

> May the Lord bless you both, you and your babe Lizaveta! You have gladdened my heart, mother. Farewell.[10]

Paul Contino astutely points out that this scene shows that Zosima is capable of receiving a gift. To this important observation I would like to add that the ability to receive a gift is one of the most enriching "skills" a practitioner of the art of ministry can cultivate.

Not only does giving thanks involve accepting gifts that are obvious gifts, but it also involves cultivating the personal and communal awareness that people give gifts in their normal, everyday interactions. Unfortunately, those of us in leadership positions often take these important but routine gifts for granted. We grow accustomed to them because of their regularity. Too often we think of the most regular, mundane gifts as happening almost by nature when they are profound acts of love and grace. A "thank you" recognizes that you know that you have been a recipient a "taste of grace." It recognizes that a bond of love exists between yourself, the giver, and the community you both serve. In many instances neglecting to say, "Thank you" for such gifts erodes this bond. The strengthening of these bonds of love may well be a heretofore unspoken dimension of the act of giving thanks for the many gifts people give. Saying, "Thank you" conveys the relationship of love in unspoken and spoken ways.[11]

Thanksgiving and Ministry

Saying, "Thank You!" is central to ministry and learning to say "Thank You" frequently can transform the communities in which these two simple words are often spoken. "Thank You" is a phrase that recognizes that a life-giving gift has been given, and it sustains the power of that gift within the community.

Small Acts of Love—The Gateway to Faith

The final person Zosima addresses in this whirlwind ministry tour is Madame Khokhlakova. She is a woman of rank, and as is the case with most people of rank, she awaits Zosima apart from the peasant women. She confesses her doubts about the afterlife and then wonders what the

---

10. Dostoevsky, *Brothers*, 51. My emphasis.

11. Thurston, *Widows*, gives us many reasons to say, "Thank You" to people whose work we often take for granted and who continue to do the work nonetheless.

elder will think of her now that she has confessed such a thing. Zosima says that she should not be concerned about his opinion and expresses his complete belief that she is suffering. He then pushes the conversation to another level and tells her that practicing active love is the way for her to recover her faith in spite of her doubts. Madame Khokhlakova, however, declares that she is not capable of active love because she demands recognition and thanks for her good deeds. To further demonstrate her need for recognition, she comically demands that Zosima recognize the quality of her confession for its honesty. In other words, she thinks it "meet and right" for Zosima to tell her she has just given "the best, most wonderful confession ever!"

Unlike the peasant woman to whom Zosima had just thanked for her gift and goodwill, Zosima does not offer thanks for Madame Khokhlakova's "overwhelmingly honest" confession. But he does not leave her where she is. Using her own words, he replies,

> If you have been talking to me so sincerely, simply to gain my approbation for your frankness, as you did from me just now, then of course you will not attain to anything in the achievement of real love; it will all get no further than dreams, and your whole life will slip away like a phantom. In that case you will naturally cease to think of the future life too and will of yourself grow calmer after a fashion in the end.[12]

His words crush her, but they prove life giving at least for the moment. Madame Khokhlakova momentarily forgets about herself and asks for Zosima to bless her daughter, and, in doing so, she makes a small step in active love.

Dostoevsky devotes an entire chapter to this encounter. His title for the chapter is "A Lady of Little Faith." This title should give us pause. Madame Khokhlakova's faith contrasts with the five peasant women who Zosima chose to address before addressing her. Her desire to be praised for the honesty of her confession is consistent with her social status and the flattery she routinely receives from others because of her status. It probably would not even cross the mind of a peasant woman that *she* should be praised and thanked for the honesty of *her* confession. It is more likely that a peasant woman rarely hears the phrase "thank you" for the truly life-giving acts of love she routinely performs, and, since the peasant women are all engaged in small acts of active love to one degree

---

12. Dostoevsky, *Brothers*, 55

or another, their presence before Zosima is an expression of their faith instead of a confession of their lack of faith.

The contrast between the peasant women and Madame Khokhlakova is stark. And yet, the title of this chapter, "A Lady of Little Faith" reminds the reader that Jesus tells us, "If you have faith the size of a mustard seed, you will say to this mountain, 'Move from here to there,' and it will move; and nothing will be impossible for you." (Matt 17:21). The next chapter illustrates that acts of active love and faith, no more than the size of a mustard seed (or an onion), move the ministries in *Brothers Karamazov*.

The Commissioning of Alyosha

After ministering to the women and after Alyosha's family leaves, Zosima, exhausted, returns to his sick bed. He looks at Alyosha and, as in all of his pastoral encounters in the hours before, Zosima discerns one thing that his apprentice needs. He tells Alyosha that he needs to leave the monastery and serve in the world, not as a celibate monk, but as a married man. This is not good news to Alyosha who desires to be a monk. He pleads for Zosima's blessing to stay in the monastery, but Zosima recognizes that Alyosha is needed among his family in the world. Zosima reiterates that after he dies, Alyosha should leave the monastery. Then he blesses Alyosha.

> I bless you for great service in the world. Yours will be a long pilgrimage. And you will have to take a wife, too, you will have to. You will have to bear all before you come back. There will be much to do. But I don't doubt you, and so I send you forth. Christ is with you. Do not abandon Him and He will not abandon you. You will see great sorrow, and in that sorrow you will be happy. Here is a commandment for you: seek happiness in sorrow. Work, work unceasingly. Remember my words henceforth, for although I shall talk with you again, not only my days but my hours are numbered.[13]

---

13. Dostoevsky, *Brothers*, 71.

5

Other Ministers Emerge

Very truly, I tell you, when you were younger, you used to fasten your own belt and to go wherever you wished. But when you grow old, you will stretch out your hands, and someone else will fasten a belt around you and take you where you do not wish to go.

—(John 21:18–19)

ALL ARTS REQUIRE MENTORS and teachers because something always remains unspoken in the transmission of an art from one generation to the next. This certain something would immediately be apparent in your culinary experience if, in anticipating a meal from a master chef, you received the "same" meal that I cooked following the chef's recipe to the letter. This "certain something" that is missing is the unspoken dimension of the culinary art that the master chef embodies. It can be taught, but it is not completely transmitted in propositional form (like a recipe). This teaching is transmitted through the unspoken assumptions, demeanor, or the body language of the mentor. Mentors and the unspoken knowledge they convey are essential to the perpetuation and flourishing of any art form and the art of ministry is no exception.

In *The Brothers Karamazov* the Elder Zosima is Alyosha Karamazov's mentor. As Alyosha matures in the art and practice of ministry, indeed, as he becomes a mature minister himself, he begins to embody the art of ministry that Zosima had cultivated in his own life and conveyed to his disciples. Zosima's transmission of his knowledge to Alyosha includes explicit teachings as well as the unspoken knowledge Alyosha absorbed by observing and helping Zosima practice the art of ministry.

Dostoevsky conveys Alyosha's effort to capture unspoken aspects of Zosima's teaching by inserting a literary fact that suggests just this. After Zosima's death and at the start of what might be called Alyosha Karamazov's public ministry, Alyosha writes "Notes of the Life in God of the Deceased Hieromonk, the Elder Zosima" by Alexy Fyodorovich Karamazov.[1] This is important because writing is a way a person begins to understand and even articulate some of the unspoken elements a mentor seeks to convey. The act of writing itself takes a writer to places he or she had not planned to go. Sometimes writing enables the writer to articulate the unspoken knowledge embodied both in the mentor and mentor's art. (In writing this book, for example, I have been able to articulate some things about the art of ministry that were once unspoken at least to me). Perhaps this is the reason teachers and mentors often direct their students and apprentices to write their thoughts and experiences. Writing helps students learn both the spoken content of their mentor's teaching as well as uncover some of the unspoken dimensions that the mentor herself had not yet been able to articulate. In writing Zosima's story, Alyosha, like those who read his narrative, made certain connections that perhaps only occur during the act of writing. Moreover, in writing his fictional account of ministry, Dostoevsky himself also becomes a teacher of some of these unspoken elements of art of ministry.

Alyosha's Growth in the Art of Ministry

The Gospel of John begins with an unparalleled cosmological poem.

> In the Beginning was the Word, and the Word was with God, and the Word was God. He was in the beginning with God. All things came into being through him, and without him not one thing came into being. What has come into being in him was life, and the life was the light of all people. The light shines in the darkness, and the darkness did not overcome it. (John 1:1–5)

---

1. Dostoevsky, *Brothers*, 248–69.

As my bishop Richard Graham once expressed in a sermon, the heights to which this cosmological poem take us are now interrupted by the mundane prose that summarize John the Baptist's ministry "There was a man sent from God, whose name was John. He came as a witness to testify to the light, so that all might believe through him. He himself was not the light, but he came to testify to the light. The true light, which enlightens everyone, was coming into the world." (John 1:6–9). The beautiful cosmological poem continues in the next verse. This movement from cosmological poetry of the highest order to mundane prose and then back to poetry expresses the idea that even though the Baptist's ministry, like most ministries, might be considered mundane and ordinary, our ministries happen on a cosmological stage that is both beautiful and teaming with light and life. This is a literary reminder that our own ministries, mundane and perhaps boring as they sometimes can be, happen within God's grandiose cosmological design.

It also gives us a clue to Alyosha's reluctance to leave the monastery. Perhaps Alyosha did not want to leave because, for him, the monastic life corresponds to the beauty of John's cosmological order, therefore, he did not appreciate it when Zosima told him that his vocation was to be carried out in the world. Zosima's "blessing" would take him to a place he did not want to go. Nonetheless, he reluctantly obeys his mentor and enters the rough and tumble, sinful world to which his mentor sent him. This world would soon include the murder of his father and the wrongful but legal conviction of his brother Dmitri for that murder.

A somewhat accurate summary of Alyosha's first foray into his attempt to practice Zosima's teaching of active love is that Alyosha has learned quite well the spoken knowledge that Zosima has taught him. He knows he should practice active love. He tries to embody active love in situations where love seldom occurs, and he is often successful in doing so. Alyosha even related to his disgusting father in a way his father had never known. In the words of the book's narrator, Alyosha had "a complete absence of contempt for him and an invariable kindness, a perfectly natural unaffected devotion to the old man who deserved it so little."[2]

In these early encounters Alyosha seems to know quite a bit even where he lacks experience. He tries to tell the truth about what he sees and understands, but he has not yet realized that knowledge is different from wisdom. Confusing the two leads him to make mistakes. He eventually

---

2. Dostoevsky, *Brothers*, 86.

learns the most important difference between knowledge and wisdom is that knowledge involves speaking the truth, but wisdom speaks the truth *at the right time*. The one who merely speaks the truth will always risk imposing the truth "from above." People who hear knowledge expressed "from above" will often resist because the way knowledge is expressed assumes the superiority of the speaker to the listener. The art of ministry requires wisdom to alleviate this inclination. Wisdom requires the ability to speak the truth at the right time, and "the right time" often requires discerning a person or group's readiness to hear the truth.

This distinction between the two spiritual gifts of knowledge and wisdom has been a blessing to my own ministry. Before understanding this difference, I was often frustrated by the fact that I "knew" what needed to be done within the congregation, but no one else would acknowledge the "facts" I thought were so obvious. Consequently, all my congregations seemed to do was talk. We never seemed to do anything. Over the years I began to understand that what seemed to be endless discussion had a purpose. Such discussion provided the time for a wise course of action to emerge. My role—a role that was never exclusive to me—was to discern the moment when a wise course of action was articulated. This articulation was seldom my preconceived notion of what we should do, but when a wise course of action was articulated and discerned, a common response was "Why did we not think of this in the first place?" Going through this discernment process made implementing the decision easier because the agreed upon action was based upon the wisdom that emerged from the group instead of the knowledge imposed from above by the leader. Excess time spent on pushing a largely unwanted agenda was avoided because more people understood and expressed the wisdom behind the agenda that patience had allowed to emerge. When wisdom guides the decision-making process, far more people are "onboard," and the common agenda is usually easier to implement.

We often learn the ability to distinguish between knowledge and wisdom through the unspoken knowledge that a mentor conveys. Alyosha was trying to follow his mentor's lead by enacting love in the situations into which he was sent, but there was still *one thing that he needed*. His understanding of Christianity had to change. Like most of us, Alyosha believed that individual acts of love were nearly impotent when faced with the need to change the world. Christians are forever tempted to jettison the small, seemingly innocuous acts of love for grandiose schemes when faced with the global issues necessities seem to impose.

Alyosha's *Malheur* (Affliction)

Simone Weil used the French word *malheur* to describe what next happens to Alyosha. English translates this word as affliction, but affliction doesn't quite convey the meaning of the French word. *Malheur* is more intense. It contains a dimension of inevitability or perhaps doom.[3] It is this sense of inevitability that enables Weil to say that affliction compels a person to "recognize as real what we do not think is possible."[4] What is real can be gracious. It can be terrifying. It can be both.

Following Simone Weil and overcoming to some degree the difference between the French word *malheur* and the English word affliction, the poet Scott Cairns contends that afflictions *might* give us a new perspective on life and living. This new perspective—known as repentance, conversion or what the Gospels call *metanoia*—is not guaranteed, but it is the best possible result of an affliction. "If we were to take greater advantage of these suddenly new perspectives, we might appreciate affliction as *the foundation of the foundation, the beginning of the beginning (...) of all that is good and beautiful*, but that is assuming we manage to respond decently, seriously, humbly and in good faith."[5]

Affliction, the kind that is "the foundation of the foundation, the beginning of the beginning of all that is good and beautiful" begins Alyosha's ministry. He emerges from his affliction differently and greatly changed. Alyosha is an example of a well-managed affliction.

Alyosha has his difficulties. At first, he succumbed to the same temptation that Jesus resisted. Alyosha believed the Christianity should involve grandiose, miraculous, displays that would erase all doubt about the high spiritual stature of the person performing these tasks. There certainly was room for small acts of love that Zosima preached and performed, but in the end Alyosha expected a grandiose miraculous display to verify Zosima's acts of active love and reveal the saintly status of his esteemed master.

Zosima's death destroyed this belief and forced him into an afflicted state. In the narrator's words, something happened that "exerted a very strong influence on the heart and soul of the chief, though future, hero of my story, Alyosha, forming a crisis and turning point in his spiritual development, giving shock to his intellect, which finally strengthened it for

---

3. Weil, *Waiting for God*, 67, n.1.
4. Weil, *Gravity and Grace*, 81.
5. Cairns *End of Suffering*, 19.

the rest of his life and gave it a definite aim."⁶ What happened was this. The "odor of corruption" began to come from Zosima's coffin. It was quite strong, and the stench soon became "in excess of nature." Although it was not official doctrine, it was commonly believed that a quick corruption of the body was God's judgment *against* the deceased, and Zosima's "quick corruption" could not be denied. Even Alyosha could not deny that the stench was "in excess of nature."

> And now the man who should have been exalted above everyone in the whole world, that man, instead of receiving the glory that was his due, was suddenly degraded and dishonored! What for? Who had judged him? Who could have decreed this? (...) He could not endure without mortification, without resentment even, that holiest of holy men should have been exposed to the jeering and spiteful mockery of the frivolous crowd so inferior to him. Even had there been no miracles. Had there been nothing marvelous to justify his hopes, why this indignity, why this humiliation, why this premature decay, "in excess of nature," as the spiteful monks said? (...) Where is the finger of Providence? Why did Providence hide its face "at the most critical moment" (so Alyosha thought it), as though voluntarily submitting to the blind, dumb, pitiless laws of nature?⁷

Alyosha, his theology of glory crushed, leaves the monastery without asking leave.

As dusk falls, Ratikin,⁸ a secularist seminarian who functions as a Satanic-like tormentor, finds Alyosha face down and asleep under a tree. He wakes him up and says that Alyosha's face has changed. It had lost its mildness. He wonders if Alyosha is angry at someone. Alyosha irritably asks to be left alone. Ratikin responds that such anger is a comedown from the angels, and then, because he "has always taken Alyosha for an 'educated man,'" asks,

> "Can you really be so upset simply because your old man has begun to stink? You don't mean to say you seriously believed that

---

6. Dostoevsky, *Brothers*, 285.

7. Dostoevsky, *Brothers*, 293.

8. Ratikin is a seminarian who has succumbed to the secular ideas that permeate mid-19th century Russia. He believes there is no God, and he is probably a nihilist who, like Ivan, believes "all things are permitted." He shows up in a variety of places in the story where the relationship between belief and unbelief is on the line. In these settings, he tries to turn people away from a Christian path.

> he was going to start pulling off miracles?" exclaimed Ratikin genuinely surprised again.
>
> "I believe, I believe. I want to believe, and I will believe, what more do you want?" cried Alyosha irritably.
>
> "Nothing at all my boy. What the devil, why no schoolboy of thirteen believes in that now. But still (. . .) ah, the devil. So now you are in temper with your God, you are rebelling against Him. He didn't promote him. He hasn't bestowed the order of merit! Eh, what a bunch!"
>
> Alyosha gazed a long while with his eyes half closed at Ratikin, and there was a sudden gleam in his eyes (. . .) but not of anger with Ratikin.
>
> "I am not rebelling against my God; I simply don't accept His world."
>
> "How do you mean; you don't accept the world?" Ratikin thought a moment over his answer. "What idiocy is this?"[9]

Like his brother Ivan, it was not God that Alyosha did not accept. He did not accept God's world. Ivan "returned his ticket" because he could not accept the torture, suffering and deaths of innocent children in God's world, and Alyosha could not accept the injustice that refused to acknowledge and even degraded the dignity of a saint like his mentor Zosima. Alyosha suffers from an affliction (*mahleur*). He is in danger of abandoning his faith, and he knows it. So does Ratikin, who continues to tempt Alyosha.

Alyosha had already succumb to Satan's second temptation of Christ. Jesus had rejected the sort of religion that Alyosha now saw evaporating, but Alyosha did not yet understand that what had happened to Zosima had also happened to Jesus. Jesus' death was even more ignominious. Jesus did not even try to glorify Himself "but emptied himself, taking the form of a slave, being born in human likeness. And being found in human form, he humbled himself and became obedient to the point of death—even death on the cross." (Phil 2:7–8). Zosima's corruption "in excess of nature" *could* have been interpreted as Zosima being allowed to follow Jesus' path, but Alyosha's demand for Zosima's glorification prevented him from understanding this.

Alyosha was in crisis. In rejecting God's world, Alyosha rejected a world in which Jesus Himself claimed that the first will be last and that great saints might be unknown, unrecognized, or even ostracized. At Alyosha's lowest point, Ratikin asks if he has eaten. Like Satan tempted

9. Dostoevsky, *Brothers*, 294.

the fasting Jesus to turn stones into bread to feed himself, Ratikin offers Alyosha the sausage that he has in his pocket, but he quickly notes that the dietary restrictions of monastic life might prevent Alyosha from accepting the sausage. Nonetheless, Alyosha "takes and eats."

> "Well now. You really are going all out! Why it's a regular mutiny, with barricades! Well my boy, we must make the most of it. Come to my place (. . .) I wouldn't mind a drop of vodka myself. I am tired to death. Vodka is going too far for you I suppose (. . .) or would you like some."
> "Give me some vodka too."
> "Well now you surprise me, brother." Ratikin looked at him in amazement. "Well one way or another, vodka or sausage, this is a jolly fine chance and mustn't be missed."[10]

But instead of going to Ratikin's place for vodka, Ratikin tries to push Alyosha's fall even further. He suggests that they go to Grushenka's place. Alyosha immediately agrees even though he believes she is a wanton woman who he "knows" is a threat to both his ministry and his salvation.

Afflictions and Their Outcome

The outcome of an affliction can never be determined in advance, but, according to Scott Cairns, the best possible result is that an affliction becomes the foundation of the foundation, the beginning of the beginning (. . .) of all this is good and beautiful. All the Karamazov brothers are afflicted. Both Dmitri and Alyosha try to make their afflictions the beginning of all that is good and beautiful.

Grushenka and Alyosha Convert Each Other

Agrafena Alexandrova Svetlova (called Grushenka) is a central and pivotal character in *The Brothers Karamazov* in two important ways. First, she is intimately involved in the action plot of the novel which centers around Dmitri Karamazov being falsely accused and convicted of murdering his father, Fyodor Karamazov. Among the overwhelming amount of circumstantial evidence against Dmitri, is that both he and his father are "in love" with Grushenka who encourages this love triangle. (Grushenka's

---

10. Dostoevsky, *Brothers*, 294.

encouragement of this rivalry was evidence enough for Alyosha's firm conviction that Grushenka is a woman of ill-repute).

Second, Grushenka is also involved in what I've called the novel's ministry plot. The ministry plot unfolds within the action plot, and it is in the dark context of the action plot that Alyosha matures and grows in the art of ministry. Grushenka is pivotal here as well. Grushenka and Ratikin were in cahoots. They had already agreed to combine forces to complete Alyosha's downfall. Grushenka had even agreed to pay Ratikin if he could deliver him to her so she could seduce him; for, she despised the way (she thought) religious people like Alyosha looked down on her.

Upon their arrival Grushenka starts to carry out her plan. She sits seductively on Alyosha's knee. Alyosha complies. Champaign is offered and accepted, but, after taking a sip of champaign, Alyosha puts his glass down. Grushenka does as well. Then something astonishing happens that changes the direction of what I have called the novel's "ministry plot." Ratikin tells Grushenka that Zosima has died. Remembering her Orthodox faith, she *crosses herself* and declares, "(. . .) what have I been doing sitting on his knee like this at this moment." She slipped off his knee and sat on the sofa. "Alyosha fixed a long wondering look upon her and a light seemed to dawn in his face."

> "Ratikin," he said suddenly, in a firm and loud voice; "don't taunt me with having rebelled against God. I don't want to feel angry with you, so you must be kinder now too. I've lost a treasure such as you never had, and you cannot judge me now. You had much better look at her—do you see how she has pity on me? I came here to find a wicked soul—I felt drawn to evil because I was base and evil myself, and I have found a true sister, I have found a treasure—a loving heart. She had pity on me just now (. . .) Agrafena Alexandrovna, I am speaking of you. You raised my soul from the depths."[11]

Both Ratikin and Grushenka intended to facilitate Alyosha's fall from a Holy man to a sinner, but by the time Alyosha had arrived, Alyosha already knew that his fall was complete. In this passage, Alyosha *confesses* that he was himself base and evil. When Alyosha comes to Grushenka's house he comes as an ordinary sinner, and he knows this about himself. He treats Grushenka as someone who is better than he is. She hardly knows what has happened, but she feels that their roles have

---

11. Dostoevsky, *Brothers*, 302.

been reversed, and she now has no reason to arrange his downfall. His downfall has already happened![12]

Moreover, when Alyosha gives her credit for raising his soul from the depths, Grushenka understands that she has done the very opposite of what she had intended. Consequently, she begins to understand herself differently as well. Instead of embodying the power of death in her interaction with Alyosha, she discovers that she has been an agent of love and life. But she still has trouble understanding herself to be an agent of God's creative word. So, to warn Alyosha of the wicked woman that she still thinks she is, she tells him a story Dostoevsky calls "The Parable of the Onion." For her, this story is a warning. She tells it as a warning. She tells it because she thinks it will conclusively demonstrate the sort of evil woman she is.

> Once upon a time there was a woman, a very wicked woman she was. And she died and did not leave a single good deed behind. The devils caught her and plunged her into the lake of fire. So her guardian angel stood and wondered what good deed of hers he could remember to tell God; "She pulled up an onion in her garden," he said, "and gave it to a beggar woman." And God said, "You take that onion then, hold it out to her in the lake, let her take hold of it, and if you can pull her out of the lake, let her come to paradise, but if the onion breaks, then the woman must stay where she is." The angel ran to the woman, and he held out the onion to her; "Come," he said, "catch hold and I'll pull you out!" And he began cautiously pulling her out. He had just pulled her right out, when other sinners in the lake, seeing she was being drawn out, began catching hold of her so as to be pulled out with her. But she was a very wicked woman, and she began kicking them. "I am to be pulled out, not you. It's my onion, not yours!" As soon as she said that the onion broke. And the woman fell into the lake, and she is burning there until this day.[13]

Grushenka concludes saying, "So that's the story Alyosha; I know it by heart, for *I am that wicked woman.*" However, her interpretation of this story as well as her interpretation of herself is about to change.

Alyosha turns Grushenka's interpretation on its head. *He recognized that he himself had been in that lake of fire, and Grushenka, his guardian angel, had pulled him out with an onion.* As Robin Feuer Miller observes,

---

12. Morson, *Onions*, 796.
13. Dostoevsky, *Brothers*, 303.

this fable, which initially functions as the last word for Grushenka, gets turned around. Observing this literary fact, Miller next reveals something of vital importance for the art of preaching when she asks, "What turns this folktale, this fable into a parable?" Alyosha has made a shift in interpretation. He did this in an instant by transforming the story from an *allegory* of Grushenka's doom into a *parable* of redemption and hope.

> The (new) emphasis shifts to memory and to the potentially great redemptive force of even a single good deed. No matter that the old woman's good deed was not enough to save her. That crucial fact is forgotten by all as Dostoevsky, with one of his typically crafty novelistic sleights-of-hand, and at the same time inspired by his potent Orthodox Christian belief, makes his characters, his readers, and perhaps himself imagine, perhaps only momentarily, that, even in the face of this contrary example, the redemptive force of the onion in each of our pasts will be enough to bring about both the salvation of the individual and the Kingdom of God.[14]

This "redemptive force of the onion" of which Miller speaks happens whenever a parabolic interpretation of a story or text occurs. Furthermore, all parabolic interpretations create a future for people (or groups) who, before the parabolic interpretation, thought they were in complete bondage to biological, sociological, psychological, technological, political, or religious necessities. When Grushenka hears how Alyosha has interpreted her story as a parable, she realizes that her perceived eternal destiny in "the lake of fire" is no longer a forgone conclusion! There are other possibilities, and, with some hesitation, she begins ordering her life in accord with these life-giving possibilities rather than the death-dealing religious necessities that her previous interpretation imposed.

At the very moment Grushenka's fable becomes a parable, a new relationship emerges and matures between Grushenka and Alyosha (and soon between Grushenka and Dmitri). This new relationship fractures their death-dealing, self-imposed dysfunction. Moreover, it is now quite difficult to determine who is giving an onion to whom (or perhaps who is ministering to whom). They seem to be caught up in a matrix of grace. Grushenka gives an onion to Alyosha when she refuses to seduce him as she had planned. Alyosha gave an onion to Grushenka when he told her that she was his sister. Grushenka gives an onion to Alyosha when she tells him the story of the onion. Alyosha gives an onion to Grushenka

---

14. Miller, *Dostoevsky's Unfinished Journey*, 84.

when he interprets her story as a parable of grace instead of an allegory about her eternal damnation.

At one point, Grushenka comes close to upsetting this new relationship when she asks Alyosha if she should forgive her former lover. In other words, she wants Alyosha to make her decision for her. Alyosha, however, does not tell her what to do. (Doing so would have re-established the illusion of superiority over her that she had once resented). Instead, he merely tells her, "You have forgiven him already."

The questions she must now answer, and answer for herself, are will she continue to forgive? Will she remember the onion?[15] Will she recognize the fact that she has herself been both an agent and a recipient of grace? Will forgiveness inform her future decisions? Will her future be open to new possibilities, or will her future once again be closed? She must always remember instances of grace such as this. Remembering the onions that she has given and received will make it more likely that her life will be open to new possibilities; that she will be free, and that she will practice the art of ministry herself.

The Transforming Power of Parabolic Interpretation

When a story is interpreted as a parable, it becomes a word of freedom to listeners who believed themselves to be in complete bondage to natural, biological, social, moral, psychological, technological, or religious necessities before they heard the story as parable. In other words, parables are life-giving phenomena that open the future and release us from bondage.

A Parenthesis on Parables and Preaching

Since the art of ministry is our concern, it is important to discuss parables. In her interpretation of "parable of the onion," Grushenka appears to think that her story can have only one moral or one true meaning. This meaning, she believed, was that she is was the woman condemned to the pit of fire and torment. The last word has been spoken about her fate. Nothing more can be said.

But, as it turns out, she is mistaken about her fate. She is mistaken because she makes an error in her interpretation. She interprets her story as an allegory instead of the parable. She is not alone in her hermeneutical

---

15. Morson, *Onions*, 793.

error. This is a common mistake made by many preachers and teachers of preachers who think that parables teach one explicit moral teaching when, in fact, parables are open ended. They often express paradox or an irresolvable duality. In fact, if a story forces those who hear it to reach moral or doctrinal closure, the story is not a parable or at least it is not being interpreted as a parable.

How a story is interpreted makes it a parable. If an interpretation closes the future of those who hear it, the story is not a parable. If it opens the future to new possibilities, it is. The same exact story can be interpreted in such a way that the future is closed, or it can be interpreted parabolically so that the future is open. The same exact story can be interpreted in such a way that the listeners can be freed from bondage, or it can be interpreted in such a way that listeners are placed in bondage. The same story can be interpreted in a way that it imparts death or gives life. Grushenka's interpretation closed her future. Her interpretation kept her in bondage. She was not free until Alyosha helped her interpret the same exact story in a way that opened her future.[16] Moreover, in the context of *The Brothers Karamazov*, the moment she hears her story interpreted as a parable is the precise moment that she begins to intentionally practice the art of ministry.

This is also the way that pastoral counseling can work. As Alyosha never denied the facts of Grushenka's story, a counselor normally does not deny the facts that the person in need of help expresses. Instead, like Alyosha did with Grushenka, the pastoral counselor tries to reinterpret the facts of the person's life-story in such a way that the interpretation opens the future and releases the person from bondage. Reinterpretations such as these are not limited to one-on-one counseling sessions. They can extend to the narratives that surround families or even large social organizations. Indeed, so long as these reinterpretations do not deny the facts, they can have life-giving consequences on a national or even a global level.

Unfortunately, we seldom interpret our biblical stories as parables even when it is expressly stated that they are parables. This has had dire, long lasting, even death-dealing consequences. The Parable of the Tenants demonstrates this contention. (It is also an important parable to discuss in preparation for a discussion of Dostoevsky's antisemitism and, by association, Christianity's antisemitism in chapters 7 and 8).

---

16. Miller, *Dostoevsky's Unfinished Journey*, 81–90.

> A man planted a vineyard, put a fence around it, dug a pit for the wine press, and built a watchtower; then he leased it to tenants and went to another country. When the season came, he sent a slave to the tenants to collect from them his share of the produce of the vineyard. But they seized him, and beat him, and sent him away empty-handed. And again he sent another slave to them; this one they beat over the head and insulted. Then he sent another, and that one they killed. And so it was with many others; some they beat, and others the killed. He had still one other, a beloved son. Finally, he sent him to them saying, 'They will respect my son.' But those tenants said to one another, 'This is the heir; come, let us kill him, and the inheritance will be ours.' So they seized him, killed him, and threw him out of the vineyard. (Mark 12:1–8)

Christians always interpret this story allegorically. In an allegory the persons, places and things in the story directly correspond to persons, places, and things in "real life." Once these direct correspondences between story and reality are made, allegories demand some inescapable conclusions that close our minds to alternative possibilities.

Most Christians know the allegorical interpretation of this story. It is simple, clear-cut, and universal once the persons, places and things in the story find their corresponding counterparts. This we have done. We probably made this allegorical interpretation in the mid-first century, and it has stuck! The owner of the vineyard is God. The vineyard represents the covenant between God and Israel. The tenants are the Jews. The slaves sent by the owner are the prophets. The son who is sent by the owner and executed by the tenants is Jesus, and the new tenants who replace the old tenants mentioned in the verses immediately following the quotation above (Mark 12:9–11) are the Christians.

Interpreted as an allegory this story reflects the emerging ideology of first century Christians regarding their Jewish brothers and sisters. They believed (as most Christians still do largely because we continue to interpret this story as an allegory) that God had a covenant with the Jews who repeatedly violated the covenant. Because God is merciful, God sent numerous prophets to get the Jews to keep their covenant with God. Finally, God had had enough, and God sent Jesus who the Jews killed. Consequently, the covenant once given to the Jews has been transferred to the Christians who understand themselves as the new Israel.

Allegorical interpretations leave nothing to the imagination. Once the connection has been made between the characters in the story and people and events in "real life," nothing more can be said. Indeed, insofar as the relationship between Christianity and Judaism is concerned, nothing more was ever said, and the Christian Church has yet to overcome the antisemitism that enabled a supreme evil like the Holocaust to occur. It might sound strange but had Christians always interpreted this story as a parable and not an allegory, there is a good chance that the Holocaust might not have happened! So much for the innocuous status most of us think literature and stories deserve.

Interpreting this story as a parable yields much different results. What follows is only one possibility. As we know, our allegorical interpretation has equated the owner of the vineyard with God! If, however, the owner of the vineyard is just a guy who planted a vineyard and left town, we no longer assume that the owner of the vineyard has divine attributes like omniscience. If the owner of the vineyard is not "all knowing" like we think God is, we are free to examine his actions more critically. When we do, we encounter the inescapable fact of this guy's absolute stupidity—a stupidity that borders on insanity. He sends a slave to collect the rent. The slave gets beaten and sent back. So, like the intellectual giant this guy seems to be, the owner sends another slave and gets similar results. The owner then appears to reason that if sending slaves does not work, the wise thing to do is to send more slaves! He does so, and "surprisingly" some slaves are beaten, and others are killed. After these failures, the owner changes his policy. His brilliant mind leads him to the conclusion that instead of sending his slaves he will send "his beloved son." What, after all, could possibly happen?

Interpreting this story as an allegory that justifies and reinforces Christian antisemitism prevents Christians from seeing just how stupid his new plan is because we wrongly assume that the owner represents an all-knowing God. Freed from our bondage to allegorical interpretations, however, we now find nothing in the story that would lead a person of even average intelligence or marginal mental health to believe his son would be treated well. As a matter of fact, everything indicates that the owner of the vineyard places his son in grave danger. Nonetheless, in his infinite wisdom, the owner sends his son, and the scene shifts to the tenants.

The reasoning processes of the tenants—who are not the Jews, but tenant farmers—also leaves much to be desired. Even though there is nearly no reason to think so, these people have unanimously concluded that they will inherit the vineyard if they kill the landlord's son (who is not Jesus but just the landlord's son). Their reasoning process reminds us that people can believe just about anything when they cut themselves off from the rest of the world. This can happen in small groups that isolate themselves, but it happens in large groups like political parties. It even happens within religions when one group of believers believes another group is worthy of death because they have slightly different doctrines. It happens in entire nations that convince themselves that building more and more armaments is the path to peace. Many cases of the reasoning processes of people and groups mimic that of the tenants. There is hardly an absurdity that if repeated often enough will not be believed and acted upon by one group or another.

Understanding this story as a parable raises a variety of questions, but I am pursuing only one line of inquiry here, namely, "Why does everyone in the parable seem to be so stupid?" In this story, it is not just the tenants and landlord who exhibit serious mental defects, but, with the possible exception of the first slave, all the slaves sent to collect the rent do not appear to have "all their oars in the water," and, the son proves that "the apple does not fall too far from the tree" when he too goes to collect the rent at his father's instruction. There is, however, at least one constant in the story that may shed some light on the mental deficiencies of the characters. That constant is the vineyard itself.

Remember, the vineyard is not the covenant with Israel. It is not the land of Israel. It is just a vineyard. Whatever else this vineyard is, it is an agricultural business, and everyone associated with this enterprise cannot think straight. The construction of the vineyard itself contributes to everyone's thinking process. It has a fence around it. The fence is designed to protect the crop from being harmed by animals and "foreign" human beings. The fence, therefore, demonstrates the existence of an adversarial relationship between anything in nature or human society that might damage or steal the crop. This implies that those behind the fence are likely to view both people and nature as potential enemies. Rather than being a part of nature or in community with other human beings, the vineyard makes us view the outside as alien. The building of a watchtower admits such fears because it enables the inhabitants of the vineyard to see enemies coming from afar and prepare a defense.[17]

Understanding this story as a parable leads us to discussions that are diametrically opposed to the conclusion Christians have reached about the Jews in the last 2000 years. Fences have been built between

---

17. Gustafson, *Biblical Amnesia*, 87–94.

Christianity and Judaism, Islam and Christianity, Islam and Judaism, Islam and Hinduism, Christianity and Islam, *et cetera*. Behind these fences people can more easily develop and implement uninformed decisions about each other. Interpreted as a parable, however, this story explains how this isolation can have death-dealing consequences. As an allegory, this story has caused, justified, and perpetuated almost 2000 years of Christian inhuman treatment of Jewish people. The same exact story has a different message if interpreted as a parable. At the very least a parabolic interpretation would not have justified antisemitism. Beyond this, the story interpreted as parable has the potential be a life-giving force. Remembering the life-giving potential of interpreting a story as a parable rather than an allegory, folktale, or fable, we can now return to other transformations about to occur in *The Brothers Karamazov*.

Alyosha's Final Conversion to the Ministry of Active Love

Having experienced the power of a parable to transform human relationships, both Grushenka and Alyosha depart. Grushenka goes to Mokroe where she is to encounter her forgiven, former love, and Alyosha returns to the monastery. He is exhausted. He is still grieving. He lays down beside Zosima's coffin and falls asleep. In his dreams he faintly hears Father Paissy read "The Wedding at Cana of Galilee" (John 2:1–11).

In the Gospel of John, Jesus' public ministry begins at The Wedding at Cana when His mother Mary tells Him, "They are out of wine." The party—a wedding feast that could last for days—was in jeopardy. Mary knows that Jesus can do something about it and tells Him, "They are out of wine." Apparently, Jesus knows that His life will change if He acts to save the party. He will become a celebrity and no longer able to go about incognito. So, Jesus responds, "Woman, what concern is that to you and to me? My hour has not yet come" (John 2:4). The phrase "my hour has not yet come" indicates that Jesus knows that saving the party (and the reputation of its hosts) will put Him much closer to the time when His hour *does* come. Nonetheless, Jesus, with the help of some servants, performs a miracle that saves the party. He changes about 150 gallons of water into wine—really fine wine at that.

There is much more that can be said about this passage, but for now we must remember that the Wedding Feast at Cana is read while

Alyosha dreams. As he dreams, Alyosha finds himself among the guests at this wedding party. Zosima is there as well, and he tells Alyosha that they, along with the myriad of guests present at the feast, are all present because each person has given only an onion, a little onion: "for what after all are all of our deeds anyway but an onion." Zosima then says to Alyosha, "And you my gentle one, you, my kind boy, you too have known how to give a famished woman an onion today. Begin your work, dear one, begin it, gentle one."[18]

This dream leads Alyosha to repentance and toward his growth in the art of ministry. Probably for the first time, Alyosha understands that he needs to repent of a religion of glory which had led to his depression regarding the saintly Zosima's corruption "in excess of nature." Alyosha begins to understand that faith must be expressed in small everyday acts of active love. Alyosha's dream reveals that even though Jesus may have come to earth to perform a great and glorious deed, He did not forsake the ordinary joys of ordinary people in their celebration of life's joyous events. Indeed, Jesus saved the party! Alyosha realized that Jesus accepts the inadequate and elementary hospitality of the poor, and Jesus even intensifies the joy inherent in their celebration. Jesus may have come to earth for the glorious act of redeeming fallen humanity, but this did not make Him an enemy of human warmth and companionship.[19]

Alyosha wakes up from his dream and goes outside where he is overwhelmed by the universe in all its glory. Following the injunctions of his teacher, he falls face down and embraces the earth. He feels connected with all of God's creation. He longs to forgive everyone and to ask to be forgiven by all.

> But with every instant he felt clearly and (...) tangibly, that something firm and unshakable as that vault of heaven had entered into his soul. It was as though some idea had seized the sovereignty of his mind—and it was for all of his life and forever and ever. He had fallen on the earth a weak youth, but he rose up a resolute champion, and he knew and felt it suddenly at the very moment of his ecstasy. And never, never, all his life long could Alyosha forget that minute. Someone visited my soul in that hour," he used to say afterwards, with implicit faith in his words.[20]

---

18. Dostoevsky, *Brothers*, 311.
19. R. Williams, *Dostoevsky*, 35.
20. Dostoevsky, *Brothers*, 312.

Alyosha, who at the beginning of this day had told Ratikin that he was not in rebellion against God but rejected God's world, now embraces the earth itself. He embraces God's world. His mind has been changed. He has repented. He understands that all things are connected, and we are responsible for all as Zosima had always said. Three days later, fortified by this new vision of Jesus, Christianity, life, and the art of ministry, Alyosha left the monastery for the last time in accord with the wishes of his mentor the Elder Zosima.

Dmitri's Conversion to the Religion of Active Love

Around the time that Alyosha and Grushenka had given each other "onions," Dmitri Karamazov was engaged in a comic quest to acquire 3000 rubles to repay a debt owed to Katerina Ivanovna Svetlova with whom he had a complicated, quite dysfunctional, love/hate relationship. Following this unsuccessful quest, Dmitri, at rock bottom, returns to his father's house. He returns to kill his father because he believes, not without evidence, that Fyodor Karamazov has romantic designs on Grushenka the woman Dmitri truly loves. Dmitri has reason to believe that Grushenka and his father will have a romantic encounter very soon. So, unobserved, and with patricide on his mind, Dmitri sneaks onto the property. He sees his father at the window. Fear and hate engulf him, but he cannot tell if Grushenka is there. Informed earlier by Smerdyakov of a special knock he was supposed to use to signal Grushenka's arrival, Dmitri uses that knock.

His father comes to the window. Dmitri's hatred rises. He is ready with pestle in hand to kill his father, but when Fyodor comes to the window Dmitri realizes that if the elder Karamazov was now at the window searching for Grushenka, she was not there. So, despite the hate rising from within, Dmitri does not kill his father. Instead, he sets off for Grushenka's house. Unfortunately, his undetected escape from the premises is thwarted by the household servant, Grigory, Smerdyakov's adopted father, as well as the person who, because of his own father's neglect, had also helped raise Dmitri himself.[21]

Grigory reached the fence just as Dmitri attempted to climb over it and escape the premises. He grabbed Dmitri and clutched his leg. His cry, "Parricide!" echoed throughout the neighborhood until, in his attempt to thwart Dmitri's escape, Grigory fell and cracked his head on the ground.

21. Dostoevsky, *Brothers*, 334–37.

Dmitri jumped down. He threw his pestle on the grass and tried to determine if Grigory was dead or alive. Unable to ascertain this, Dmitri left Grigory for dead and continued to Grushenka's house. On the way, he is seen running through town with blood on his hands, but it is Grigory's blood and not his father's.

We must briefly pause our account of this fateful evening to recognize that everything in Dmitri's life—his lustful passions, his undisciplined nature, his hatred of his father, his immaturity, the beliefs he held about his father being a rival for Grushenka, the decisions he was making that very evening (secretly going to his father's house, carrying a weapon, etc.), and his intention to murder his father—would lead anyone "in their right minds" to conclude that Dmitri killed his father when Fyodor Karamazov was found murdered that night. But Dmitri does not kill his father. He does not commit parricide as Grigory had mistakenly shouted. In other words, in a context in which the psychological, emotional, and sociological necessities afflicting Dmitri should have led him to kill his father, Dmitri chose life instead. This is a profound indication that, at least as far as Dostoevsky is concerned, any person, with any background, in any situation no matter how dire, can choose life over death.

How this choice of life manifests itself depends on the context and the character of the individual making the choice. Alyosha, for example, would never have had to choose to murder his father because his character, demeanor, and training would have prevented him from being at his father's house contemplating the act. Dmitri, however, is different. His character was consistent with him waiting for the opportunity to kill his father, yet, even in this context—a context created by his own character and foibles—Dmitri expresses the freedom to choose life instead of death. In Dmitri we can see that there is no necessity that an act of active love cannot overcome. Resisting necessities is seldom likely, but it is, in Dostoevsky's view, always possible.

When Dmitri arrives at Grushenka's house, he is informed that Grushenka had left for Mokroe to see her former love. Hearing this, Dmitri resolves to see her one last time if only to publicly step aside. He consciously meant no harm to Grushenka and her former lover, but the same cannot be said for intending to harm himself. He ponders suicide after stepping aside.[22]

---

22. Dostoevsky, *Brothers*, 337–38.

Dmitri hires a coach driven by a very wise peasant Andrey who acts as Dmitry's confessor on the twelve mile trip to Mokroe.[23] The conversation begins with Dmitri expressing his fear that when he arrives Grushenka might already be asleep and in the arms of her lover. He gets quite agitated at this thought, but Andrey assures him that they are likely to be awake because Dmitri is only about an hour and a half behind. Andrey, who will demonstrate that the art of ministry can be mastered by anyone despite his or her station in life, now pushes the conversation to another level.

He expresses his concern that in transporting Dmitri to Mokroe, he might be serving as an accomplice to murder. From the perspective of ministry, this is a difficult but artistic move. Rather than a direct question, Andrey takes a less threatening route. He expresses his feeling, namely, fear. If, for example, Andrey had asked, "You're not going to involve me in murder, are you?" Dmitri might become defensive, lie or just be unresponsive. The same thought expressed as Andrey's feeling, however, led Dmitri to assuage Andrey's fears. He assures Andrey that there will be no murder. Taking Andrey by the shoulder, Dmitri says that he intends to punish himself by committing suicide. He then asks his coachman, "Andrey, simple soul, will Dmitri Fyodorovich Karamazov go to hell or not. What do you think?"[24]

Andrey's response is threefold. First, he says that he does not know the answer to this question because it depends on Dmitri who is free to take this path to hell or not. This response indicates that Andrey himself is a master of the art of ministry, for, a "Yes" or "No" response would have ended the conversation. Answering "Yes" surely would have closed the future of the relationship between the two men. One of the first things a practitioner of the art of ministry must accomplish is to refrain from saying the last word. The conversation must be ongoing rather than truncated by a dogmatic statement like a simple "Yes" or "No."

Second, Andrey reminds Dmitri of a basic belief they both share, namely, that Christ's death, descent into hell and His resurrection frees "all" sinners who are infernally tormented in hell. Andrey does not say so but he, like every Christian, cannot answer Dmitri's question because God's grace means that no one can possibly know the ultimate status of even the most grievous sinner or glorious saint. A practitioner of the art of ministry must keep in mind that God's grace means no human being

---

23. Contino, *Dostoevsky's Incarnational Realism*, 117–18.
24. Dostoevsky, *Brothers*, 352.

can say the final word about the eternal destiny of anyone. Since we cannot know, we can never speak the ultimate "No." Only God can do this. Only God can determine if there is a limit to grace and love.

Third, Andrey distinguishes Dmitri from the proud and mighty who are in hell "until Christ comes again" (not forever but until Christ comes again) when he says that Andrey and his people think of Dmitri as a little child. This too might give Dmitri some hope because children are not deemed as culpable for their crimes and misdemeanors as are adults. In the language of heaven and hell, this might mean that an act that sends the proud and mighty to hell might not do the same if done by a child. Here too, Andrey gives Dmitri hope. As far as Andrey is concerned, Dmitri's fate is not settled. For a variety of reasons Dmitri's future remains open even if he commits suicide.

Andrey has turned his carriage into a confessional, and while this confessional has not persuaded Dmitri to refrain from suicide, it has given him some hope that even if he commits suicide there still might be some hope that he can avoid hell.[25] As they come into the town of Mokroe, Dmitri prays this prayer.

> Lord, receive me, with all my lawlessness, and do not condemn me. Let me pass by thy judgment (. . .) do not condemn me, for I have condemned myself, do not condemn me, for I love Thee, O Lord. I am a wretch, but I love Thee. If Thou sendest me to hell, I shall love Thee there, and from there I shall cry out that I love Thee forever and ever (. . .) But let me love to the end (. . .) Here and now for just five hours (. . .) till the first ardent ray of Thy day (. . .) for I love the queen of my soul (. . .) I love her and I cannot help loving her. Thou seest my whole heart (. . .) I shall gallop up. I shall fall before her and say, "You are right to pass on and leave me. Farewell and forget your victim (. . .) never fret yourself about me.[26]

Dmitri's prayer does not exactly prepare him for what is in store for him because shortly after his arrival in Mokroe, he experiences the miraculous. Grushenka has come to realize her love for him, and they vow to begin their lives together. Perhaps, sometimes, prayers work in ways beyond expectation. Who knows?

---

25. Contino, *Dostoevsky's Incarnational Realism*, 188.
26. Dostoevsky, *Brothers*, 352.

There Is Always Hope

Dmitri Karamazov's character is not of the sort that one might want to emulate, but he demonstrates that no matter one's character or circumstance a person can resist the death-dealing consequences of any necessity. Such resistance is an act of Christian freedom that serves life in the midst of necessities that try to enslave or destroy us. Had Dmitri been thoroughly determined by the necessities governing his life, he would have killed his father. He did not. He chose to be free. He chose life.

Prayer and Confession as Acts of Christian Freedom

It is difficult to proceed with Dostoevsky's narrative without some reflection on the significance of prayer in ministry. We see subtle acknowledgement of prayer's significance at crucial points throughout *The Brothers Karamazov*. Alyosha often offers a short prayer before proceeding to what he knows will be a difficult encounter. Grushenka crosses herself and leaps from Alyosha's knee after told of Zosima's death. Now Dmitri prays before what he perceives as a closed future that might result in his suicide. Here we see that prayer can be an expression of freedom in the face of necessity. In this case, Dmitri's prayer expresses such freedom because in the act of praying Dmitri acknowledges his inability to control his situation as well as his dependence on the grace of God. Dmitri's prayer expresses his faith that God's grace which can create new, unforeseen possibilities can overturn what appears to be an inevitable, and closed future.

Prayer's relationship to freedom is exposed in this scene because Dmitri's prayer is a prayer of a person "who stands naked before God with nothing in his hands."[27] A prayer like Dmitri's is a prayer of freedom because nothing is held back, and nothing other than dependence on God is asserted. He recognizes that he is not a righteous person in a world where religious necessities often demand that only the righteous ones can successfully pray to God.

Like Dmitri's prayer, many prayers are acts of Christian freedom in the sense that they ask God to violate one necessity or another in response to the prayer. A prayer for healing, for example, asks God to circumvent the natural or biological necessities that create disease and

---

27. Ellul, *Ethics of Freedom*, 126–27.

the natural progression of a disease. Prayers that the nations of the world act justly ask God to violate political necessities that compel every nation to oppose justice if justice conflicts with the necessity to universalize a nation's power. Dmitri's prayer is made despite the religious necessities that often demand that only the prayers of the righteous will be answered (for no one, not even Dmitri himself, would call Dmitri righteous). A person who prays recognizes, perhaps only in an unspoken way, that the necessities of nature, religion, society, psychology, and politics are neither universal nor absolute. Prayer is an act of hope that God can free us even from the strongest of necessities (even the biological necessity of death) that enslave us.

Dmitri prays for forgiveness—even forgiveness for the unforgivable act of suicide he thinks he is going to commit. Forgiveness can only be requested. It can never be demanded or deserved. The one who, like Dmitri, asks for forgiveness without giving reasons why he or she should be forgiven comes before God "with nothing in his hands." The one who prays for forgiveness is praying for something life-giving in the face of one death-dealing necessity or another. The one who, like Dmitri, prays for the capacity to love realizes that true love is beyond his reach and depends on an external power. In short, Dmitri's prayer is an act of Christian freedom, and this act of freedom supports him in his ongoing affliction; for, Dmitri, like Alyosha, undergoes affliction here. What is happening to Dmitri might also be "the foundation of the foundation, the beginning of the beginning (. . .) of all that is good and beautiful."[28]

The ensuing scene could be interpreted as the power of prayer to change the world and make the impossible possible. Even though Dmitri had not prayed for Grushenka to change her mind and declare her love for him, this happens! Nonetheless, their joy is short lived. Officials have followed Dmitri to Mokroe. He had left a trail of evidence leading directly from Fyodor Karamazov's murdered body to Dmitri himself. They tell Dmitri that he is wanted for murder, and Dmitri responds, "I un-der-stand." But he thinks he "un-der-stands" because he believed he was being arrested for Grigory's murder. Until now he did not even know his father had been murdered. The officials, on the other hand, think that when Dmitri said, "I un-der-stand," it is a confession of his guilt and one more piece of incriminating evidence against him.

---

28. Cairns, *The End of Suffering*, 19.

But even as he is interrogated, Dmitri undergoes a decisive moral and spiritual transformation that may also be an answer to his prayer. According to Joseph Frank, Dostoevsky suggests a further transformation of Dmitri's spirituality with the title chapters that encompass Dmitri's interrogation. Book VIII, chapter 3, is titled "The Soul's Journey through Torments: First Torment," and chapters 4 and 5 are simply titled "The Second Torment," and "The Third Torment." These titles reflect the Orthodox teaching that as the soul ascends to heaven, it is subject to a period of torments by various evil spirits.

Dostoevsky has secularized these torments in Dmitri's interrogation, but Dmitri clearly is tormented, and afflicted just as his brother Alyosha was afflicted by the circumstances surrounding Zosima's death. Under the questioning of the police, prosecutors and other officials, Dmitri begins a process of self-scrutiny and self-understanding that would eventually lead to Dmitri's metamorphosis. He admits, for example, that he himself is not very beautiful and concludes from this that he did not have the right to even consider his father repulsive.[29]

Finally, worn down by the overwhelming evidence of his guilt, being treated by his interrogators as a vile and despicable human being, and possibly in doubt of Grushenka's expressed love, a fatigued and disheartened Dmitri asks to say something to Grushenka in the presence of his interrogators. He stands and says, "'Agrafena Alexandrovna have faith in God and me. I am not guilty of my father's murder.' At this, Grushenka stood up, *crossed herself before an icon* and said, 'Thanks be to Thee, O Lord,' (. . .) she said in a voice thrilled with emotion, and still standing, she turned to Nikolay Parfenovich (one of Dmitri's interrogators) and added, 'As he has spoken now, believe it! I know him. He'll say anything as a joke or from obstinacy, but he'll never deceive you against his conscience. He's telling the truth. You may believe it.' 'Thanks, Agrafena Alexandrovna, you've given me courage,'" (Dmitri replies).[30] The officials allowed Grushenka to leave. Dmitri, looking calm and more cheerful, was soon overcome with fatigue. He laid down on a large chest and immediately fell asleep.

As Alyosha, who perhaps at this very moment dreams about the Wedding Feast at Cana, Dmitri dreams as well. He dreamed he was somewhere in the Russian steppes on a cold November night in a carriage

---

29. Frank, *Dostoevsky*, 890–91.
30. Dostoevsky, *Brothers*, 427.

being driven by a middle-aged peasant. They came upon a village with half its huts destroyed by fire. On the outskirts of the town, they encountered many emaciated peasant women. One woman held a crying baby that could not be comforted.

> "Why are they crying? Why are they crying?" Dmitri asked as they sped by.
> "It's the babe," answered the driver, "the babe is crying."
> (. . .) "But why is he weeping?" Dmitri persisted stupidly, "Why are its little arms bare? Why don't they wrap it up?"
> "The babe's cold, its little clothes are frozen, and don't warm it."
> "But why is it? Why?" stupid Dmitri persisted."
> "Why, they're poor people, burned out. They've no bread. They're begging because they are burned out."
> "No, no," Dmitri, as it were, still did not understand, "Tell me: *why* it is those poor mothers stand there, *why* are these people poor, *why* is the babe poor, *why* is the steppe barren, *why* don't they hug each other and kiss, *why* don't they sing songs of joy, *why* are they so dark from black misery, *why* don't they feed the babe?"[31]

The reader will recall that when Ivan confronted Alyosha with the unjust and unmerited suffering of children in a world created by the all-powerful and loving God, Ivan "refused his ticket" and rejected God's world. Rejecting God in this way, Ivan plunged himself into the ravages of nihilism which would result in his mental illness that would undermine his testimony that Smerdyakov, not Dmitri, had murdered Fyodor Karamazov. Dmitri's response to suffering children is different. Unlike his brother Dmitri persistently asks "Why. Why is it that those poor mothers stand there? Why are they poor? Why is the babe poor?"

Dmitri asks, "Why?" when confronted with evil, and this question incites Dmitri to action. It begins his ministry. *He wants to do something for everyone so that the babe and the mother will weep no more and so that no one will shed tears.* In contrast to Ivan, Dmitri does not understand the existence of evil to be an intellectual problem that is "resolved" by reason. Evil is an ethical problem instead, and ministry alone addresses the ethical problem of evil. But, in Dmitri's typical "Karamazov" recklessness, he wants all that needs to happen to happen immediately.

---

31. Dostoevsky, *Brothers*, 428. Emphasis mine.

Still dreaming, Dmitri's resolve for this nearly impossible task was strengthened by Grushenka's tender voice, "And I am coming with you. I won't leave you now for the rest of my life." Awakening, he sees his interrogator, Nikolay Perforovich, standing over him suggesting he should hear and sign the deposition they had prepared, but Dmitri's only question is "Who put that pillow under my head? Who was so kind?" An unknown person had extended Dmitri "an onion." His entire soul quivered with tears. He signed the disposition and was led to the carriage that would take him back to the scene of his alleged crime.[32]

As he climbs aboard Dmitri expresses his new self-understanding prompted by his interrogation, dream, and by Grushenka's new expression of love.

> Gentlemen, we're all cruel, we are all monsters, we make all men weep, and mothers and babes at the breast, but of all, let it be settled here, now, of all I am the lowest viper! I've sworn to amend every day of my life, beating my breast, and every day I've done the same filthy things. I understand now that such men as I need a blow, a blow of destiny to catch them as with a noose and bind them by a force from without. Never, never could I have risen by myself! But the thunderbolt has fallen. I accept the torment of accusation, and my public shame, I want to suffer and by suffering be purified. Perhaps I shall be purified, gentlemen what? But listen, for the last time, I am not guilty of my father's blood. I accept my punishment not because I killed him, but because I meant to kill him, and perhaps I really might have killed him. Still, I mean to fight it out with you, I warn you of that. I'll fight it out with you to the end, and then God will decide.[33]

These words are Dmitri's public confession before God and his audience. When a person like Dmitri makes a true confession—a confession that is not designed for the ultimate approval of God or other human beings, but to merely confess—his utterance is factually accurate as far as the one confessing is concerned. In Dimitri's view, he is, in fact, one of the lowest of vipers that make up the human race. He wanted to kill his father but did not kill him. He wants to suffer because he thinks that in his case at least his suffering might purify him. He confesses even though he also knows that his audience might not understand or even believe his words.

---

32. Dostoevsky, *Brothers*, 428–29.
33. Dostoevsky, *Brothers*, 429.

Paradoxically, however, a true confession like Dmitri's makes a new person of the one who confesses. While this is a process and might take time, Dmitri must come to understand things in such a way that he owns his acts. He must abandon his vanities and self-absorption. He must reorient his life away from himself toward God by a divinely instituted process the Gospels call *metanoia*. This process, as Dmitri admits, cannot be accomplished alone. An external thunderbolt like Dmitri's interrogation or an underserved but received expression of faith and love like Grushenka's pledge can be the external force that leads to a true confession. In any case, a true confession can, if remembered and consistently acted upon, enable a person to accept consolation, forgive others, and accept the love and forgiveness from others as well as from God. True confession can be the beginning of a new life. It is an act of freedom that is necessary for his new life to begin.[34]

---

34. Tilley, *Evils of Theodicy*, 198–201.

6

Alyosha and Dmitri's Transgressions

God's call to Abraham is also a call to transgress. Abraham's transgressions begin when, because of God's promise, he leaves Ur and crosses the Euphrates. This act gives his descendants the name "Iurium" (Hebrew) which means those who cross over.

—Jacques Ellul, *The Ethics of Freedom*[1]

MONTHS LATER AND SHORTLY before his trial, Dmitri is still experiencing the affliction which began on the night of his arrest. He is, however, well on the road to making this affliction "the foundation of the foundation and the beginning of the beginning" of all that is good and beautiful. He understands that, in *his* case, his suffering is a product of God's grace. He reports to Alyosha that he is now a new man.

In accord with Zosima's contention that a person is responsible to all, for all and for everyone, Dmitri tells Alyosha that he wants to embody his newly found responsibility for all people by suffering for others. What haunts him, however, is the fear "the new man" he has become will leave him if he faces the many trials and tribulations that he is sure to

---

1. Ellul, *Ethics of Freedom*, 347.

experience in prison. Yet, Dmitri hopes he will find another convict and revive his frozen heart even in the mines of Siberia. "It is for the babe I'm going. Because we are responsible for all. For all those 'babes' for there are big children as well as little children, All are 'babes.' I go for all for somebody must go for all. I didn't kill father, but I've got to accept it."[2]

Still fearful that the "new man" will leave him if he is convicted and goes to prison, Dmitri tells Alyosha a secret. Ivan has arranged for Dmitri and Grushenka's escape to America. Dmitri thinks that he cannot live without Grushenka, and both he and Ivan doubt that the authorities will allow Grushenka to follow Dmitri to Siberia. "And without Grusha what would I do there underground with a hammer? I would only smash my skull with the hammer."

Dmitri asks for Alyosha's advice. On the one hand, he cannot face Siberian captivity without Grushenka, but on the other hand, his conscience tells him that if he rejects the suffering of his Siberian imprisonment, he will be running away from suffering. Since the suffering that awaits him may well be a source of grace that he now experiences, Dmitri faces a dilemma. He trusts Alyosha to decide this for him, but, wisely, he wants Alyosha to put off his decision until after the trial.

Dmitri informs Alyosha that he is troubled because Ivan did not even ask him if he agreed with the plan. Ivan does not even seem to care to know his opinion about his own escape. "He insists terribly. He doesn't ask me but orders me. He doesn't doubt my obeying him, though I have showed him all my heart as I have you."[3] Dmitri then informs Alyosha that Ivan had told him not to tell anybody, particularly Alyosha, because he feared that Alyosha would become his conscience in the matter and persuade Dmitri to reject the plan.

Dmitri does not trust Ivan to make this decision for three reasons. First, Ivan does not believe in God. Consequently, Ivan does not seriously consider Dmitri's contention that an escape might undermine "the new man" he has become. This fear led Dmitri to believe that Ivan was *not listening* to him. Second, since Ivan does not listen to what is important to Dmitri, Ivan *imposes* his decision on Dmitri, and in doing so, Ivan speaks the last word on Dmitri's fate. Finally, Dmitri thinks Ivan does not believe that he is innocent (Neither Ivan not Alyosha has yet heard Smerdyakov's confession that he killed Fyodor Karamazov). Dmitri, however, is

2. Dostoevsky, *Brothers*, 499.
3. Dostoevsky, *Brothers*, 503.

confident that Alyosha can make the decision for him. But Alyosha, in his growing wisdom and mastery of the art of ministry, merely repeats Dmitri's own words, "You're right. It's impossible to decide anything until the trial is over."

Alyosha's First Transgression?

But now the conversation takes an unexpected turn. Dmitri asks Alyosha,

> "Tell me the whole truth, as you would before God. Do you believe I did it? Do you, do you in yourself, believe it? The whole truth, don't lie."
> Everything seemed to heave in front of Alyosha, and he felt something like a stab at his heart.
> "Hush! What do you mean?" he faltered helplessly.
> "The whole truth, the whole, don't lie," repeated Dmitri.
> "I've never for one instant believed that you were the murderer!" broke in a shaking voice from Alyosha's breast, and he raised his right hand in the air, *as though* calling God to witness his words. Dmitri's whole face was lit up with bliss.
> "Thank you (. . .) Now you have given me new life. Would you believe it, till this moment I've been afraid to ask you, you, even you. Well go! You've given me strength for tomorrow. God bless you!"[4]

The narrator of the story proceeds to say that Alyosha leaves tearfully because of Dmitri's lack of confidence in him, and he was overwhelmed by an intense, infinite compassion for his brother and his brother's grief. But as is the case in many of Dostoevsky's novels, it is very possible that the narrator misinterprets Alyosha's feelings and thoughts. Dostoevsky's narrators are often quite wrong about the facts.[5]

Neither narrator nor the author himself is omniscient in Dostoevsky's fiction. This means that there is a good chance, contrary to the narrator's opinion, Alyosha is deliberately lying when he says. "I've never for one instant believed that you were a murderer." When this conversation takes place, Ivan has not yet told Alyosha that Smerdyakov had confessed to the murder, and all Alyosha has to go on is the mound of evidence that has been compiled against his brother. This means that it is possible that Alyosha is lying to Dmitri. Alyosha lying is not inconsistent

---

4. Dostoevsky, *Brothers*, 503–4, emphasis mine.
5. Tunimanov, "The Narrator," 145–75.

with "everything seemed to heave in front of Alyosha" when Dmitri asked him if he thought Dmitri was guilty. Dmitri's question obviously surprised him, and Alyosha did not know what to say. Alyosha bought himself time stammering, "Hush! What do you mean?" Perhaps this time was necessary for Alyosha to decide if he should lie. Only when Dmitri asks again does Alyosha in a shaking voice raise "his right hand in the air *as though* calling God to witness his words" and tell his brother that he has never for one instant thought Dmitri was guilty of murdering their father. The *"as though"* introduces some doubt as to the veracity of Alyosha's assertion.

Frankly, no one can know why Alyosha feels the way he does. He is, after all, a character in a novel who does not have feelings in the first place. But even in the fictional world Dostoevsky has created, Dostoevsky has introduced much ambiguity about what his character is or is not feeling. We must, nevertheless, entertain the notion that Alyosha is lying because the dialogue now occurring between Alyosha and Dmitri takes place in the context of a chapter on transgression. This dialogue between Dmitri and Alyosha begins a decision-making process designed to determine if the Karamazov brothers and their compatriots are going to transgress the law of the land (the law being a legal or political necessity) and help Dmitri escape from the law's judgment. Lying is often a transgression as well. Since lying transgresses the moral, political, or social imperatives to tell the truth, the possibility that Alyosha is transgressing here enables us to explore in more detail the relationship between transgression, freedom, and the art of ministry.

The narrator does not even consider the possibility that Alyosha is lying because, as the narrator mentions, Alyosha is the hero of his story, and if someone is your hero, you tend to tell the hero's story in the most positive way possible.[6] This is done, not by design, but simply because they are your hero. Saying or even expecting that your hero is lying is difficult. Moreover, most people would have the same disposition with respect to Alyosha because he is understood to be a "Holy Man," and conventional wisdom might think that such a man does not lie. In this case lying would be a religious transgression that would, if discovered, severely undermine the perceived character of a spiritual or holy person. Nonetheless, on occasion, a person who is practicing the art of ministry must transgress this limit and lie.

---

6. Dostoevsky, *Brothers*, 21.

Remembering the Apostle Paul's contention that all things, including lying, are lawful. Also remember that, contrary to popular belief, there is no commandment against lying *per se*. The commandment we think opposes all lying just opposes a certain type of lying, namely, bearing false witness against one's neighbor. Alyosha is not bearing false witness against his neighbor. *If* he is lying, Alyosha is lying about what he himself in fact feels or thinks when he is asked if he thinks Dmitri is guilty. On an even deeper level, Alyosha's lie may indicate his growing mastery of the art of ministry.

When a person is engaged in ministry, he or she ministers to a particular person or group. The minister does not minister to a doctrine or embody a moral absolute (as Job's friends mistakenly thought). Ministers often think it best to refrain from expressing their own feelings or thoughts on a particular issue and perhaps *should avoid doing so* even if asked. There are many reasons for such avoidance. In the first place, a mature minister knows from experience that these personal thoughts or feelings, no matter how convinced he or she might be about their veracity, may not be true. Second, the minister knows that her mind has changed on several things in the past, and it might change on this particular issue in the future. Third, and maybe more important, the expression of certain "true" thoughts and feelings at the wrong time might completely undermine one's ability to minister to someone. These "true' thoughts and feelings might be so objectionable that expressing them could close the conversation (and relationship).

While this does not mean a minister should never express her true thoughts and feelings, if their expression is not deemed beneficial or helpful to the life of the community, a minister might decide (because "all things are lawful, but not all things build up") that it is best to transgress the religious or spiritual obligation to be truthful about everything and lie so the relationships are not undermined. If, for example, Alyosha truly believed that Dmitri was guilty of their father's murder and had told Dmitri the truth about how he felt, Dmitri would have been crushed, and Alyosha's ministry to his brother would have been seriously undermined if not destroyed. Lying is a transgression, and sometimes such transgressions are necessary for any ministry to occur in the future. If Alyosha is lying to his brother in this instance, it could reflect the maturing judgment of a Christian to transgress from time to time.

Nonetheless, confusion and uncertainty will always be present when pondering a transgression, and this uncertainty probably cannot be resolved apart from the final judgment of God; for, as has been discussed, "all things are lawful" is difficult to distinguish from Smerdyakov and Ivan's belief that since there is no God "everything is permitted." "Everything is permitted," as used by Ivan and Smerdyakov and the atheistic Russian intelligentsia of Dostoevsky's time, contends that "everything is permitted" because we are all isolated and alone, and there is no God who judges our acts.

In the context of ministry, however, "All things are lawful" means that an action or a transgression is subject to judgment, and until God's ultimate judgment, we will never really know if what we thought was a transgression is a legitimate expression of our Christian freedom or if it is something else. Does this transgression open someone's future, or does it close it. The transgression's suitability as an act of ministry or active love can be debated and judged penultimately by human beings, but they should all know in doing so that God is the ultimate judge of transgression. Before such a judgment is made clear, no last word can be given about a transgression. If Alyosha lied to Dmitri, he chose to transgress a moral norm for the sake of building-up his neighbor, his brother Dmitri, rather than telling the truth to demonstrate his own righteousness. Indeed, if he is crestfallen because he makes a transgression on behalf of his brother, he is dismayed because of the uncertainties that accompany all transgressions.

Transgression as an Act of Christian Freedom

Even if Alyosha is not lying, this discussion of transgression allows us to discuss the nature of a transgression in a less controversial setting than Ivan's proposed transgression to help Dmitri escape the law of the land. Most of us would admit to lying at certain times, but few of us plan a prison break. Both, however, are transgressions. If we were only to talk about planning Dmitri's escape, we would be less likely to understand how certain desperate circumstances might force anyone to contemplate a transgression.

Transgression is an extreme act of freedom because transgressions violate the boundaries imposed by the necessities under which we live. These boundaries are not evil *per se*. In fact, these limits make normal, everyday life possible. These boundaries can even be life-giving. Nonetheless, transgression means passing beyond. On this side of the frontier life as we know it is possible. The other side offers us the unknown. Those who transgress do not know what the future will bring, but, like Abraham, they go elsewhere in the hope (not the knowledge) that life will be better if they transgress the frontier.

Christian freedom itself is quite possible on this side of the frontier. But Christian freedom may not be a visible and explosive act if the frontier is never transgressed. For example, Rosa Parks engaged in an act of transgression when she refused to give up her seat to a white person on a Montgomery Alabama bus. This transgression turned out to be a visible and explosive act of Christian freedom that still has far-reaching social and political consequences in American life. Although her act demonstrates how a transgression can reveal Christian freedom, we should always keep in mind that the outcome of her act was neither certain nor determined. She did not know in advance what would happen. She might have simply been arrested for her transgression. She might have just served her time and paid her fine.[7] Transgressions always involve such uncertainty. They are always a step into the unknown.[8]

When confronted with the real limits imposed by the necessities present in nature, politics, economics, the law, morality, family, health or even death itself, and when these limits undermine the life and freedom of people, a Christian is forced to decide whether to transgress. Since all things are lawful, she can decide to live within the limits that necessities impose. If she chooses this, she still could be choosing freedom (all things are lawful), but she will never be quite certain that she is not supporting or even establishing social necessities, technological constraints, or even organizations that keep people in bondage. On the other hand, she can transgress the boundaries necessities impose for this too is lawful. When she does so, she will pass into a region where outcomes are uncertain. As Rosa Parks transgressed when she refused to obey the Jim Crow law, Dmitri's proposed transgression would also place Dmitri and Grushenka in unknown territory.

The Bible is full of transgressions. It is full of people who cross the limits or boundaries imposed by law, religion, culture, geography,

---

7. Rosa Parks' success was not an individual effort. She was an officer in the NAACP who had attended workshops on nonviolent resistance. Months earlier the Black Women's Political Council made plans to distribute 50,000 notices calling people to boycott the buses should someone do what Rosa Parks did. Hearing about Parks' arrest, they put their plan in motion. The next day, every man, woman, and child in Montgomery knew of the bus boycott. Douglas, *The Nonviolent Coming of God*.

8. Ellul, *The Ethics of Freedom*, 345–55.

politics, morality, family, or nature. The people of Israel find their origins in transgression. When Abraham leaves his home in Ur and crosses the Euphrates, he is transgressing. This act gives his descendants the name "*Iurium*" (Hebrew) which means those who cross over.[9] The Hebrews understood their existence to be the consequence of Abraham's transgression. Other biblical transgressions followed: the Passover, the crossing of the Red Sea, the Good Samaritan's transgression of the social order, the transgression of the Sabbath day religious laws, the transgression of the idea of equal pay for equal work in the parable of the Laborers in the Vineyard, the transgression of the Temple's sanctity in Jesus' Cleansing of the Temple and the transgression of the biological limits of death itself in Jesus' crucifixion and resurrection.

Transgressions Test Christian Freedom

Transgressions are extreme acts of Christian freedom that violate the boundaries necessities impose. The most obvious boundaries that transgressions violate are moral and legal necessities. Transgressions can be explosive acts that have far reaching consequences, but they can be ridiculed or ignored by society at large. Moreover, from any perspective other than God's (a perspective we do not have), it is impossible to determine if an act that claims to be a transgression is an act of Christian freedom or just a stupid thing to do. This is why people who commit transgression never know the outcome of their acts. They do not know where their "leap of faith" will take them.

Dmitri's Planned Transgression

There has been much debate concerning the morality of Dmitri's proposed escape.[10] Generally speaking, however, these debates do not recognize that Dmitri's proposed escape is a transgression—an act of Christian freedom. Any transgression, while debatable, *always* violates one sort of morality or another. Given that Christians freedom means "all things are lawful, but not all things are beneficial," debates concerning this episode should center on whether the proposed transgression will be beneficial; whether the proposed transgression will build up; whether the proposed transgression is made on behalf of the neighbor rather than the

---

9. Ellul, *The Ethics of Freedom*, 347.
10. Contino, *Dostoevsky's Incarnational Realism*, 128–36.

self. This is precisely the sort of reasoning Alyosha employs in supporting Dmitri's escape.

Dmitri is conflicted concerning whether to transgress because he is afraid it will kill the "new man" he has become. At the same time, he also realizes that this "new man" might be destroyed by 20 years spent in the mines. Dmitri does not trust Ivan to resolve his dilemma because Ivan does not believe in God. Ivan does believe "everything is permitted" because God does not exist, and his analysis seems to end there. For Ivan, this is as far as his reasoning goes because "everything is permitted" is not subject to any external scrutiny by God or human. What is permitted is determined only by the power of the lone, isolated individual to do what is proposed.

Alyosha believes that "all things are lawful," but because God exists, we are not isolated beings. Instead, we are communal human beings, and, in choosing among all things that are lawful, our actions are subject to the criterion of whether these actions are beneficial to the other, build up the community, or are done for others rather than the self. After Dmitri is found guilty, he asks for Alyosha's opinion about the proposed transgression of Russian law.

> Listen brother, once and for all (. . .) This is what I think about it. And you know that I would not tell you a lie. Listen: you are not ready, and such a cross is not for you. What's more, you don't need such a great martyr's cross when you are not ready for it. If you had murdered our father, it would grieve me that you should reject your cross. But you are innocent and such a cross is too much for you. You wanted to regenerate another man in yourself by suffering, I say only remember that that other man always, all your life and wherever you escape to; and that will be enough for you. Your refusal of that great cross will only serve to make you feel all your life an even greater duty, and that constant feeling will do more for your regeneration, perhaps, than if you went *there* (. . .) If other men would have to answer for your escape, officials or soldiers, then I would not have "allowed" you. But they declare—the superintendent of that stop told Ivan himself—that if it's well managed there will be no great inquiry, and that they can get off easily. Of course bribing is dishonest (it's a transgression) even in such a case, but I can't undertake to judge about it, because if Ivan and Katya commissioned me to act for you, I know I would go and give bribes. I must tell you the truth. And so I can't judge your own action. But let me assure you that

> I shall never condemn you. And it would be a strange thing if I could judge you in this. Now I think I've gone into everything.[11]

In this passage, Alyosha understands that they are contemplating a transgression. In even discussing Dmitri's escape as a possibility, Alyosha agrees, at least implicitly, that "all things are lawful"—even things that violate the laws of his country. He recognizes the proposed transgression as a potential act of Christian freedom, and he agrees to transgress the law because the freedom of the Gospel allows him to try if such a transgression is, in Zosima's words, an act of active love.

Next, Alyosha evaluates the proposed transgression. He believes Dmitri should escape because Dmitri has not grown enough in the Spirit to withstand what he will endure in Siberian captivity, therefore, Dmitri will not be able to minister in the Siberian mines. Note, Alyosha's opinion is not imposed on Dmitri "from above" as Ivan's opinion had been. Alyosha's judgment is based on Dmitri's own words. Alyosha has *listened* to Dmitri's fear that he could not survive the treatment he would receive in the mine and might kill himself. Even so, Alyosha qualifies his opinion. It would be one thing if Dmitri were guilty, but he is not, so this transgression would be beneficial to Dmitri. Escape would allow Dmitri's "new man" to mature and develop. Just as Zosima declared that the monastery was not to be the place for Alyosha's ministry to mature and grow, Alyosha, now in the same position in relationship to Dmitri as Zosima was to him, declares that a Siberian mine is not the place for Dmitri to serve God.

Alyosha then says that even if Dmitri's escape is successful, in the planned American exile Dmitri's "new man" is in jeopardy unless he *remembers* that he has escaped for the purpose of performing acts of active love to those he and Grushenka encounter. If he forgets, he will regress, and his transgression, his act of Christian freedom, will come to naught. Alyosha also says that he would not be in favor of this transgression, and the dangers of Dmitri regressing, if other men were punished for his escape. If others suffer because Dmitri has transgressed, then this would not be an act of freedom but one of self-preservation. To put it in Ivan's words, "too high a price would be paid" for Dmitri's transgression if others suffered because of it. This concern also meets the criteria of transgression because it is done to benefit others and not the self.

Assured to his satisfaction that others will not suffer if Dmitri's escape is engineered, Alyosha involves himself in this transgression. If

---

11. Dostoevsky, *Brothers*, 636.

asked to aid in the plot, he says he will give out the bribes to the officials himself to aid in the plot. In other words, Alyosha is also prepared to transgress the law along with those engaged in the plot. He insists that his own involvement indicates that he cannot possibly judge Dmitri whatever he does (even if Dmitri does not agree to take part in the escape) because Alyosha also is involved. He too is engaged in transgression. He too will be "guilty."

The Brothers Karamazov ends before we even know if Dmitri's escape is successful. This too is important because the outcome of a transgression is always uncertain. The escape party could be arrested. Dmitri and Grushenka might not make it to America. The officials could just take the bribes and do nothing. The conspirators would have little recourse. Moreover, we can never adequately judge or evaluate a transgression this side of the kingdom because this side of the kingdom a transgression can always be confused with the acts of political revolutionaries who just want to substitute their rules and their own necessities. Alyosha agrees to the transgression because he believes that this particular action is life-giving, beneficial, and builds up. Nonetheless, both Ivan the atheist and Alyosha the former monk join in this conspiracy. Ambiguity abounds in acts of transgression. A practitioner of the art of ministry must discern whether a particular transgression is an act of Christian freedom or something else.

7

The Church of Active Love

For where two or three are gathered in my name, I am there among them.
—(MATT. 18:20)

IN THE FIRST FOUR books of *The Brothers Karamazov*, Dostoevsky introduces all important characters in the novel. Most of them have been mentioned already. The few who remain will be mentioned in this chapter. The characters about to be introduced combine to form what I have come to understand as The Church of Active Love. Alyosha is its founder, its evangelist, and its most mature practitioner of the art of ministry. Nearly all of the members of this congregation are, however, victims of the "old" Dmitri's dubious character and actions.

Katerina

Katerina Ivanovna Verhovtseva is one of the first "members" of the Church of Active Love. A translation of her name describes her quite well. *Verkh* means upper, supreme, and proud and *verkhovnyi* means superior.[1] Throughout most of the novel, her goal is to remain superior

---

1. Dostoevsky, *Brothers*, xx.

and supreme to those she encounters. When the story opens, she is engaged to be married to Dmitri Karamazov.

Unusual circumstances led to her engagement (there were always unusual circumstances in any encounter with the "old" Dmitri). At one time her father was Dmitri's commanding officer. He was in danger of being exposed as an embezzler, which caused great consternation to Katerina and her sister. His books were soon to be audited, and if he could not account for 4500 rubbles he had misappropriated, he would be arrested and discharged without a pension.

Dmitri lusted after Katerina (the "old" Dmitri lusted after all women), and her lack of attention infuriated him. So, when he heard of her father's problem, and in recent possession of a 6000-ruble inheritance from his father—money Fydor Karamazov thought fulfilled all his financial obligations to his son Dmitri—Dmitri notified Katerina's older sister that he would give them the needed 4500 rubles in exchange for Katerina's sexual favors. After much consternation, Katerina agrees to "sell herself" to Dmitri. She comes to him. She offered herself to him as was the "deal," but he gives her the money without taking advantage of her. Katerina bows to Dmitri, but she soon realizes that Dmitri now knows that she would have sold herself. He knows she has "a price." At first Dmitri tells no one. (He later tells Grushenka much to Katerina's chagrin). In any case, Katerina is embarrassed. Her "superiority" would forever be in jeopardy with respect to Dmitri.

There is little communication between Dmitri and Katerina immediately following this episode. Her father dies, but he dies with military honors. The family moves to Moscow and Katerina inherits a small fortune. Only then does she repay Dmitri the money she owes him, but she knows that Dmitri still "knows" that she would sell herself if the price were right. The only way that Katerina can imagine that she might restore her virtue in Dimitri's eyes is to offer to become his wife. She does so and pledges her love for him. She promised that even if he did not love her, she would be his furniture, the carpet on which he walked, adding that she wanted to save him from himself.[2] Dmitri accepts the engagement offer, but soon he realizes that he has made a big mistake and tries to get out of the engagement.[3]

---

2. Dostoevsky, *Brothers*, 101–5.

3. Their relationship is even more complicated and dysfunctional than this, but its ridiculous dysfunction is not all that unusual. Unfortunately, I have been privy to several that I think are even worse, and Abraham and Sarah's biblical family was just as

The Schoolboys

Alyosha encounters other future members of the Church of Active Love when he comes upon six or seven young schoolboys who are throwing rocks at another child who returns their fire. Alyosha engages the group with a simple question. He asks one of the boys "When I used to wear a satchel like yours, I always used to carry it on my left side, so as to have my right hand freed, but you've got yours on your right side. So it will be awkward for you to get at it." The narrator points out that Alyosha begins his conversation with a practical remark, "which, incidentally, is the only way for an adult to begin if he needs to enter right into the confidence of a child, and especially with a group of children. One must begin in a serious businesslike way so as to be on a perfectly equal footing. Alyosha understood it by instinct."[4]

Alyosha is informed that the one who carries his bag on his right side is left-handed. Alyosha probably knew this but chose to ask an apparently ignorant question in order to be "enlightened by the boys." If so, his question placed him on an equal footing with the boys who he now could engage more readily because of his dumb question. After talking to the group in this manner, Alyosha admonishes them saying, "Six against one, why you'll kill him," and Alyosha runs forward to screen the boy being attacked. The boys respond by telling Alyosha that he does not know what a beast this boy is. They tell him that he stabbed (Koyla) Krasokin with a pen knife. At this moment, however, the boy begins to throw rocks at Alyosha himself! The rest of the boys return fire and hit their adversary on the chest. He screams in pain and runs out of striking range. He stops and looks back. Apparently, he is waiting for Alyosha.

The boys notice this and tell Alyosha to ask him "does he like a disheveled bathhouse wisp of tow." A boy named Smurov warns Alyosha that he should not go too close because the boy will hurt him. Alyosha is baffled because he has no idea who this boy is, yet he approaches the young boy despite the warnings. The boy waits. The two engage in a short conversation where Alyosha unsuccessfully tries to get the boy to tell him why he is so angry at him and insists that he has never seen the boy before. Alyosha turns to walk away, and the boy hit him in the back with his biggest stone.

---

seriously dysfunctional.

4. Dostoevsky, *Brothers*, 156.

Certain that Alyosha was now going to attack him, the boy attacked Alyosha biting him on the finger. Alyosha, still responding non-violently and refusing to "return evil for evil" takes time to wrap his bleeding finger in a handkerchief.

> "Very well," he said, "you see how badly you have bitten me. That's enough isn't it? Now tell me what I have done to you."
> The boy starred in amazement.
> "Though I don't know you and it's the first time I've seen you," Alyosha went on with the same serenity, "yet I must have done something to you, you wouldn't have hurt me like this for nothing. So what have I done? How have I wronged you?"

The boy did not respond but broke down into a tearful wail and ran away. Alyosha made up his mind that he would get to the bottom of this.[5]

In this episode Alyosha skillfully opens a dialogue with the boys and refuses to act in such a way that the dialogue will be closed. With the group of boys, he engages them practically so the discussion can be about something familiar. Instead of shouting, as a "responsible" adult might, for the boys to quit throwing rocks at each other, he erroneously but perhaps knowingly comments on how one of the boys carries his satchel. His apparent ignorance is quickly corrected, and only then does he tell them that they might kill their adversary.

The boys try to justify their actions, and they try to help Alyosha with the knowledge, correct knowledge as it turns out, that the boy is going to hurt him if he is not careful. Nonetheless, Alyosha does not return violence for violence when he is in fact attacked by the boy. Had he done so his future with the young man might have been cut off. Instead, his non-violence keeps open the possibility of a future relationship with the boy even though Alyosha had no idea of what this future relationship might entail. Alyosha was soon to learn much more.

Captain Snegiryov's Family

When Alyosha encountered the boys, he was on the way to Katerina's house. There he learned the reason for the boy's animosity. Katerina told him that about a week ago Dmitri lost his temper with a former army captain and had publicly humiliated this man by dragging him by his beard throughout town. His son and his friends from school came upon

5. Dostoevsky, *Brothers*, 158–59.

this humiliating scene. His son pleaded with the crowd for someone to help him defend his father, but his plea was met by the crowd's laughter. Katerina tells Alyosha that this man was a former Captain named Snegiryov, and he and his family have become destitute since his less than honorable discharge from the army.

As Captain Snegiryov himself later described them, this family consists of three ladies. His wife, Arina Petrovna, is crippled and weak-minded. One daughter, Nina Nikolaevna, is crippled and a hunchback. His other daughter, Barbara Nikolaevna, is a student who desires to get back to Petersburg to work for the emancipation of women. Finally, there is his son, Ilyusha. It was this boy who was throwing stones and who had hurt Alyosha. Ilyusha became sick after his encounter with the boys because he was hit in the heart by a rock thrown by the boy named Smurov.

Katerina wished to assist Captain Snegiryov's family, and she gave Alyosha two hundred rubles to give to the captain. She thinks Captain Snegiryov might reject the gift out of pride, so she rapidly explains to Alyosha that he should tell him that this is not a recompense for the insult he received at Dmitri's hands. Instead, she extends this money to him because she too has also been insulted by Dmitri who had broken off their engagement. She rapidly shoves the money into Alyosha's hand and withdraws from his presence leaving Alyosha with no time to refuse this difficult mission. Nonetheless, Alyosha, who now realizes that the young boy who hit him with a rock and bit his finger for no apparent reason was Snegiryov's son Ilyusha. Alyosha takes up the mission bequeathed to him by Katerina and seeks out Captain Snegiryov and his family.

Upon arrival, Alyosha encounters the entire family living in a small apartment under squalid conditions. Upon hearing Alyosha announce his name, everyone in the family had something to say and nothing was very flattering. Alyosha asked the captain if they could go outside and talk. Captain Snegiryov ushered him outside, and they began to walk.

Captain Snegiryov told Alyosha of his embarrassing encounter with his brother Dmitri. The encounter was all the more embarrassing and destructive because, following the insult, Dmitri challenged the Captain to a duel. In the presence of Ilyusha, and a laughing crowd, Dmitri said, "'You are an officer, and I am an officer, If you can find a decent man to be your second, I will give you satisfaction though you are a scoundrel.' That's what he said, sir. A chivalrous spirit indeed. I retired with Ilyusha, and this genealogical family picture is imprinted forever on Ilyusha's soul."[6]

Much to his further embarrassment, the captain goes on to say that he could not do what codes of personal honor demand; for, what becomes of his family if he is killed, and if he is not killed but crippled, who was there to feed his family? They would perish without him. Snegiryov could only promise his son that he would not suffer any more indignations; never forgive Dmitri and never take money from him for any reason.

Alyosha, however, is still quite conscious of his mission to give Captain Snegiryov and his family two hundred rubles. So, when he and the captain find an isolated spot, Alyosha tells him that Dmitri has insulted others as well, and one of those who Dmitri has insulted is Katerina Ivanovna Verkhovtseva. She is offering him two hundred rubles in solidarity with Snegiryov's suffering. Alyosha tells him that no one will ever know of this transaction. When he hears the offer Snegiryov is ecstatic! In glee he recounts the things this money will do for his family. He can take care of the medical and physical needs of his wife and daughter Nina. He can hire a servant, send his daughter Barbara back to school, buy beef and properly feed his family. He can even move to a place where his disgrace is not known and start a new life. But, when he remembers his promise to his son, his demeanor suddenly changes. He accuses Alyosha of tricking him. Throwing the money to the ground he shouts, "What should I say to my boy if I took money from you out of shame?" and runs away. After he was out of sight, Alyosha picked up the notes and went to report to Katerina what had happened.

Dostoevsky calls actions like these self-lacerations. Self-lacerations are a common phenomenon. Many, many people inflict unnecessary pain on themselves in life. It happens for many reasons. Pride and shame are operative in this story, but many self-lacerations are the consequence of a person's inability to envision alternatives because they mistakenly equate the way things currently are with reality itself. Self-lacerations are difficult to witness because the minister knows that alternatives are possible, but the person or persons engaged in their self-destructive practices are doing so largely because of the false conviction that things must be the way they are, and, as a result, there is no way out of the difficulty (when there really is). Alyosha was "inexpressibly grieved" by Snegiryov's refusal for this reason.

---

6. Dostoevsky, *Brothers*, 177.

When self-laceration happens, it is important for the minister to wait until a more favorable moment. Knowing when that moment has occurred takes patience, time, and the spiritual gift of discernment, but when that moment happens intervention can help a person broaden his limited understanding of what is possible. This broadening often happens when the self-lacerating ones discover that they are not alone. (In this case, Snegiryov and his family will discover they are members of the Church of Active Love). When we next encounter Alyosha amid the Snegiryov family, Captain Snegiryov knows he is not alone. He has accepted Katerina's help, and most of the obstacles that led to his self-laceration have been overcome. Unfortunately, another more formidable obstacle tragically remains.

Kolya Krasokin

Two- or three-months later Captain Snegiryov has accepted Katerina's generosity. He was able to send Barbara back to Peterburg to continue her education, provide food, medicine, and help for Arina, Snegiryov's wife, and Nina his physically disabled daughter. He even got a doctor to see his son Ilyusha, who, unfortunately, is now gravely ill. Katerina's much needed assistance was not limited to the two hundred rubles. She gave money for a specialist to visit Ilyusha and eventually she would pay for Ilyusha's funeral. (This was in addition to her donation of ten thousand rubles to finance Dmitri and Grushenka's upcoming escape to America). While Katerina's generosity does not come close to the Christian community in Acts 4—a community where the resources were held in common and distributed according to need—Katerina is the source of much needed funding for the Church of Active Love that is growing in numbers and spiritual maturity.

Another change that has occurred in the last three months is the boys who once had mercilessly teased and attacked Ilyusha now visit him. Even as Ilyusha's condition deteriorates, they routinely gather around his bed. The only exception is that the oldest member of the group and its leader, Kolya Krasotkin, had yet to appear. Dostoevsky does not say how the boys transformed from enemies to friends, but this transformation has occurred. These boys now practice "active love" to a boy they had once bullied and tormented.

Moreover, each boy who now gathered around Ilyusha's deathbed thought that he had gathered of his own accord as described by this conversation between Smurov and Kolya. Referring to his upcoming initial visit, Kolya tells Smurov that *his* visit must be distinguished from the rest of the boys because "(. . .) I am going on my own because I choose to, but you've all been hauled here by Alexy (Alyosha) Karamazov—there's a difference you know." But Smurov denies this saying,

> It's not Karamazov at all; it's not his doing. Our fellows began going there of themselves. Of course they went with Karamazov at first. And there's been nothing of that sort—no silliness. First one went, and then another. His father was awfully pleased to see us. You know he will simply go out of his mind if Ilyusha dies (. . .) he seems so glad we have made up with Ilyusha (. . .) You know he's a very decent man. We made a mistake then.[7]

Alyosha's ministry had been quite delicate. He got Captain Snegiryov to accept Katerina's financial aid. He slowly gathered the boys around Ilyusha's bed, and the boys who gathered thought they each had decided to do so on their own. They had to admit that Alyosha was there too, but he was more a part of the group than its acknowledged leader. Finally, one must remember the place where they gathered was composed of Ilyusha's mother Arina who is mentally ill and unable to walk, Nina, Captain Snegiryov's hunchback daughter and Ilyusha who was rapidly approaching his death. Already in cramped quarters, the addition of seven or eight boys and a former monk for a few hours a day could not have eased the apartment's congestion. In general, though, the added congestion in the apartment was pleasantly accepted. Nothing in the story so far tells us how Alyosha had managed to pull this off, but the family appreciated the presence of the boys—boys they all knew to have once been their beloved son's antagonists.

Alyosha's conversations with Koyla are the only literary evidence of how Alyosha moved the boys from a violent, adversarial relationship with Ilyusha to becoming ministers of active love. Being a couple years older than the rest of the boys, Koyla had, in fact, once intervened to prevent the younger ones from teasing and bullying the poverty stricken Ilyusha. Ilyusha had grown remarkably close to Koyla. But Ilyusha had somehow gotten to know Pavel Smerdyakov, the actual murderer of Fyodor Karamazov.

---

7. Dostoevsky, *Brothers*, 444.

Smerdyakov diabolically told Ilyusha to take a piece of bread, stick a pin in it, throw it to a hungry dog, and see what happens. Ilyusha prepared the bread and threw it to a dog named Zhucha who swallowed it. Naturally, Zhucha began to squeal and ran away in pain. Ilyusha thought he had killed the dog and remorsefully confessed his sin to Kolya. Kolya did not accept Ilyusha's confession very well. He told him that he would have no more to do with him because of this crime. This devastated Ilyusha who had now lost the support of his best friend and protector. After falling ill, Ilyusha longed for Koyla to visit, but Koyla had yet to visit even though he knew that Ilyusha's strength was faltering.

Kolya Krasokin is a young man who is incredibly conscious of what other people think about him. In particular, he wants everyone else to recognize that he is very smart and autonomous; however, he is also aware of some of his defects. As is the case with many people, however, Koyla only considers things to be defects if others think they are as well. For example, he tries to hide the fact that he enjoys playing with young children because he thinks some "important" role models might not approve. Kolya is also a pest around town because he is always trying to demonstrate his superior knowledge through his pranks. Kolya uses these outrageous pranks to hide his vulnerability.

After he finally visits Ilyusha, Kolya's conversations with Alyosha demonstrate Alyosha's growing mastery of the art of ministry. One conversation occurs when a specialist doctor from Moscow, paid for by Katerina, comes to see Ilyusha. The apartment is vacated, and Kolya and Alyosha meet in the hallway. Kolya wants to appear mature beyond his years to Alyosha so he presents a philosophy that mimics Ivan's rationalist, atheistic philosophy. As was the case with Ivan, Kolya fears that he will be rejected by Alyosha for expressing these views and demands that Alyosha tell him immediately if he has contempt for him.[8] Looking at him in wonder, Alyosha responds, "I have contempt for you? (. . .) What for? I am only sad that a charming nature such as yours should be so perverted by all this crude nonsense before you have begun life."[9]

One must note the skill that is implicit in Alyosha's response. He says that he has no contempt for Kolya himself, but he is "sad" that his charming nature is clouded by an external source before he even begins life. This response reflects Alyosha's growing mastery of the art of ministry.

---

8. Contino, *Dostoevsky's Incarnational Realism*, 172.
9. Dostoevsky, *Brothers*, 468.

He does not deny that he disagrees with Kolya's philosophy. He is just "sad" about it. (Alyosha has told Kolya how it makes him feel). Moreover, Alyosha does not blame Kolya for his philosophy or even the things he does because of his philosophy. Alyosha just thinks that these actions are against his charming nature which is in danger of being perverted by this worldview.

Because Alyosha responds in this non-adversarial way, Kolya can listen, and he takes this as an opportunity to make an adjustment in his life. Rather than try to rationally justify himself and his immature philosophy, Kolya talks about Alyosha's "sadness" instead. Kolya says that Alyosha should not be anxious about his nature, and, surprisingly, Kolya finds the freedom to confess that he is sensitive—crudely sensitive. Gradually Kolya's thoughts turn to Ilyusha. He realizes that the doctor has taken a long time and wonders if the doctor is "examining the 'mamasha' and the poor cripple Ninochka. I like that Ninochka, you know. She whispered to me suddenly as I was coming away, 'Why didn't you come before?' And in such a voice, so reproachfully! I think she is awfully nice and pathetic."

Upon hearing this, Alyosha expresses one of the most essential social functions of the church, namely, to bring socially diverse people together. Such gatherings get people talking to one another and these conversations benefit everyone. Alyosha also uses Kolya's own words—the fact that he likes Nina—to invite Kolya into the gathering saying, "Yes, yes! Well, you'll be coming often, you will see what she is like. It would do you a great deal of good to know people like that, to learn to value a great deal which you will find out from knowing these people (. . .) That would have more of an effect on you than anything."[10] In this dialogue we have one of the best descriptions of the Church at its best in theology or fiction!

Alyosha's words open the future for Kolya, and his first act upon hearing Alyosha's words is to confess his sins saying, "Oh, how I regret and blame myself for not having come sooner." Alyosha does not minimize this confession. He does not say, "Don't worry about it," or "Your actions were not that bad" or "It doesn't matter that much." In a case like this, such statements are no more than lies designed to say the last word in an uncomfortable conversation. Instead Alyosha agrees with what Kolya has said. "Yes, it's a great pity. You saw for yourself how delighted the poor child was to see you and how he fretted for you to come." Kolya hears these tough words, but since they merely reiterate his own words

---

10. Dostoevsky, *Brothers*, 469.

and thoughts, Alyosha's words force the conversation to an even deeper level. Kolya confesses his truth.

> "Don't tell me! You make it worse! But it serves me right. What kept me from coming was my conceit, my egoistic vanity, and beastly willfulness, which I can never get rid of, though I have been struggling with it all my life. I see now, I am a scoundrel in many ways Karamazov."
>
> "No you have a charming nature, though it has been distorted, and I quite understand why you have such an influence on this noble, morbidly sensitive boy." Alyosha answered warmly.
>
> "And you say that to me!" cried Kolya, "and would you believe it," I thought (. . .) that you despised me. If only you knew how I prize your opinion."[11]

Alyosha's mastery of the art of ministry is clear in this conversation. He listens to Kolya, and, as all true listeners do, he adjusts or responds because of what he hears Kolya say. Kolya's future is now open. He moves from a boy who feels that, by his own nature, he is trapped in his conceitful, egoistic and beastly willfulness to a boy who, by virtue of Alyosha's words, now understands that these flaws can be overcome. Alyosha has opened Kolya's future. Kolya sees new life-giving possibilities before him because of Alyosha's rapidly emerging mastery of the art of ministry.

Moreover, Alyosha's carefully chosen words—words that are not Alyosha's but given to him by Kolya himself—push their conversation and their relationship to deeper and more profound social, psychological and spiritual levels. For example, when Alyosha hears Kolya say that he likes Ninochka *even though she reproached him* for not coming sooner, Alyosha's response opens the conversation to the exploration of at least three different arenas. On the social level Alyosha notes that Kolya's admiration for Nina should lead him into this community that has emerged around the bed of a dying boy. This is hardly unrelated to the spiritual level because, in my opinion at least, this community should be called The Church of Active Love. Moreover, belonging to this gathering will enable Kolya to work on his ongoing psychological/social issues like his vanity or his egoistic desire to be the center of attention because such a community—such a church—will lovingly oppose the isolated individualism that might promote the sins that Koyla has confessed to Alyosha.

---

11. Dostoevsky, *Brothers*, 469

Following his confession, Kolya expects Alyosha to condemn him, but Alyosha does not do so. He does, however, *reinterpret* Kolya's sin. Koyla believed that his egoistic vanity was embedded in his nature, but Alyosha tells him that he has a charming but externally distorted nature. Kolya experiences grace when he hears this re-interpretation, and Alyosha invites him to live as a recipient of grace for the rest of his life. But living in grace, Alyosha warns, means that Kolya will be different from everyone else because "you are not ashamed to confess to something bad and even ridiculous." Finally, echoing Zosima's blessing to him, Alyosha tells Kolya, "You know Kolya, you will be very unhappy in your life (. . .) But you will bless life on the whole all the same."[12]

Alyosha's final words remind us of the relationship between freedom and happiness that was first expressed in The Grand Inquisitor. Freedom and happiness will always be in conflict because both demand universality. The person who seeks happiness must be happy in all spheres of life and will not count his life successful if there is something about his life that makes him unhappy. Freedom also demands universality. Freedom can be practiced anywhere even amid necessity and bondage, but people will ways be tempted to abandon freedom and submit again to the many forms of slavery that necessities offer. (Gal 5:1). When Kolya hears this, he responds, "Harrah!" He says Alyosha is a prophet and discloses his understanding of the reason his ministry is so effective. "Do you know, what delights me most, is that you treat me quite like an equal. But we are not equals, no, we are not, you are better."

Alyosha's Church of Active Love is coming into being. Kolya, the schoolboys, Katerina, the Snegiryov family, Grushenka and even Dmitri are in the process of abandoning their egocentric, isolated antagonism toward others. They practice Zosima's version of active love in a church that is being assembled by Alyosha and the Holy Spirit.

Alyosha the Evangelist

Alyosha uses the skills in the art of ministry in founding The Church of Active Love. He listens to people and uses their own words to help them gain profound insights that they may in fact already know but in an unspoken way. In Koyla's case, Alyosha uses an event—the communication and feeling expressed by Koyla concerning Nina—not only to invite him to participate

---

12. Dostoevsky, *Brothers*, 470.

in this church but also to demonstrate to Koyla that an essential function of the church is to bring socially diverse people together in ways that can help everyone who gathers.

Ilyusha's Funeral

Ilyusha dies shortly after this conversation, and his funeral is both the end and fulfilment of *The Brothers Karamazov*. Much of the novel is recapitulated here, but in a different key.

In contrast to Zosima, Ilyusha's corpse had hardly decomposed at all, "there was practically no smell there was practically no smell from the corpse."[13] This fact might be a critique of the theology of glory that Alyosha had abandoned in favor of onions and active love. A young schoolboy like Ilyusha could never be confused with a saint like Zosima. The surprise is, however, that both Zosima and Ilyusha are founding saints of The Church of Active Love. Some might even give Ilyusha precedence, but this would only be thinking in the hierarchical ways the world thinks.

Flowers had been sent, but Captain Snegiryov, stricken with grief, would not give even one flower to his wife saying that they were all Ilyusha's flowers. This act isolates the grieving husband and wife from each other, but later, Alyosha encourages Captain Snegiryov to take some flowers back to his invalid wife which he does. This recapitulates the scene were Zosima encounters Nastasya, the mother grieving the death of her last living child After listening and spending time with her, Zosima counsels that she should return to her husband so that they can grieve the loss of their child together.

Alyosha had learned from his mentor that while we may think we need to grieve in isolation, proper mourning is done corporately. In fact, the overwhelming feeling of grief we all experience at the death of a loved one—a feeling we neither desire nor seek—compels us to feel the interconnectedness of life at its most profound, natural, and fundamental level. Judith Butler describes grieving quite well writing, "It is not as if an 'I' exists independently over here and then simply loses a 'you' over there, especially if the attachment to 'you' is part of what composes who 'I' am (. . .). Who am I without you? When we lose some of these ties by which we are constituted, we do not know who we are or what we do."[14]

13. Dostoevsky, *Brothers*, 640.
14. Butler, *Precarious Life*, 22.

Through his own experience of his mentor's death, Alyosha had learned this often-unspoken truth, that mourning, if it is to grant the comfort that Jesus promises in the Beatitudes, must be a corporate phenomenon.

As her brother and his coffin are removed from the home, Nina kisses her brother on the lips. This might recapitulate Jesus' kissing The Grand Inquisitor and Alyosha's kissing Ivan. Both the Inquisitor and Ivan had chosen a death-dealing path. In both cases a kiss from Jesus and Alyosha rejected their death-dealing path without rejecting the person on that path and without leaving the person to the finality of death. Nina's kiss may also reject the finality of death itself. It also expresses the belief that what seems to be so (death's finality) is not so. Nina's kiss recapitulates this rejection of death as our ultimate fate.

There also may be a recapitulation of Alyosha's transforming dream at the Wedding Feast at Cana. Before the funeral, the boys have what might otherwise be considered a strange discussion of the possibility that after the funeral, they will gather to eat pancakes and maybe even salmon! During Alyosha's dream of the Wedding Feast at Cana—a human gathering that celebrates the joy of a wedding—Alyosha realizes that even though Jesus came to perform the glorious act of saving us from our bondage to sin and death, He did not distain the celebrations and gatherings of everyday life. Now, on a far more somber occasion—yet still a common occasion—Kolya almost comically comments, "It's all so strange Karamazov, such grief and suddenly pancakes." But even here amid profound grief, essential, natural, fundamental needs like nourishment and human fellowship are not distained. This reinforces the fundamental truth that human presence is a faithful response to the extreme highs and lows of life.

It is after the discussion of the meal of pancakes and salmon that Smurov exclaimed, "There's Ilyusha's stone under which they wanted to bury him!" Reminded of this fact, Alyosha felt his soul shaken and asked the boys if he could say something. He tells them that he will be leaving soon (he does not tell them that he is going to help his brother escape) and proposes that they make a compact before Ilyusha's stone *to never forget* each other, Ilyusha, and how "we buried the poor little boy at whom we once threw stones (. . .) And even if we are occupied with most important things, if we attain honor or fall into some great misfortune—still let us *never forget* how good it was once here (. . .) united by a good and kind feeling which made us for the time we were loving the poor boy, better perhaps than we are."[15]

Alyosha goes on to tell the boys how important such memories are; for, if a person carries a good memory such as this one for his or her entire life, these memories can serve us for our salvation. In other words, a good memory can function as an onion. As Alyosha explains, even if we grow wicked later on "yet we recall how we buried Ilyusha, how we loved him in his last days, and how we have been talking like friends altogether, at his stone, the crueler and most mocking of us—if we do become so—will we not dare to laugh inwardly at having been kind and good at this moment."

Alyosha is extremely realistic in this sermon. It is indeed possible, in fact it is more than possible, that life's necessities will divert us in such a way that we will fulfill their demands and forget freedom and love. To one degree or another, this happens to all of us. But Alyosha is just as realistic about the power of good memories. Remembering, even for just an instant, that things in your life were not always the way they are now and remembering, just for an instant, that you did not believe, think, or act in the ways you do now, demonstrates that these good memories are like "onions." They always have the power to transform lives (as mere "onions" did for Alyosha, Grushenka and Dmitri). Alyosha's sermon says that our memories of these gracious and loving moments have the power to resurrect lives. In the end, the very end of the novel, the discussion turns to eternal life and the salvation that awaits us all when Kolya cries out,

> "Karamazov! (. . .) Can it really be that what religion says that we shall all rise from the dead and shall live, and see each other again, everyone and Ilyushechka?"
> Certainly, we shall all rise again, certainly we shall see each other and gladly, joyfully will tell each other all that has happened." Alyosha answered half laughing, half ecstatic.
> "Ah, how good it will be," broke from Kolya.[16]

But Alyosha, now a master of the art of ministry, reminds his congregation that even though they would one day be reunited with Ilyusha and all the saints, and despite their desire to maintain this moment of ecstasy, they all had a job to do in the real world—a world still permeated with injustice, grief, suffering, sorrow and evil. Right now, in this

---

15. Dostoevsky, *Brothers*, 644–45.
16. Dostoevsky, *Brothers*, 645.

real world, they all had to go to the funeral dinner to help the family and themselves mourn the death of their beloved Ilyusha. So, like Peter, James, and John after witnessing Jesus' transfiguration, they had to come down from the mountain top and continue their ministry in the world of necessities, brokenness, and death.

8

The Death-Dealing Power of Unconfessed Sin

Evil is live spelled backwards.
—M. Scott Peck, *People of the Lie*[1]

THE LAST CHAPTER ENDED on a high note. It is Dostoevsky's best statement of how small instances of active love can revive relationships, create communities, bring diverse people together, bestow hope on the hopeless, experience resurrection even in the presence of death, and emancipate us from the many things that keep us in bondage. Dostoevsky believed that these individual acts of love—these onions—could be enough to address the evil that he knew ran rampant throughout the world if only enough people performed these acts.

While it is true that if everyone focused on performing acts of active love it might change the world, it is also true that the likelihood of that happening is remote (remote but not impossible). Furthermore, small acts of active love seem to stop sort of addressing the systemic evil that permeates the world. To even begin to address such evil, Zosima's second component of ministry—we are responsible to all people, for all people and for everything—must also be adopted. It is only by following this

---

1. Peck, *People of the Lie*, 42.

admonition that we can even begin to address the global evils that have plagued us since the dawn of civilization.

Antisemitism, racism, sexism, and institutional poverty compose the core of these evils. Each appears to be autonomous. Each is death-dealing, and there appears to be little we can do about them in the long run. For example, once the evil of racism is addressed and maybe even eliminated in one arena, it often emerges elsewhere. The same might be said about sexism, antisemitism, and institutional poverty as well. So, before explicitly addressing Dostoevsky's unabashed antisemitism in the next chapter, it is necessary to explore how antisemitism and other "isms" receive their seemingly autonomous death-dealing power from the sort of evil that Scott Peck has called "human" evil. It will be argued below that *human evil is the consequence of unacknowledged and unconfessed sin*. Since Dostoevsky believes that ministry is the way we combat evil, understanding the source and foundation of these global evils is also important if we are to seek a remedy.

How Evil Emerges from Unconfessed Sin

Evil is not the opposite of good. Evil is the opposite of life. It is always death-dealing. Nevertheless, almost everyone thinks evil is the opposite of good. The Bible, however, suggests otherwise. Those who recognize that Adam and Eve's first sin was eating the forbidden fruit, rarely register that fact that the name of the tree from which Eve plucked the fruit was "The Tree of the Knowledge of Good and Evil." This story appears to be saying that the first or original sin is our knowledge of good and evil. That is to say that morality—our knowledge of good and evil—is the source of our sin. It is not the remedy for our sin that it is often taken to be. In fact, our penchant for thinking that evil is the opposite of good could be the source of much of our malaise.[2]

Evil, the opposite of life, has a variety of sources, but the Principalities are largely the source of the kind of evil now under consideration. This evil can also be called human evil because human beings, living but mostly dead created the Principalities and perpetuate their power. Human evil can be as brazen as torture and murder, or it can be as subtle and mundane as an office memo. It can have global ramifications like the destruction of the climate, oppression of the poor, and the Holocaust,

---

2. Gustafson, *Behind Good and Evil*, 37–47

or it can occur on the personal or familial level. In all cases, *human evil happens because of our refusal or inability to acknowledge and confess our own sins or to recognize our responsibility for the sins of our predecessors.* It is *human* failure to acknowledge and confess our sins that creates human evil—the seemingly autonomous force that emerges whenever our sins go unacknowledged and unconfessed.

In his book *The People of the Lie: Hope for Healing Human Evil*, M. Scott Peck tells a haunting story that describes the emergence of evil from unconfessed sin. The courts assigned a teenaged car thief to Peck for therapy. As is customary in cases like this, Peck interviewed the boy's parents. Like most "good" parents, they expressed their willingness to help their son with "his" problem in whatever way the doctor deemed appropriate. As therapy progressed, Dr. Peck discovered that eighteen months before the theft of the car his client's brother had killed himself with a twelve-gage shotgun. Weeks later and in a different context, Peck heard the shocking news that at the Christmas *immediately after* his brother's suicide, the parents had given their only living son a twelve-gage shotgun! Dr. Peck, astonished and shocked, said, "Do you mean to tell me that your parents gave you a gun just like the one your brother killed himself with!?!" To this the boy sullenly replied, "Not the same *kind* of gun (. . .) *It was the same gun*."[3]

One need not be a trained psychiatrist to know that something was seriously wrong with this family's dynamic. When Peck confronted the parents with the fact that they may need more help than their son, the parents tried to justify their diabolical Christmas gift. They complained that they were a little short of money that Christmas. They said they did not want to deny their son gifts at Christmas, and they noted that the gun was, after all, a perfectly good gun. (Perhaps it had only been fired once. They did not say). The parents were blind to the fact that their actions might have an adverse effect on their child, and they refused to even entertain the possibility that their actions might have something to do with their son's crime. Rather than examine themselves, repent, confess, and acknowledge their sin, they preferred to believe that their son's case was hopeless. Indeed, they appeared to prefer the death of both sons to the prospect of acknowledging the existence their own sin.

This tragic account reveals how unconfessed sin releases the death-dealing power of human evil. This power appears to be autonomous. Its

---

3. Peck, *People of the Lie*, 51–52. Emphasis mine.

consequences are unpredictable. In this case, the death-dealing power of unconfessed sin may have promoted the suicide of one son and the criminal activity of the other. Other outcomes were, however, quite possible, but, without repentance, all possible outcomes would likely be death-dealing in some way.

But make no mistake, human evil only *seems* to be autonomous. Confession can reassert our control over human evil. It is, however, a long, arduous process that becomes more arduous the longer the sins remain unconfessed. *Since sins like antisemitism, racism, sexism, and institutional poverty have gone unconfessed throughout human history, the power of these unconfessed sins persists from generation to generation and consequently are extremely difficult to eradicate.*

Controlling the death-dealing power of human evil not only depends on the acknowledgement and confession of our own personal sins, but also on the acknowledgement and confession of our responsibility for the sins of our predecessors—particularly those sins from which those with higher social status such as myself still receive economic, social, and political benefit. These unconfessed sins are still present among us in the form of the Principalities that continue to rule. In any case, our responsibility for the current existence of human evil is the unspoken knowledge behind the second axiom of Father Zosima's teaching on ministry—"everyone is really responsible *to* all (people) *for* all (people) and for everything."[4] This adage now emerges as an important guide. We are responsible because we are the ones who are alive, and, as a consequence of being alive, we are the only ones capable of beginning a process that one day might destroy evil's death-dealing power.

Before proceeding to discussions of institutional poverty, racism, and antisemitism as example of how unconfessed sin has already released the seemingly autonomous power of human evil in the undeniable facts of human history, it should be said that the unconfessed sin that releases evil is unspoken. Its unspokenness is, however, a consequence of a self-imposed amnesia that is often a by-product of sins that we do not confess. It is because of self-imposed amnesia that we refuse to listen to stories about the religious origin of antisemitism, the political origins of racism, the biological origin of sexism, and the economic origins of institutional poverty. Unconfessed sin enables us to forget what we once knew, and our forgetfulness is often deliberate. (Witness the fear in some sectors of American life

---

4. Dostoevsky, *Brothers*, 250.

regarding the mere knowledge of American slavery. Rather than upset our children and their parents with this knowledge, we prefer a version of history that minimizes slavery and refuses to consider its terrors).

The unspoken knowledge that our amnesia creates is very different from the unspoken knowledge present in all artistic knowledge. Artistic unspoken knowledge is not a product of deliberate amnesia. It is the consequence of the fact that in the act of creation there is still much more we can discover. The articulation of the unspoken knowledge that is necessary to all arts opens the future to many unforeseen possibilities. The unspoken knowledge that is a product of our deliberate forgetfulness and amnesia closes the future because there is no way we can even begin to address human evil without acknowledging and confessing our responsibility and often our continued guilt for the unconfessed sins of our human past.

Evil Is the Opposite of Life

All evil is the opposite of life. All evil is death-dealing. Human evil is the seemingly autonomous, death-dealing power that emerges when human sins are unacknowledged and unconfessed. Moreover, the longer these sins remain unconfessed (this can be for centuries) the longer these unconfessed sins appear to be natural or even God-given. The confession of these unconfessed sins and the acknowledgement of our responsibility for the unconfessed sins of our human predecessors is how we can begin to oppose and perhaps eliminate the evils created by human sin.

How Unconfessed Sin Enables Institutional Poverty

The Gospels record several stories and parables in which people are oblivious to their sins against others probably because these sins may have gone unconfessed for generations and have become a part of "the way things are." Those who "benefit" from "the way things are" do not even consider the fact that their way of life contributes to the dehumanizing of others.

> There was a rich man who was dressed in purple and fine linen and feasted sumptuously every day. And at his gate lay a poor man named Lazarus, covered with sores, who longed to satisfy

his hunger with what fell from the rich man's table; even the dogs would come and lick his sours. The poor man died and was carried away by the angels to be with Abraham. The rich man also died and was buried. In Hades, where he was being tormented, he looked up and saw Abraham far away with Lazarus by his side. He called out, "Father Abraham, have mercy on me and send Lazarus to dip the tip of his finger in water and cool my tongue; for I am in agony in these flames." But Abraham said, "Child, remember that during your lifetime you received your good things; but now he is comforted here, and you are in agony. Besides all this, between you and us a great chasm has been fixed, so that those who might want to pass from here to you cannot do so, and no one can cross from there to us." He said, "Then, father, I beg you to send him to my father's house—for I have five brothers—that he may warn them, so that they will not also come into this place of torment." Abraham replied, "They have Moses and the prophets; they should *listen* to them." He said, "No, father Abraham; but if someone goes to them from the dead, they will repent." He said to him, "*If they do not listen* to Moses and the prophets, neither will they be convinced even if someone rises from the dead." (Luke 16:19-31, emphasis mine)

In his life on earth the Rich Man is oblivious to the plight of Lazarus as well as the fact that he bears some of responsibility for his plight. It is only when he is tormented in Hades that the Rich Man begins to suspect that his torments have something to do with his treatment of Lazarus. As this suspicion dawns on him, he requests that Father Abraham send Lazarus to tell his brothers of the torment that awaits them if they do not repent and help the poor. Father Abraham's response gives the Rich Man a further surprise. He hears that he and his brothers *were* properly informed. The Law and the Prophets repeat this message time and time again. His torment is because he and his brothers did not *listen* to the Law and the Prophets. They knew of their responsibility to the poor, but they chose to forget. Not listening enabled them to practice voluntary amnesia with respect to the poor. Because they did not listen, the rich man had lived, and his brothers still live as if the Law and the Prophets have no meaning or truth.

The story of the Rich Man and Lazarus is a biblical example of how human evil—the sort of evil usually employed by Principalities like the Grand Inquisitor—perpetuates its death-dealing power in the economic, social, and intellectual constructs that human beings build to mask and "disremember" the human evil inherent in these constructs. The human evil present in these constructs then receives a "life" of its own. It appears to be autonomous. Our socio/economic necessities are perpetuated in these constructs and necessities where human evil resides and perpetuates itself in unpredictable ways. It doesn't matter if this economic order is religious, monarchist, socialist, or capitalist. Since the dawn of civilization, the fact that evil is embedded in these structures makes it easy, and I might add socially acceptable, for the Rich Man to routinely ignore Lazarus and his plight.

There was no social apparatus or civil law to *make* the Rich Man listen to Lazarus' cries, and there continue to be few such structures that nudge the rich to heed the cry of the poor. As the Rich Man faced no social consequences for treating Lazarus as he did, the rich of our generation also face few consequences for their "unknowing" neglect of the poor and their plight. This fact alone indicates the power of Principalities (the rulers and institutions of human design) to perpetuate the death-dealing power of unconfessed sin.

The Principalities continue to create relationships between the rich and the poor like that relationship between Lazarus and The Rich man. Ideology is an important way this happens. These economic ideologies perpetuate and support the belief that the current relationship between the rich and the poor is natural or God-given. They rationalize poverty in such a way that absolves the rich of their responsibility for the poor. Once absolved, the rich can go about their true "calling." They can make and spend money with the ideological certainty that their actions have nothing whatsoever to do with God or perpetuating the plight of the poor.

In the nineteenth century, a very radical source of such "ideological certainty" was provided by Social Darwinism, an economic ideology attributed to Herbert Spencer (1820–1903). According to Social Darwinism, rich people like the Rich Man cannot be condemned (as he was in the biblical story) because the rich are rich because nature and perhaps God "Himself" has "selected" them for survival. Conversely, the poor are poor because nature had "selected" them for extinction. Social Darwinism maintained that the rich are not responsible for poverty. Poverty is a fact of nature, and no one can do anything about it. Since poverty has its roots in nature itself and since nature's "will" cannot be thwarted, Social Darwinism considered it immoral for a rich person to help the poor in their plight; for, *caring for the poor was contrary to natural law.*

Without mentioning Social Darwinism *per se*, America's first billionaire John D. Rockefeller (1839–1937) articulated Social Darwinist theory to his *Sunday School Class (!)* saying, "The growth of a large business is merely the survival of the fittest (. . .) The American Beauty rose can be produced in the splendor and fragrance which bring cheer to its beholder only by sacrificing the early buds which grow up around it (. . .) This is not an evil tendency in business. *It is merely the working-out of a law of nature and a law of God.*"[5] Here Rockefeller "Christianizes" Social Darwinism saying that the rich serve nature and, in Rockefeller's words, serve God Himself by continuing to do whatever makes the rich people richer. The rich are in no way responsible for the poor's plight except, ironically, when they make charitable donations to relieve the suffering of the poor. Charity merely delays the inevitable. It prevents the "pruning" necessary for economic growth.

I have often wondered if Herbert Spencer received a large stipend from the rich American men of the late nineteenth and early twentieth centuries. If he did, whatever he may have received was hardly enough because it enabled the rich of his day to continue the legacy of social numbness to the plight of the poor revealed in the biblical story of The Rich Man and Lazarus. Not only did this ideology justify the rich in their refusal to listen to the plight of the poor, but it is also an example of the death-dealing legacy of unconfessed sin. It supports the perpetuation of institutional poverty over the ages.

Since people began to see that there "might be" something wrong with Social Darwinism asserting that charity violates nature's design, Social Darwinism is no longer an acceptable economic theory. This, however, merely means that the unconfessed sins that promote institutional poverty must hide behind different ideologies. Adam Smith's "Invisible Hand" now gives the rich our cover. Like some kind of divine providence, "The Invisible Hand" guides the selfish economic behavior of the economic marketplace in such a way that all selfish behavior leads to the best possible social outcome.[6] This belief has led expert economists and politicians alike to deduce that any restriction on self-interested economic behavior by government, religion, ecological concerns or morality undermines the best possible social outcome and should, thereby, be avoided.

---

5. Galbraith, *Affluent Society*, 56
6. Smith, *Wealth of Nations*, 572.

Once again, we see "The Invisible Hand" provides a very convenient ideology for rich people because they are only required to continue their selfish economic behavior because it is now the best way to help the poor. This contention provides the rich with moral justification that Social Darwinism lacks. Furthermore, "The Invisible Hand" is not complete baloney. It does express an economic fact that makes it a more convincing ideology; for, self-interested economic activity does have some social benefit. A businessman might start a business only motivated by the possibility of his own personal gain. He might even be very successful and make a great deal of money. The businessman might remain a totally selfish person in this regard, but nonetheless and even though he did not intend it to be so, the businessman's success can and does support the lives of hundreds or even thousands of men, women, and children. The social benefit of this self-interested activity cannot be denied.[7]

In changing this economic fact into an ideological absolute, however, we forget that unencumbered self-interest in the pursuit of profit can also be socially damaging, particularly on a macro scale. Economic history contains many disastrous examples of unbridled economic self-interest run amok.

- The Dutch Tulip Bulb Debacle of 1636
- The South Sea Bubble of 1720
- The Mississippi Bubble of 1720
- The Stock Market Crash of 1929
- The Japanese Bubble in Stocks and Real Estate 1985–1989
- The U.S. Savings and Loan Crisis of the Late 1980s
- The Asian Stock and Real Estate Bubble 1992–1997
- The Mortgage and Housing Bubble and Crash 2004–2009

If the unrestricted self-interested pursuit of profit is in any way responsible for these economic debacles, the assertion that the pursuit of one's economic self-interest *always* benefits society is inaccurate.[8]

---

7. The phrase "The Invisible Hand" is the centerpiece of Capitalist ideology, and a much-quoted idea from Adam Smith's economic masterpiece *The Wealth of Nations*. This is an extremely lengthy book. My copy is 1208 pages long. Surprisingly, the phrase "The Invisible Hand" occurs only once in 1208 pages. In my copy this occurs on page 572. Smith, *Wealth of Nations*, xvi.

8. Gustafson, *At the Altar*, 42.

When the fact that in some instances the pursuit of one's selfish economic advantage has positive social consequences becomes an absolute, an absolutist ideology emerges that conceals any responsibility that the rich might have for the plight of the poor. Moreover, when government policies adopt the absolute status of "The Invisible Hand" theory, they strengthen the institutionalization of poverty; for, why do we need legislation that helps mitigate the plight of the poor if "The Invisible Hand" is performing this providential task? Shielded by this ideology, the rich can continue to ignore the poor and the plight of the poor without disruption to their lives, and institutional poverty remains buttressed by another ideology. It is here, buttressed by ideology and other dynamics, that evil remains to unleash its seemingly autonomous death-dealing power.

Deliberate Amnesia

As strange as it may seem to the victims of unconfessed sin, people may not even be aware of their unconfessed sin. Often this is a product of what might be called deliberate amnesia—the deliberate and successful attempt to obscure the existence of our yet to be acknowledged or confessed sins. When these attempts to obstruct the truth are successful, we who benefit from the existence of unconfessed sin falsely believe that there is nothing we can do about evils like racism, sexism, antisemitism, and institutional poverty because these "isms" are just the way things are.

How Unconfessed Sins Empower Racism[9]

Racist ideologies also obscure our responsibility for racism, but this is not the entire story. In recent years institutional poverty has been used to obscure and hide racism so that our responsibility for racism can hide behind the science of economics. In an age where most people acknowledge the evil of racism but cannot believe that they are racist in any way, hiding our racism behind institutional poverty (which nearly everyone considers to be natural or inevitable in some way) enables the evil of racism to evolve and manifest itself in different, less obvious ways. How

---

9. Any discussion of race must realize that race is an *idea* developed by Europeans to justify their enslavement of African people. The *idea* of race enabled Europeans to say that some "races" were by nature inferior to other "races," and that the "inferior races" *might benefit* from their enslavement. Gossett, *Race*, makes this point in all 17 of the book's chapters.

racism now hides behind poverty will be discussed below after the following considerations.

The ideology undergirding both slavery and racism emerged in North America in the eighteenth century when some prominent eighteenth and nineteenth century American slaveholders offered their justifications for slavery. These justifications helped obscure much of the death-dealing activity directed against African Americans in the United States. The story that follows demonstrates how the Principalities that rule America control the unrepentant American mind. Rationalizations of slavery and racism help create a world in which those who uncritically inherit these racist ideologies can avoid responsibility and repentance. This enables us to "unknowingly" participate in the death-dealing power of the human evil we call racism.

We can begin this story with Thomas Jefferson (1743–1826) who famously wrote about the institution of slavery, "I tremble for my country when I reflect that God is just; that his justice cannot sleep forever."[10] Despite this clear-eyed assertion, Jefferson decided to reject God's justice and justify slavery. Disregarding the fact that slavery is itself an act of extreme deadly violence, Jefferson called the institution of slavery "a necessary evil" because, he believed, slavery *prevented the violence* that was sure to happen if the slaves were freed. In other words, Jefferson confessed that slavery was evil, but immediately justified this evil. (One "wonders" if his position as a man who owed his opulent life and leisure to the slaves he owned and exploited in every way had anything to do with his reasoning process).

In response to abolitionists' criticisms, slaveholders pushed Jefferson's belief to a more deadly place. They began to disagree with Jefferson's assertion that slavery was even evil or wrong! In fact, they explicitly called slavery a good thing! Thomas R. Dew (1802–1846) of William and Mary College, for example, justified slavery saying that since slavery is a "necessary stage in human progress" it cannot be evil. South Carolina governor George McDuffie (1790–1851) pushed the envelope a little further. Arguing from the perspective of *divine providence*, he said "Africans were destined by God to be slaves as evidence by their color and intellectual inferiority." In 1837, John C. Calhoun (1782–1850) furthered this argument saying that slavery was not only a good thing but the best possible arrangement of society. "I hold that in the present state of civilization

---

10. As quoted, Eze, *Race and Enlightenment*, 96.

where races of different origin and distinguished by color and other physical differences, as well as intellectual, are brought together, the relations now existing between the two is, instead of evil, a positive good."[11]

During the first centuries of American life, racism became more and more entangled in the social order, and the rational justifications for slavery strengthened its death-dealing presence. Moreover, our refusal to confess this sin made the evils manifested by American racism increasingly unpredictable. When slavery ended, courtesy of the American Civil War (another violent manifestation of the death-dealing power of unconfessed sin that should not go unnoticed), the evil perpetuated by racism became more and more subtle and out of control because the sin of racism was never confessed. Since we have never confessed this sin, the death-dealing power of this unconfessed sin still wreaks havoc on our social order.

The consequences of our failure to confess took on a life of its own. Jim Crow segregation emerged as another manifestation of the seemingly autonomous death-dealing power of unconfessed sin. Through racist laws and terrorism, white supremacists tried to keep African Americans and other people of color in "their proper place." After nearly a century, we abolished Jim Crow, but once again we did not confess our racism, so the death-dealing power of this unconfessed sin emerged in other unpredictable ways. New laws and policies like "The War on Drugs" incarcerated a disproportional number of African Americans making certain that a large percentage of African American men are imprisoned, placed on probation, and their civil rights legally denied.[12] Both Jim Crow and "The New Jim Crow" demonstrate how our inability to confess our sin unleashes human evil—the death-dealing power that Principalities use to infiltrate our social policies, ideologies, and social constructs whenever our sins remain unconfessed. The actual death-dealing policies that emerge are not preordained or certain. What is certain is that, unless our racism is confessed and thereby explored and understood, a death-dealing power will emerge that largely benefits the dominant, mostly white people at the expense of people of color.

---

11. Frederickson, "Slaves and Race," 34–58.

12. Reading a few of the following books might help begin a process of repentance for the sin of racism: Alexander, *The New Jim Crow*, Diangelo, *White Fragility*, Fredrickson, *Racism*, Gossett, *Race*, Wilkerson, *Caste*. For histories of the relationship between global Capitalism, slavery and racism Baptist, *The Half Has Never Been Told*, Beckert, *The Empire of Cotton*, and Mintz, *Sweetness and Power* could prove helpful.

Even when a nation explicitly designs itself in such a way that racism might be purged, racism can still find a place to hide. This was revealed in South Africa's abolition of apartheid. The new anti-apartheid South African government was extremely deliberate in its attempt to abolish the racism behind apartheid. Their only historical guides, however, were the blanket national amnesty that occurred after the American Civil War and the Nuremburg trial of Nazi war criminals. South Africans rejected both approaches. A Nuremburg-like trial was designed to prosecute and punish Nazi leaders. If the many people who were involved in apartheid had been tried and punished, it may have led to a bloody civil war. On the other hand, following the American Civil War (1861–1865) a blanket amnesty was granted to most Confederate soldiers, officers, politicians, and plantation owners on the condition that they would never again take up arms against the Federal Government. Those who received amnesty only had to pledge that they would never take part in an armed insurrection against the Federal government. They did not have to confess their sin of racism. The South African government thought the lack of such a confession allowed the Old Confederate states to institute racist policies that sustained a racist climate even though slavery had been abolished. (These racist Post-Civil War policies, many say, provided the old South African government its model for apartheid).

The new government of South Africa chose a third option that was concisely summarized by Bishop Desmond Tutu, "(. . .) that third way was granting amnesty to individuals in exchange for a full disclosure (confession) relating to the crime for which amnesty was being sought. It was the carrot of possible freedom in exchange for truth and the stick was, for those already in jail, the prospect of lengthy prison sentences, and for those still free, the probability of arrest and prosecution and imprisonment."[13] The South African anti-apartheid government looked at human history, learned from it, and tried to do something different. But even within the ingenious solution that the South Africans meticulously and expertly employed, racism found a place to hide.

When Nelson Mandela (1918–2013) was released from prison in 1990, he and his African National Congress (ANC) believed in nationalizing South African businesses; but, after a trip to the World Economic Forum in Davos, Switzerland, Mandela was "persuaded" (how he was persuaded is subject to great debate) to support an economic framework

---

13. Tutu, *No Future Without Forgiveness*, 10.

based on capitalism and globalization. "They changed my views altogether," Mandela reported to Anthony Sampson the author of his authorized biography. South Africa, to the consternation of many of Mandela's supporters, opened itself to globalization and free markets, big money came into the country and South Africa became the fastest growing economy in Africa in terms of Gross Domestic Product (GDP).[14]

But the thing about the GDP is this. The GDP will grow by the same amount if one person makes $1 billion or if 1000 people make $1 million or if 100,000 people make $10,000. The amount of money is the same. A billion dollar increase in the GDP is a billion dollar increase no matter how it is distributed. The GDP does not measure *how* money is distributed. It does not measure where the money is spent. The GDP does not measure economic inequality, and as of 2013, the gap between the haves and have-nots in South Africa—the inequality gap—was greater than it was when Mr. Mandela became president. Economic inequality in South Africa has been on the rise since Mandela led his country into the global economy of capitalism. Furthermore, if economic inequality in South Africa is like it is in the United States, it becomes a good place for racism to hide. When any government cedes its understanding of the public good solely to the mathematical formulae that measure the GDP, the human evil of racism can still exert its death-dealing power.[15]

The inequalities inherent in modern economies help us remove explicit racist language from our speech and, at the same time, perpetuate the death-dealing consequences of racism. This is important because, today, explicit racist language is one of the few ways we determine if something or someone is racist. Since some white people are also strangled by poverty and since some people of color are not, we avoid discussing racism by discussing economic inequality instead. The unconfessed sin of racism and its death-dealing power hide here under disguise. Nonetheless, the death-dealing power of our unconfessed racism embeds itself in poverty and economic inequality and, therefore, remains a death-dealing power within American society. Embedding racism within poverty gives cover to those of us who are "unaware" of our racism and thereby can conceal their racism from themselves. Racism, they think, is over. The inequalities of our current age concern class and these difficulties apply regardless of race—so we think.

14. Sorkin, "How Mandela Shifted Views."
15. Klein, *Shock Doctrine*, 245–74.

In 1981, specific acknowledgement the use of economic language to distance ourselves from explicit racist language was articulated by an uncommonly candid Lee Atwter (1951–1991), a Republican political strategist and advisor to Presidents Reagan and George H.W. Bush. In explaining what is called "The Southern Strategy," Atwater discussed how to appeal to the racism of white Southern voters using cover language that allows us to deny our racism. (Such a rhetorical device is not limited to American Southerners. It is designed to appeal to Northerners as well, but they are just not a part of "The *Southern* Strategy.")

> You start out in 1954 by saying "(N word), (N word), (N word)." By 1968 you can't say, "(N word)"—that hurts you. Backfires. So you say stuff like forced busing, states' rights and all that stuff. You're getting so abstract now [that] you're talking about cutting taxes, and all these things you're talking about (are) totally economic things and a byproduct of them is [that] blacks get hurt worse than whites. And subconsciously maybe that is part of it (. . .) But I'm saying that it is getting that abstract, and that coded, that we are doing away with the racial problem (*Sic!*) (Or maybe just sick) one way or the other. You follow me—because obviously sitting around saying, "We want to cut this," is much more abstract than even the busing thing, and a hell of a lot more abstract than "(N word), (N word)."[16]

The consequences of our refusal to acknowledge and confess the sin of American racism has enabled racism to maintain its control over American life, but it does so in more "abstract" and "coded" ways than the oppressive realities of slavery, lynching, bombing churches, and Jim Crow. Today we disguise our racism under drug laws, language, and economic policies that enable white people to claim, "we are not in the least bit racist," or "we are not against people of color in the least!" We are only against crime, criminals, and busing. We are in favor of lower taxes and budget cuts to social programs (never defense) to pay for these tax cuts. These cuts, when implemented, remove social support for poor people who are a much higher percentage of African Americans than are poor white Americans a percentage of white Americans. These disguised policies are not fool proof, but they are effective (if effective means the maintenance of white control). From 2016–2017, for example,

---

16. As quoted, Diangelo, *White Fragility*, 33. Lee Atwater was not revealed as the source of this quotation until 1990. Right or wrong, I have substituted "N-word" for the word Atwater actually used.

- All ten of the richest people in America (7 of the richest in the world) were white.
- 90% of Congress was white. 96% of American governors were white.
- U.S. House Freedom caucus was 99 % white.
- 91% of the US cabinet officials were white.
- 93% of the people who decide what television shows we see were white.
- 90% of the people who decide what books we read were white.
- 85% of those who decide what news to report were white.
- 95% of those who decide what music to produce were white.
- 82% of our teachers were white.
- 84% of the full-time college professors were white.
- 97% of the owners of professional football teams were white.[17]

If accurate, these statistics reflect the insidious nature of the American sin of racism.

The death-dealing power of the unconfessed sin called racism controls our society in ways we cannot foresee, see, or understand until we (white people) begin to confess this sin. Moreover, since racism is so insidious, since it has dominated United States since its origins (slavery was written into the Constitution), it will take a long time for white Americans to fully confess because confession involves doing many things that we prefer remain undone. We must listen to the victims of racism. We must recognize the terrible fact that we have been complicit with the violence and death associated with our racism. Confession will involve many years of painful study of history and the social sciences. It is quite probable that such study will continually reveal the sad fact that even the most "enlightened" of white Americans have yet to comprehend the depth of our common sin. Confession and repentance of our racism is no small task. It will take generations to adequately repent, but it is the sole task of white people to do so. It is our problem. It is not "the black problem." The issue is so important that understanding the unconfessed sin of our racism continues to undermine the art and practice of ministry.

Racism (and antisemitism, sexism, and poverty) are the work of Principalities. Principalities largely have their source in the unconfessed

---

17. Diangelo, *White Fragility*, 31.

human sin of our forebearers. In the case of white people in the United States, these unconfessed sins have granted many white Americans considerable economic benefits that might dwindle if these sins are confessed. For this and many more reasons we do not confess our national sin. But as Matt Fitzgerald pointed out in an article in *The Christian Century*

> The sin of slavery is still alive.
> > If it were not still alive,
> > > the net worth of a typical white family
> > > > would not be ten times greater than a black family.
>
> If slavery were not still alive,
> > Black activists would not have had to coin
> > > the phrase that sets the bar so low
> > > > Black Lives Matter.
>
> To object to that sentiment is
> > to be confronted with your inhumanity.
>
> It is to discover that your inhumanity
> > has an undead demonic quality, that keeps
> > > the values of a 500-year-old slaveholder
> > > > alive in your twenty first century mind.[18]

How Unconfessed Sins Created and Empowers Antisemitism

The previous section attempted to document how the unconfessed human sin of racism unleashes evil. Antisemitism is an example of another way the death-dealing power of unconfessed sin manifests itself. The death-dealing power of *this* unconfessed sin is manifest in the Holocaust. Indeed, the Holocaust itself might not have happened if Christians—Protestant, Catholic and Orthodox—had begun to confess our antisemitism and begin the process of repenting of this terrible sin that still persists throughout Europe and America.

It might also be acknowledged that both World War II and the Holocaust might have been avoided if the allies had been able to confess a different sin. This failure also had death-dealing consequences. It is a commonly held belief that the Treaty of Versailles was in some sense responsible for the Holocaust. This treaty made Germany and Germany alone accept responsibility for the unprecedented carnage of World War

---

18. Fitzgerald, "What Should We Pray For?" 34. I have taken the liberty of placing Fitzgerald's prose in semi-poetic verse.

1. Germany was deemed absolutely evil, and the victors deemed themselves pure, innocent, and good. France, England, and the United States admitted no responsibility for the war. Refusing to accept even one iota of responsibility, the Allies felt justified in imposing gigantic reparations on the Germans. This enormous debt put Germany's economy in shambles, and the economic devastation that ensued undermined Germany's fledgling democracy. Many think that this created a political climate that allowed Hitler to come to power. If France and England had confessed a shared culpability for the war, however, Germany's economic plight might have been mitigated, and Hitler's vile, antisemitic reign might have been avoided.[19] If this common wisdom resembles the truth, it follows that France and England's failure to confess their own sins for World War I helped to unleash the horrific death-dealing force of antisemitism throughout Europe in World War II.

What this account does not disclose, however, is that if Orthodox Christianity, Catholicism and Protestantism had begun to repent of their antisemitism at any time in the previous 1000 years, Hitler's rise to power and the ensuing Holocaust might have been avoided. The Holocaust relied on a population primed to accept Nazi claims about "Jewish Evils" and "Jewish inferiority." These false claims were first perpetuated by Christian priests and pastors, parents, schools, arts, literature, and civil authorities. For centuries nearly all Christians accepted these falsehoods as undeniable truth. This fact created a "favorable" climate for the Nazi attempt to kill every Jew in Europe—a goal they nearly accomplished.

We see the power of the unconfessed sin of Christian antisemitism the moment the overt and aggressive antisemitic Nazis took control of the German government. Their policies gave top priority to purging Jews from German society, and these policies were enabled by people who believed in the antisemitic tenants of Nazism long before Hitler rose to push these death-dealing beliefs to their horrific extremes. The Nazis relied on the German peoples' own antisemitism to pursue their death-dealing agenda. Along with The United States and the rest of Christian Europe, the German Christians basically agreed with antisemitic assertions of the Nazis. Few opposed Nazi policies. Indeed, along with the rest of Europe, the Germans did not consider Hitler's policies particularly disturbing—at least if they were not Jews themselves; for, they mistakenly

---

19. Andelman, *Shattered Peace*.

believed that the tenants of antisemitism were mostly true, and their sin remained unconfessed as a consequence.

What happens next is an extreme and well documented historical example of how human evil is truly a death-dealing power that emerges when we do not acknowledge and confess our sins. As Hannah Arendt (1906–1975) apply recognized, the power of such evil occurs in banal, everyday events that were largely the result of mundane bureaucratic processes.[20]

Germany's modern bureaucracy made the murder of 6 million Jews a reality. Its first task was to distinguish the Jew from the non-Jew. In the United States the difference between most African Americans and white Americans was simply a matter of sight, but in Germany a Jew might not be distinguished from a non-Jew by sight alone; hence, the Nazis made everyone who its bureaucracy determined to be a Jew embroider a yellow Stars of David into their clothing. This made the distinction between Jew and non-Jew visible. Everyone who wore this badge was marginalized. All who wore this badge were in grave danger.

The great historian of the Holocaust, Raul Hillberg, articulates the downward spiral into genocide as

- Definition (Wearing the Star of David badge)
- Dismissal of Jewish Employees and Expropriation of Jewish Businesses.
- Concentration
- Exploit Jewish Labor until death by overwork and starvation.
- Annihilation
- Confiscation of Personal Effects.[21]

The first thing to note is that this agenda can easily be transformed into a bureaucratic flow chart. Each task can be efficiently performed by any modern bureaucracy should it somehow be so motivated. As is the case with any bureaucratic task, the tasks are broken down into smaller and smaller tasks. Each small task contributes to the entire process, but its banality often prevents the one performing the task from recognizing his or her role in the outcome (not that a person could not discover his or her role in this death-dealing process should this be desired).

---

20. Arendt, *Eichmann In Jerusalem*.
21. Hillberg, *The Destruction of European Jews*, 267.

In most cases the functionary would not need to be concerned with the ultimate outcome of the task at hand. Bureaucratic language, the language of expertise, further removed the functionary from any concerns with the ultimate outcome of the bureaucratic enterprise as the following quotation from a German technician ironically named Willy "Just" indicates.

> A shorter, fully loaded truck could operate much more quickly. A shortening of the rear compartment would not disadvantageously affect the weight balance, overloading the front axle, because "actually a correction in the weight distribution takes place automatically through the fact that the cargo in the struggle toward the back door during the operation always is preponderantly located there." Because the connection pipe was quickly rusted through the "fluids," the gas should be introduced from above, not below. To facilitate cleaning, an eight-to-twelve-inch hole should be made in the floor and provided with a cover opened from the outside. The floor should be slightly inclined, and the cover equipped with a small sieve. Thus all "fluids" would flow to the middle, and the "thin fluids" would exit even during the operation, and the "thicker fluids" could be hosed out afterwards.[22]

Apparently, Mr. Just used his expertise to perfect a certain kind of vehicle that was not operating as efficiently as it might. His memo discussed flaws in the previous design. He accounted for the "cargo" that would shift during the "operation." He effectively addressed the near automatic expulsion of the "thin fluids," and the "unfortunate" fact that there would be the need to hose out the "thicker fluids" that were the result of "the cargo's" reaction to the "operation." Willy Just probably could sleep well at night because the bureaucracy and its language enabled him to design a mobile chamber of death without even considering the morality of his actions.

Such moral considerations would be the concern of the functionary's immediate supervisor who also could avoid thinking about the moral consequences of the mandated outcome. This is a common way human evil operates. One might say that unconfessed sins have the power to organize us in such a way that there is little place in our institutions for a moral concern to emerge. Under the sway of unconfessed sin, the bureaucratic process itself becomes its own moral code. A functionary

---

22. Browning, *Fateful Months*, 64–65.

is no longer concerned with the good or the evil, the right or the wrong, the life giving or the death-dealing. The functionary's only concern is whether he or she is doing a "good" job. "Good," of course is defined by the bureaucratic organization. It is no longer defined by the individual, the church, the family, or any other value external to the system.

In Nazi Germany the bureaucratic process was the moral code. As the flow chart above indicates, the bureaucratic process first established the divide between the "good" people (Aryan Germans) and the "evil" people (the Jews). Second, it then isolated the victimized Jews (by making them wear the Star of David) and set them apart as a separate bureaucratic category. Isolation assured those not categorized as Jewish that they were immune from whatever might happen to the Jews. Third, the Nazi bureaucracy established a process whereby Jews were dismissed from their jobs and their businesses were expropriated. Fourth, the Jewish population was rounded up and concentrated into ghettos or concentration camps. This removed them from sight. Out of sight, Jews were not encountered in everyday life which made it less likely that anyone would hear stories of their suffering. Sympathy and empathy for these now unseen victims became much less likely than ever. No one had the opportunity to listen to their plight. Without the opportunity to listen, ministry became less and less likely, and the lives of the Jews were dangerously threatened.[23]

Concentration completed this distancing process by completely removing the victims of oppression from society. They were no longer encountered. They were not personally known by those in the dominant class. The public only knew the victimized group through abstract categories, and Nazi propaganda supplied the content for these categories. Moreover, concentration camps made Nazi propaganda regarding the Jews more difficult to resist and refute. A German was unlikely to accept propaganda that claimed the Jews were "sub-human vermin" if he or she socialized with Jewish people, but consigning the Jews to concentration camps or ghettos meant that the average German would have no experience of a Jew that would contradict Nazi propaganda. Absent the empirical evidence provided by everyday association, vile Nazi propaganda became even easier to believe.

Exploitation and starvation further disguised the humanity of the Jewish victims who, emaciated by slave labor, starvation, and other

---

23. Hilberg, *The Destruction of the European Jews*, 41–44.

death-dealing forms of oppression, began to look as sub-human as the propaganda declared them to be! After treatment that was beyond inhumane, annihilation did not appear to be a great step at all! *It was the simple "logical" outcome of a banal bureaucratic process. A process created to a large extent by our unconfessed sin of antisemitism. This unacknowledged and unconfessed sin allowed the political leadership to implement its antisemitic horror.*

The Holocaust and Unconfessed Sin

The Holocaust is the most extreme example of how a regime of death can quickly emerge from unconfessed sin. It is also the most documented because the Nazi's were quite proud of what they were doing and wanted to leave a record. This process reveals that our unconfessed sins have the death-dealing power to organize us in such a way that there is little place in our institutions for ethical concerns to emerge. The bureaucratic process itself becomes its own moral code. Its functionaries only concern is whether he or she is doing a "good job," and "a good job" is defined by whether or not the functionary is carrying out the institution's mission. In the case of the Holocaust the institution's mission was the extermination of the Jews.

Why Repentance and Confession Are not the Same for Everyone

It is very important to say that what needs to be confessed by people like The Rich Man, Dostoevsky, and other members of the dominant culture such as myself is very different from what, *if anything*, needs to be confessed by the *victims* of racism, sexism, antisemitism, and institutional poverty. In fact, I, a person of social status, cannot tell any victim of racism, sexism, antisemitism, or institutional poverty what, *if anything*, they need to confess. That would only maintain my status in the social hierarchy that the Principalities perpetuate. All I can do is report on what the victims have said they need to confess. I make no judgment on the accuracy of these reports, but I do know that they are more accurate than any such judgment I might make.

In her article, "The Human Situation: A Feminine View," Valerie Saiving reminds us that it is *only from the perspective of male dominance* that sin manifests itself as the prideful concern for the self and its accomplishments, and that love—understood as self-giving that takes no thought for its own interest but seeks only the good of the other—is the opposite of sin.[24] For example, telling a woman experiencing domestic violence that love demands that she should not be concerned for her own interests (in this case her own life and limb) but only for the good of the other (in this case her abusive husband) not only perpetuates violence and endangers her life, but, more often than not, makes her, in the name of love and usually God, responsible for her husband's evil acts. If she accepts this definition of love—a definition derived from the male experience—she places her life in danger. Nonetheless, those who try to make this radical self-giving the universal definition of love cite Philippians 2:6–7. Here The Apostle Paul and perhaps Jesus himself appear to endorse the universality of self-emptying love saying, Jesus "who though he was in the form of God, did not regard equality with God as something to be exploited, but emptied himself, taking the form of a slave."

What is lost on people who would universally apply this description of self-emptying love is the fact that this understanding of love cannot be meant for slaves themselves or many others who are marginalized. These men and women cannot empty themselves because in many cases, they literally have nothing to empty! Jesus was "emptying Himself" of divine status! We with high social status are often called to empty ourselves of riches, power, or prestige in imitations on Jesus' love. Acts of love might be described differently by someone who cannot empty herself because she has nothing to empty. As is the case with a slave, if everything has already been taken from you, you are already empty!

James Cone, a patriarch of Black Liberation Theology, agrees. He states that the repentance required of marginalized African Americans is to repent of the *definitions* imposed on them by the socially dominant group or class. For him, the principal and most fundamental sin of black Americans is assuming the social position and the social definitions that the dominant white society assigns.

> But the real sin of the black church and its leaders is that they even convinced themselves that they were doing the right thing by advocating obedience to white oppressors as a means of entering, at death, the future age of heavenly bliss. The black church identified white words with God's Word and convinced its people that by listening in faithful obedience to the great white father they would surely enter the pearly gates. Thus, the

---

24. Saiving, "The Human Situation," 25–42.

The Death-Dealing Power of Unconfessed Sin

creativity of black churches which characterized the pre-Civil War period is missing after the war.[25]

Both Saiving and Cone remind us that while self-emptying love might be something the dominant group consistently needs to do if *we* are to confess and repent of our sin, this is only very rarely the path the oppressed should take. If self-emptying love is universally applied to all without respect to social context, urging a marginalized one to perform "virtues" like sacrificial love will probably benefit their "masters" and oppressors far more than it benefits them. Truly, there may be instances where a marginalized person might decide to practice self-emptying love, but this cannot be demanded of them by the dominant group. Only a socially marginalized person is in the position to understand when self-emptying love is life-giving rather than death-dealing.

Indeed, many African American Womanist theologians cogently argue that black liberation theology and feminist theology only partially reflect their life experiences. Delores Williams, matriarch of African Womanist theology, concisely summarizes this difference,

> (...) womanist theology especially concerns itself with the faith, survival and freedom-struggle of African-American women. Thus, womanist theology identifies and critiques black male oppression of black females while it also critiques white racism that oppresses all African Americans, female, and male. Like white feminist theology, womanist theology affirms the full humanity of women. But womanist theology also critiques white feminist participation in the perpetuation of white supremacy, which continues to dehumanize black women. Yet womanist theology is organically related to black male liberation theology and feminist theology in its various expressions.[26]

One difference Williams exposes is that while black women are concerned with liberation, they are often more concerned with the survival and "the quality of life" of those for whom they care. This is the core value for black women who tried to survive under slavery and still try to survive under other forms of racial oppression.[27] In many circumstances, black women, constrained by sexual and racial oppression, nonetheless adopted a stance of self-emptying love for the sake of survival of those under their

---

25. Cone, *Black Theology*, 107.
26. Williams, *Sisters in the Wilderness*, xvii.
27. Williams, *Sisters in the Wilderness*, 19–21.

care. (Those under their care have been white as well as black). This loving tactic, however, was not primarily chosen to benefit their "masters." They chose self-emptying love when it increased the chance of survival and/or enriched the lives of those for whom they cared.

Social context is an important key to understanding what, *if anything*, needs to be confessed. For the victims, confession involves the refusal to accept the definitions and limitations that the dominant culture tries to impose. What these definitions are can only be discovered by the victims. But for those who benefit from our privileged position in the dominant culture, "self-emptying love," which often involves abandoning one's social advantages and position, is vital. Only through our meager attempts at self-emptying love can we even begin to confess the sins of racism, sexism, antisemitism, and the benefits we receive from institutional poverty. Only with such confession can we even begin to oppose the evil that emerges as a by-product of unconfessed sin.

For those with social status, confession and repentance begins with *listening* to what those marginalized by the death-dealing power of sin have to say. The very least such listening requires is that we make changes in our lives because of what we hear. Moreover, even when we *think* we have made an adjustment, we cannot be the ones who determine if the adjustment we think we made is acceptable. We must "empty ourselves" of the social status that enables us to define what a proper adjustment might be. We must listen to the victims—the Jews, victims of racism, the poor, American Indians, women, the mentally ill, and others who are marginalized—to see if our perceived adjustments are, in fact, acceptable and how we can improve them.

For members of the dominant groups, confession and repentance also ask us to help clear, protect, and maintain an arena in which the voices of the marginalized are heard without, at the same time, controlling the content of the discussion. Confession and repentance also imply that members of the dominant group educate themselves concerning the breadth and scope of sexism, racism, antisemitism, and institutional poverty so that we might discover more sins to confess and thereby oppose the evil that is the consequence of unconfessed sin. Through disciplined study we become aware of what we were once unaware. In some important ways this newfound awareness might help us discover and articulate how the dominant culture hides what it is doing to marginalize the marginalized.

Racism, antisemitism, sexism, and institutional poverty are examples of the consequences of unacknowledged and unconfessed sin. They are embedded in the Principalities whose works are so engrained in civilization that our first impulse is to equate them with "the way things are," think of them as God-Given, or understand them as a product of nature. We are wrong when we do so because they are, in truth, a consequence of our unconfessed sin and the unconfessed sins of our predecessors. Moreover, these unconfessed sins have death-dealing consequences as our brief accounts of the workings of Nazi antisemitism, American racism, institutional poverty, and sexism indicates. It will probably take many human lifetimes to purge these evils. But in the process of our confessions, we can diminish their death-dealing power. Engaging in this process is ministry's profound and fundamental task for people with high social status.

The next chapter is about Dostoevsky's antisemitism as it was reflected in both his fiction and journalistic writings. It ends by discussing how Dostoevsky's relationship to Russian peasants and serfs changed during his lifetime. This emerging relationship illustrates how he *could* have addressed his own antisemitism had he acknowledged and confessed this sin. His relationship to Russian serfs and peasants also discloses how we too might begin to come to terms with our unconfessed sins embodied in racism, sexism, institutional poverty, and antisemitism—unacknowledged and unconfessed sins that continue to plague humanity and the rest of God's creation with the unnecessary evils that our confessions have the power to destroy.

This grim account of the death-dealing power of the unconfessed sins of racism, antisemitism, and institutional poverty demonstrate how evil emerges from our continued refusal to acknowledge and confess our sins and assume responsibility for the sins of our predecessors. These evils appear to be autonomous. They remain unstoppable as long as the sins that make them possible remain unconfessed. Left unchecked, they destroy communities and cultures. The Holocaust, slavery, apartheid and Jim Crow are concrete, historical examples of their power.

9

Dostoevsky's Unabashed Antisemitism

Why do you see the speck in your neighbor's eye, but do not notice the log in your own eye? Or how can you say to your neighbor, "Let me take the speck out of your eye while the log is in your own eye?" You hypocrite, first take the log out of your own eye, and then you will see clearly to take the speck out of your neighbor's eye.

—(MATT 7: 3–5)

DOSTOEVSKY'S ANTISEMITISM COMPLETES MY meditation on his contribution to the theology and practice of the art of ministry, but unlike the many beautiful and positive contributions discussed in previous chapters, his deep-seated antisemitism is an obstacle to ministry. As we know too well, antisemitism is not confined to Dostoevsky. It is a constant feature of Christianity itself. It dominated Europe, and this unconfessed sin was and remains an integral feature of American life.

Dostoevsky's unabashed antisemitism rejects one of Zosima's guides to ministry, namely, "everyone is really responsible to all people for all people and for everything,"[1] Responsibility does not necessarily mean

---

1. Dostoevsky, *Brothers*, 250.

guilt, but it can mean guilt. A white person living in the United States is not guilty for the *institution* of slavery that plagued the country's past. We did not create it. But we still benefit from it and have the clear responsibility to oppose and try to set right the continuing death-dealing consequences of American slavery and racism—a racism for which we are still quite guilty. Repentance is necessary to even begin to acknowledge our responsibility as well as our guilt.

Dostoevsky's antisemitism also violates Zosima's admonition to active love. Active love requires listening—making an adjustment because of what is said. Refusing to listen means no adjustments are made. Not adjusting to what someone says is a concrete manifestation of the fact that the speaker means nothing to you. Treating a person as if they mean nothing to you is the near equivalent of treating her as if she is dead. This chapter seeks to explore how sins like antisemitism, racism, sexism, and institutional poverty are often the product of refusing to love and refusing to accept responsibility. The two central dictums of Zosima's understanding of ministry.

Not only does Dostoevsky refuse to listen to his most significant characters, but he also carried this refusal to listen into "real life" where evidence from his journalistic writings demonstrate his consistent refusal to listen to and learn from the Jews. Despite this, however, Dostoevsky leaves ample information that helps us find a way to struggle not only with his antisemitism, but our own antisemitism, racism, and sexism as well; for, Dostoevsky's growth in his own personal understanding of Russian peasants might be a way to begin to overcome his and our own racist and antisemitic attitudes and actions.

Dostoevsky's Antisemitism in His Fiction

In his fictional works, there is only one character of consequence who is Jewish. Isay Fomich Bumstein is a prisoner in *The House of the Dead* which is a semi-fictional account of Dostoevsky's real-life imprisonment at Omsk prison in Siberia in the late 1840's and early 1850's. Bumstein is stereotypically presented in contradictory terms. He is the "only Jew among us who everyone laughed at and derided" but "accepted" even though he was a Jew. In accord with many stereotypical accounts of Jews,

Bumstein is presented with contradictory characteristics of being lazy but tireless, rash but cowardly, and a bit of an idiot but very shrewd.[2]

When Bumstein is first placed with the other inmates, he appears frightened and sits pensively at the edge of one of the common beds. In silence, he stays in this position until another convict approaches him. The convict spreads out some tattered garments and asks if Isay Fomich might loan him a silver ruble using these rags as collateral. Isay visibly perks up. He looks at the rags and, to the delight and amusement of his fellow convicts, the first words the convicts hear Isay Fomich utter are, "A silver ruble, no, but seven kopecks maybe." Everyone roars with laughter at these words. The convict agrees, but Isay next negotiates the terms, namely 3 kopecks interest to be paid monthly not yearly as was first surmised by the recipient of the loan—again much to the amusement of the crowd.[3] Even when incarcerated, the only Jew in custody is introduced as a usurious moneylender. Furthermore, Isay Formich Bumstein is the only source of comedic relief in a dire and morbid book about the miserable lives of convicts in a Russian prison. This book is not titled *The House of the Dead* for nothing.

Early in *The Brothers Karamazov*, the narrator tells us that after his first wife's death and before Ivan and Alyosha were born, Fyodor Karamazov spent several years in Odessa. There he became acquainted with "a lot of low 'Yids', 'Yiddels', 'Yidkins', and 'Yidlets', and finally ended up being received not only by 'Yids' but even Jews as well." The narrator goes on to comment, "It may be presumed that in this period of his life he developed a particular faculty for making and hoarding money."[4] The narrator proceeds to associate Fyodor Karamazov with the Jews as they are stereotypically portrayed saying that in this period Fyodor "acquired"—perhaps like someone who might "catch" a communicable disease—a particular faculty for making and hoarding money. The implied source of this "particular faculty" is, of course, the Jews; for, what else could possibly be the source of Fyodor's miserly behavior? The Russian reader would likely "understand" this to mean that at least one of the elder Karamazov's vile vices was "acquired" from the Jews because no Russian could be a miser unless influenced by the Jews. In a very subtle way, therefore, the narrator of *The Brothers Karamazov* suggests that Fyodor Karamazov's many vices are not part of normal Russian society. Their source resides

2. Dostoevsky, *House of the Dead*, 69.
3. Dostoevsky, *House of the Dead*, 118–19.
4. Dostoevsky, *Brothers*, 25.

in the Jews who "infect" Russian society.[5] *Statements of the dominant group being "infected" by a socially subordinate group are the near universal language of antisemites and racists.*

David Goldstein recognizes that late in his life, Dostoevsky imputed the basest of his antisemitic notions to Alyosha Karamazov himself—the person who we have employed herein as a prime exemplar of the art of Christian ministry! In the last encounter between Alyosha and Liza Khokhlakova (the daughter of Madame Khokhlakova who had wanted a compliment from Zosima because of the "honesty" of her odd confession) an overly excited Liza asks Alyosha if it is true that around Easter the "Yids" steal a child and kill it. Alyosha responds, "I don't know."[6] Rightly outraged at this antisemitic response, Goldstein writes,

> Alyosha's evasive reply is not justifiable on either human or artistic grounds (. . .) and (. . .) in betraying Alyosha, Dostoevsky betrayed himself. Driven by a blind hatred against a people, ostracized and execrated in the country of their adoption—the only homeland they knew—Dostoevsky, humanist and Christian, in the twilight of his life, did not shrink from endorsing, with all the authority he commanded as both a man and writer, an ignominious myth and odious lie. Thus, he knowingly and willfully incited his people (. . .) against the "people of the book."[7]

In his greatest novel Dostoevsky pedaled one of the greatest antisemitic falsehoods that Christians have long repeated—that each Easter Jews recapitulate "their role" in the crucifixion of Christ by kidnapping and crucifying a Christian child. The perpetuation of this falsehood helped further justify the persecution of the Jews through the Holocaust and beyond.

The only disagreement I may have with Goldstein is that, as strange as it may seem to victims the death-dealing power of unacknowledged and unconfessed sins like antisemitism, Dostoevsky, and his character Alyosha may not, in fact, "know" the answer to Liza's inquiry. Like most Christians who grew up with these antisemitic stories, Dostoevsky chose not to question the veracity of these vile lies even though these lies have absolutely no basis. By now I hope this voluntary amnesia and ignorance in no way justifies Dostoevsky's antisemitism. It does, however,

---

5. Goldstein, *Dostoevsky and the Jews*, 155.
6. Dostoevsky, *Brothers*, 492.
7. Goldstein, *Dostoevsky and the Jews*, 156.

demonstrate that many antisemites choose "not to know" they are antisemites. There are many racists who also choose "not to know" they are racist. There are many misogynists who choose "not to know" they hate women, and many rich people neither "know" they are rich nor care about the poor. Despite their voluntary ignorance of their sins, these people are responsible for continuing the death-dealing power these sins unleash.

Many modern antisemites, racists, sexists, and those who are oblivious to the plight of the poor are like the Rich Man in the story called The Rich Man and Lazarus. They do not believe that they are in the least bit antisemites or racists even though they are! Their antisemitism or racism may be obvious to the victims of these perennial sins, but, like Dostoevsky and Alyosha, they are oblivious. These sleepwalkers "know" that racism, sexism, and antisemitism are "wrong," but, instead of examining their possible culpability, they go to great lengths to justify themselves and "prove," at least to their own personal satisfaction, that they cannot be painted with the brush of these sins. Furthermore, it is not that the victims have not told them. Like Dostoevsky, they simply refuse to listen to the victims of these human sins.

What Dostoevsky "Did Not Know" Hurt Us All

Like many others Dostoevsky may have chosen "not to know" he was an antisemite, and like many others, he tried to justify himself when confronted with his antisemitism. But more than almost anyone of his generation, he should have known because he made his living examining the consequences of many of the ideas of his generation, and he found them wanting after such an examination. Had he thought about antisemitism with the depth of artistic imagination and reflection that he devoted to other social and intellectual issues of his day, he may have had the power to alter the trajectory of world history. Dostoevsky's deliberate amnesia regarding his own antisemitism was more than tragic!

Dostoevsky's Antisemitism in His Journalism

In *A Writer's Diary* Dostoevsky is a man who is completely blind to his antisemitism. He cannot understand why some of his Jewish correspondents place him among the "Haters of the Jews." But, instead of *listening* to an interlocutor's criticism and making an adjustment because of what he said, Dostoevsky refuses to listen. He refuses to take the accusation as an opportunity to reflect on the truth of his beliefs. Instead, Dostoevsky, indignant at this "insult," tries to justify himself. He asks his correspondents, "Where and how did I declare my hatred for the Jewish people?" Rather than listening, he wonders,

> Might they not be accusing me of "hatred" because I sometimes call the Jew a "Yid"? But in the first place, *I never thought this was so offensive*, and in the second place, as far as I can recall, I always used the word "Yid" to denote a well-known idea: "Yid, Yid-ism, the Kingdom of the Yids," etc. These designate a well-known concept, a tendency, a characteristic of the age. One can argue with that idea, one can disagree with it, but *one should not take offense at a word*.[8]

Now, I must admit, that when I am subject to unfavorable criticism my first reaction—a reaction that I have tried, with limited success, to train myself to avoid—is to try to justify myself just like Dostoevsky. If I can stop myself from justifying myself, however, I will try to explain myself instead. While we may not recognize it, an explanation is different from a justification. The distinction is simple. Self-justification seeks the high moral ground. It is an effort to demonstrate why your action is morally good, and, indeed, far more morally good than the proposal of your critic. In contrast, an explanation merely tries to give the reason for what you have said or done without laying claim to the high moral ground. It merely attempts to convey information concerning your position.

While it is very easy to distinguish between an explanation and a self-justification abstractly, in practice, it is quite difficult for your interlocutor to recognize the difference. Usually, my critics will think I am trying to justify myself when I am trying to explain myself. At my best, I try to avoid this confusion by repeating phrases like "I might be wrong, but (. . .)" or "This might have been a dumb thing to do, but (. . .)" or, even better (if you can honestly say so), "Because of what you just said, maybe I should have (. . .)." Such statements help someone see that you are not seeking the high moral ground; are willing to entertain the fact that you might be wrong; and that you are at least trying to listen to their criticism.

I try to intentionally make this distinction because self-justification is an impediment to ministry. Think about it for a minute. If you think

---

8. Dostoevsky, *Writer's Diary*, 350, emphasis mine.

you have successfully justified yourself, your conversation partner has limited options. He can accept your reasoning process, and bow to your intellectual and moral superiority. Perhaps you gain a loyal follower who now follows because you have demonstrated that he was a fool to question you, however, your future conversation on the subject is now quite restricted. At least with respect to the topic, the last word has been uttered. Another possible outcome is the conversation partner remains in disagreement and on this subject at least thinks that she is not the fool, but you are. This response also truncates your future relationship. Another is the person recognizes that you refuse to take her concerns seriously and simply drops out of your life, for what is the point in being around a person who thinks the way you think? All these possibilities are obvious impediments to ministry that self-justifications create.

Dostoevsky is "shocked" that certain Jews believe that he is a "Jew Hater." Apparently, he believes that he might have a moral defect if the charge is true, so his response is to claim the high moral ground in his defense. Clearly, he had options other than self-justification. He could have recognized that a victim of antisemitism might have some insight into the nature of antisemitism that he (Dostoevsky) does not possess. Whenever a Jew charges a Christian with the sin of antisemitism, the Jew courageously does the Christian a favor. The Jew gives the Christian an opportunity to examine this sin, understand it more deeply, and perhaps confess his or her antisemitism. For Christians, however, this is a road that is less travelled. Dostoevsky takes a more well-travelled route. When accused of the sin of antisemitism, Dostoevsky, like most of us, tries to justify himself. He tries to demonstrate by "reasonable" means that the accuser is wrong and the accuser, not Dostoevsky, should apologize.

Like many people accused of making a racist, sexist, or antisemitic remarks by victims of these unconfessed sins, Dostoevsky does not say, "I am sorry this offended you and I will try not to speak in this fashion in the future because I know it offends you." (*One need not yet understand why a statement or act offends. One needs only know that it does offend*). Dostoevsky, however, refuses to acknowledge that his words gave offense! Instead, to justify himself, he says that he never thought that calling someone a "Yid" could offend anyone. (Despite what he thought, it did offend someone, namely, the person to whom he was responding). His rather stupid defense does not even end here. He goes on to say that the words "Yid, "Yidism" "Kingdom of Yids" *denote a well-known idea*! He goes on to haughtily say that you can disagree with the idea, but "one should not take offense at a word." It is socially respectable for Dostoevsky to say something like this because *members of the dominant culture not only get to define the parameters of "rational discourse," they also get to instruct those who are not members of the dominant culture in the rules of engagement.*[9] This is the essence of capturing the High Moral Ground that self-justification seeks.

As a member of the dominant group, Dostoevsky thinks he can define the terms of the debate. In this case, he, not a Jewish person, gets to define what it means to be an antisemite. According to the perch provided him by his dominant antisemitic culture, Dostoevsky is not a "Jew Hater." Despite what the victims of such hatred say, Dostoevsky's culture told him that he could not be a "Jew Hater" because he never *intended* to offend anyone. Absence of intent exonerates him from the charge of antisemitism regardless of anything a *victim* of such hate might say.

Relying on the definitions provided by his social status, Dostoevsky admonishes his accuser saying that this person has no reason to be offended, and that this argumentative Jew should get over it. Words, Dostoevsky lectures, represent ideas. You can disagree with the ideas, but Dostoevsky, certain of his perceived right to set the rules of proper debate, continues, you *cannot* take offense at words. His response takes no regard of the thoughts and feelings of his Jewish interlocutor whose feelings do not matter to Dostoevsky. Indeed, Dostoevsky ridicules these feelings because he has the social status to do so. He goes on to lecture this Jew saying that reason demands that he jettison these "false" feelings and thoughts he "irrationally" holds about poor Dostoevsky's hatred of the Jews.

As deliberately noted on many occasions already, Dostoevsky's refusal to listen to this Jewish critique is more tragic than an more average person's refusal. His fiction has been widely acclaimed for his uncanny ability to use his characters to push popular philosophical ideas to their logical and extreme conclusion. In *Notes from the Underground* Dostoevsky pushed the Russian intelligentsia's belief that we live in a thoroughly determined world to its logical extreme in the person of The Underground Man. In *The Possessed* he did the same pointing out the violence inherent in socialist ideas that prefigured Leninism. In *Crime and Punishment,* he took on the radical individualism inherent in capitalism and demonstrated

---

9. Long, *Significations*, is a classic expression of how the dominant culture establishes conventional and often unquestioned symbols, images, ideas, and definitions that govern all "rational' social discourse.

the death-dealing capacity of this idea. In these writings he, more than anyone else, demonstrated the capacity to take a contemporary idea and push that idea to its logical, death-dealing extreme.

In this journalistic endeavor, however, he did not even attempt to push this "well known concept" represented by the words, "Yid," "Yidism" and "the Kingdom of the Yids" to the level that his art had accomplished in his dramatizations of nihilism, utopianism, rationalism, individualism, utilitarianism, and materialistic socialism. It is beyond unfortunate that we no longer need the genius of Dostoevsky's fiction to perform this task with respect to antisemitism. Reality itself pushed this this "idea of 'Yidism'" to its logical, death-dealing conclusion. The Nazis did this in the Holocaust, and the Holocaust is not fiction!

The "idea" that is represented by Dostoevsky's racial slurs associates Jews with moneylending and capitalism. Dostoevsky expresses this stereotypical idea on many occasions writing tirades like, "One would think that it is not they (the Jews) who rule Europe, not they (the Jews) who at least control the stock exchange there, and, accordingly the policy, internal affairs and morality of the states."[10] Dostoevsky thought that radical capitalism has its origin with the Jews. He thought that it was in direct contradiction with Russian Christianity, and because of this contradiction Dostoevsky thought there was a cosmological conflict between Judaism and Russian Orthodoxy. For him this was a struggle between good and evil that Russia must win to save the rest of humanity. Dostoevsky asserts that should the Jews reign over Russia, "Would they (the Jews) not turn (the Russians) directly into slaves? Even worse: would they not strip them utterly bare? Would they not massacre them altogether, exterminate them completely, as they did more than once with alien peoples in times of old in their ancient history?"[11] Apparently, *this is the "great idea" of "Yidism" that Dostoevsky repeats without criticism.*

In his introduction to *A Writer's Diary*, Gary Saul Morson recognizes that Dostoevsky's antisemitic claims—claims that are the "great idea" behind "Yidism" and Dostoevsky's racial slurs—belong to the tradition of antisemitic thought in Russia and Europe that led to the infamous Russian forgery *The Protocols of the Elders of Zion*. This collection of words alleges a universal Jewish conspiracy to enslave the world. Dostoevsky does not suggest, as *The Protocols* do and as the Nazis nearly accomplished, that

---

10. Dostoevsky, *Writer's Diary*, 352.
11. Dostoevsky, *Writer's Diary*, 357.

we should exterminate the Jews before they enslave us. Yet, there is but a "small step" in logic from Dostoevsky's "idea of 'Yidism'" to the Nazi policy of extermination. Dostoevsky was "incapable" of understanding the radical consequences of his antisemitic idea because he was blind to his own antisemitism and refused to even entertain the notion that his words and fictional characters were antisemitic at their core. This error, this inability, this refusal to acknowledge and confess his (and our own sin) had implications even more dramatic than the refusal of the parents of Scott Peck's client to acknowledge and confess their sins. Had Dostoevsky confessed and pushed the "idea" behind "Yidism" to its logical extreme, he might have been able to diminish the worldly power of this diabolical "idea." This being done, he may have changed the future just enough to prevent the Holocaust. Who knows? He was a great and popular writer, but his inability to confess his antisemitism may have had far reaching death-dealing consequences.

Dostoevsky's Antisemitism—Against His "Better" Judgment[12]

Had Dostoevsky managed to listen to his character Father Zosima, he might have been able to address his own antisemitism and help Russia do so as well. Listening to Zosima would mean remembering the two important themes of his ministry. The first, small acts of active love, have been discussed at length. Dostoevsky intends these acts of ministry to be the way to oppose evil, and they are, but only in small ways. If performed enough they can have a ripple effect throughout culture, but they are small. Their small, seemingly insignificant status has often led critics to argue that Dostoevsky's use of these small acts—these onions—to oppose the entirety of evil in the world comes up short. The magnitude of the world's evil and its complexities are just too great if all we are doing is giving people a "few onions."

Had Dostoevsky remembered and embraced Zosima's second theme of ministry, however, Dostoevsky's teaching on the art and practice of ministry might have gained a more global scope. His second theme—a

---

12. Gritsch, *Martin Luther's Antisemitism: Against His Better Judgment*. The title of this section is an adaption of the title of this book in which Gritsch first demonstrates beyond a shadow of a doubt that Luther was an antisemite, and then goes on to argue that if Luther had followed his own train of thought, he might have overcome his antisemitism which Luther, like Dostoevsky, did not do.

theme he received from his dying brother Markel—is *"everyone is really responsible to all (people) and for all (people) and for everything."* The social implications of this admonition could be enormous. Had Dostoevsky seen the implications of this admonition, he might have begun to address antisemitism as well as the human sin embodied in Principalities that continues to unleash the death-dealing power of unconfessed sin throughout civilization.

It is interesting to note that Zosima does not say we are guilty. He says we are *responsible*. Those of us on the upper rungs of society often are guilty as well as responsible because we continue to take advantage of the social status bequeathed to us by our predecessors and the Principalities they created. In the United States white people, for example, are never subject to the same obstacles our laws and mores place in the path of people who are not deemed white. Furthermore, those who are "unaware" of this nonetheless rely on these advantages in everyday life. For instance, we white people "belong" everywhere. The police are not "out to get us." We receive the benefit of the doubt from authorities. We are rarely incarcerated for crimes like having small amounts of illicit drugs in our possession. We rely on these advantages. We obviously had no appreciable role in setting society up the way it is. (We do have a role in keeping it this way). We are not guilty for the culture into which we were thrown at birth, but we are responsible. We are responsible because in many and various ways, we seek to perpetuate the system that benefits us at the expense of others. Our refusal or inability to accept responsibility *to* all people, *for* all people and *for* everything (like global warming and political unrest) rests at the core of the human sins of antisemitism, racism, sexism, and institutional poverty.

Like most of his Russian culture, Dostoevsky never dreamed that his responsibility to all people and for all people could possibly include the Jews. This was the source of his antisemitism. But when it came to the Russian serfs and peasantry, Dostoevsky's attitudes did change markedly. Somehow, he was able to listen. He tried to repent of his sins with respect to the Russian underclass, and, eventually, he began to treat Russian peasants as human beings of vital importance to Russian society.[13] He listened to their voices, and, in the process of listening, Dostoevsky found that Russian peasants had much to teach. He came to this insight during four years of hard labor in Siberia.

---

13. Miller, *Dostoevsky's Unfinished Journey*, 2–21.

In 1849 Dostoevsky was arrested for being a member of the Socialist Petrashevsky Circle. After eight months in solitary confinement, Dostoevsky was unceremoniously removed from his cell and, along with his comrades, marched out to be executed by a firing squad. On the brink of execution, the Tsar commuted their death sentence, and instead Dostoevsky and his fellow prisoners were sentenced to hard labor in Siberia. Dostoevsky's near execution had a tremendous influence on his life. Quite understandably he felt reborn. For the first time he understood that "life itself is the greatest of all goods and blessings, and that (each person) has the power to turn each moment into an eternity of happiness."[14] Beginning with this re-awakening, and proceeding throughout his imprisonment and subsequent freedom, Dostoevsky began to understand the peasants differently. He began to understand them iconically. He began to see right through their gruff surface appearance, and, in doing so, he found a "jewel" at their core. Dostoevsky listened to them, and by listening he developed ideas and beliefs that influence the fictional worlds he created.

Unable to communicate with his family during his four years of hard labor, Dostoevsky wrote a letter to his brother Mikhail upon his release. Here he describes his first impression of Russian peasants that is "unvarnished" by his later thoughts and literary efforts. He wrote, "and here in Omsk, I settled down to living with them (the peasants) for four years. They were coarse, ill-natured, cross-grained people. They're hatred for the gentry knew no bounds, and therefore, they received us, the gentlemen, with hostility and malicious joy in our troubles. They would have eaten us alive if given the chance."

Even in this letter, however, Dostoevsky begins to express certain socio/political reasons for the peasants' hatred of the gentry. He understood their hatred contending that it was as if they were saying, "You are noblemen, iron beaks that used to peck us to death. Before the master used to torment the people, but now he is lower than the lowest, has become one of us." This was the theme that the peasant convicts played in many variations throughout Dostoevsky's four years of incarceration. Yet, by the end of this letter, Dostoevsky displays a change in attitude saying, "Men, however, are everywhere men. In four years in prison, I came at least to distinguish men among criminals. Believe me, there are deep,

---

14. Frank, *Dostoevsky*, 183.

strong, beautiful characters among them, and what joy it was to discover the gold under the course, hard surface."[15]

Nearly a decade after his release from prison, Dostoevsky published *The House of the Dead*, his slightly disguised autobiographical account of his life in prison. This account demonstrates a change in his attitude toward Russian peasants while in prison that continues during the years following his release. Upon arrival he was immediately thrown in with peasant convicts, and, for four years, he lived among them in close quarters. He was threatened with violence, and, to one degree or another, this threat of violence remained throughout his incarceration. At first, he could not endure their irrational, violent, drunken behavior. He could not see beyond their surface behavior until he recalled an incident from his youth. As a nine-year-old boy, he was playing in the forest and thought he saw a wolf. Fleeing the forest in terror he saw the Peasant Marey working in a field. He ran to him for protection, and seeing the child's terror, Marey smiled, made the sign of the cross on the young Fyodor's head, comforted him and sent him home promising to watch over him to make sure the wolf does not get him. Although this story is not told in *The House of the Dead*, years later Dostoevsky remembers (that he remembered) this very incident while in prison, and, remembering this event, his attitude toward the peasants began to change. He writes,

> And so when I climbed down from my bunk and looked around I remember I suddenly felt I could regard these unfortunates in an entirely different way and that suddenly through some sort of miracle, the former hatred and anger in my heart had vanished. I went off, peering intently into the faces of those I met. This disgraced peasant, with shaven head and brands on his cheek, drunk and roaring out his hoarse, drunken song—why he might also be that very same Marey; I cannot peer into his heart after all.[16]

After this event, Dostoevsky's attitude toward the Russian peasants was forever transformed. He began to understand the peasants as icons. Their new iconic status enabled Dostoevsky to find beauty in the Russian peasant. In iconic fashion, he found this beauty beneath the surface on which "only abominations were evident." Remembering Marey, Dostoevsky came to understand that these "surface abominations" were a consequence of centuries of oppression and deprivation. He saw that the Russian

---

15. Dostoevsky, *Pisma*, 1. 135—7, in Frank, *Dostoevsky*, 188—90.
16. Dostoevsky, *Writer's Diary*, 135.

peasants should not be judged by what they appear to be on the surface, but by the ideals they embody; for, "these ideals have fused with the People's soul since time immemorial and have conferred upon it the blessings of frankness, honor, sincerity and broad mind, receptive to everything; and all this is combined in the most attractive harmonious fashion."[17] Although this short quotation was written years after *The House of the Dead*, it testifies to the fact that the full implications of a life transforming event can take time to unfold. *The House of the Dead*, however, testifies to Dostoevsky's emerging understanding of Russian peasants, and this new understanding begins to gradually emerge from his prison experience.

For instance, much to his surprise, Dostoevsky discovered that the peasants believed that there was an insurmountable chasm between Russian gentry and peasants. The gap was so great that Russian peasants could not even conceive of any Russian gentry as one of their comrades. "This is not the result of conscious prejudice but comes about of itself, quite sincerely and unconsciously."[18]

> I understood that they would never accept me as a comrade, however much I might be a convict, not if I were in for life, not if I were in the special division. But I remember most clearly Petrov's face at that minute. His question, "how can you be our comrade?" was full of such genuine simplicity, such simple hearted perplexity. I wondered if there were any irony, any malicious mockery in the question. There was nothing of the sort, simply we were not their comrades and that was all. You go your way, and we go ours; you have your affairs, and we have ours.[19]

This gap between the peasants and gentry persisted even within the close quarters of prison life. This fact, undisputable in Dostoevsky's view, undermined the commonly held beliefs among the Russian Socialist intelligentsia that the peasants would heed the revolutionary call to revolution by the educated Russian gentry. Prison life enabled Dostoevsky to know the peasants as few of his class could, and this knowledge greatly influenced Dostoevsky's mature, post-Siberian writings particularly his lifelong suspicion of materialist socialist movements—particularly the "myth" that the peasants would join the cause at the instigation of the leaders of the intelligentsia and submit to the intelligentsia's leadership.

17. Dostoevsky, *Writer's Diary*, 128.
18. Dostoevsky, *House of the Dead*, 32.
19. Dostoevsky, *House of the Dead*, 271.

Second, Dostoevsky's daily contact with criminals revealed one aspect of human nature that Joseph Frank has called "a spirit of perverseness." This too undermines the socialist agenda, or any social agenda with utopian goals—which predicts that humanity, on its own and certainly without God's help, can create a rational, utopian society where everyone receives what they need. Dostoevsky thought such projects were doomed by the spirit of perverseness which is inexplicable irrationalism, sadism or masochism directed toward someone, something or even oneself.

> The Prison authorities are sometimes surprised that after leading a quiet, exemplary life for some years, and even being made a foreman for his model behavior, a convict with no apparent reason suddenly breaks out, as though he were possessed by a devil, plays pranks, drinks, makes an uproar and sometimes positively ventures on serious crimes—such as open disrespect to a superior officer, or even commits murder or rape. They look at him and marvel. And all the while possibly the cause of this sudden outbreak, in the man from whom one would least have expected it, is simply the poignant hysterical craving for self-expression, the unconscious yearning for himself, the desire to assert himself, to assert his crushed personality, a desire which suddenly takes possession of him and reaches the pitch of fury, of spite, of mental aberration, of fits and nervous convulsions.[20]

The spirit of perverseness is not limited to prisoners. It probably pertains to all of us. It resides in the human craving for self-expression, which is consistently thwarted in prison. Moreover, a job, a marriage, a family, an education or just about any institution might thwart or need for self-expression which leads to the spirit of perverseness of which Frank speaks. No matter how wonderful a social community might be—even in the most beautiful utopian dreams of the egalitarian societies of socialists and communists—there would always be someone who, in the grip of the spirit of perverseness, will do the unexpected and oppose such rational expressions of human well-being. It is for these reasons that Dostoevsky opposed nearly all utopian agendas (capitalist or socialist) of the mid-nineteenth century Russia intelligentsia.

This theme, essential to his writing projects, emerged because Dostoevsky, in the language of Russian Orthodox Christianity, began to treat Russian peasants as icons. For something to function as an icon it must be available in the ordinary world. When treated iconically, an abundance

---

20. Dostoevsky, *House of the Dead*, 83–84.

present in the ordinary can open us into a larger world that exists beyond what our normal perceptions convey.[21] When Dostoevsky perceives "the gold under the course hard surface" of the Russian peasants, he asserts their iconic status.

If Dostoevsky's iconic understanding of the peasants represents Dostoevsky's "better judgment," it could well be that had he understood the Jews in the same iconic way, his feelings and his relationship to the Jews would have been transformed. In the process of such reflection, he could have acknowledged and confessed his antisemitism and begin to address the death-dealing consequences of this sin. There were, however, some important things that appear to prevent Dostoevsky from developing an iconic vision of the Jews. Two will be listed here not to offer an excuse, but because they still may be obstacles to our own attempts to acknowledge and confess our own sin.

First, like most Russians, he rarely encountered Jews in everyday life. Dostoevsky was able to view peasants as icons largely because prison gave him the opportunity to see them every day. In Russian culture, however, Jews normally lived in a ghetto and day to day contact was limited. Accordingly, Dostoevsky did not have much opportunity to see beyond the surface of a Jew because he never had a "surface" to see. The way his culture was arranged with respect to the Jews made it very unlikely that the average Russian gentleman or peasant would encounter very many Jews. Not seeing or encountering Jews made it difficult if not impossible to visualize them as icons.

Second, his understanding of the Bible was largely limited to the New Testament. (This is related to the fact that we do not encounter Jews in everyday life). In fact, he was given a *New Testament* (not the entire Bible) when he entered the confines of his Siberian prison. As the New Testament was the only book a convict was allowed in the Siberian prison, Dostoevsky read it again and again.[22] Had convicts been allowed to possess and read the entire Bible, Dostoevsky's attitude toward the Jews might have been much different.

Dostoevsky was far more creative, imaginative, and insightful than nearly all human beings who have ever walked this earth. If he could have read the Old Testament regularly and with some understanding, he might have understood the Jewish people iconically like he understood

---

21. R. Williams, *Dostoevsky*, 207.
22. Frank, *Dostoevsky*, 187.

the Russian peasants. Had he achieved this vision, maybe he could have recognized that the biblical God had emancipated the Jews from Egyptian captivity. He would have seen that God stuck with them even when they deviated from God's ways. He might have seen that after their exodus from Egypt the Jews attempted to be develop a society that was unlike other nations and live without a king. Maybe he would have seen that even when, against God's wishes, they demanded a king, God stuck with them. He might also have seen that the biblical God sent them prophets so that the word of their King would not be the only word that the Jewish people heard. Maybe he also would have recognized that Jesus himself was a Jew, and his Jewish mother was selected by God to birth him into the world.

Knowing and remembering these biblical events, Dostoevsky might have listened to his Jewish critics who said he was a "Jew Hater," and, rather than trying to justify himself against this charge, he could have become responsible, confess his sin, and begin the process of repentance. He failed to do this. He, along with all of Europe and North America, remained profoundly antisemitic, and the unconfessed sin of antisemitism continues to exert its death-dealing power—a power revealed in the Holocaust and still persists throughout Western civilization.

A Concluding Literary and Biblical Postscript

From now on, therefore, we regard no one from a human point of view (...) So if anyone is in Christ, there is a new creation: everything old has passed away, see, everything has become new! All this is from God, who reconciled us to himself through Christ, and has given us the ministry of reconciliation.

—(2 Cor 5:16–18)

GRACE IS AN EVENT in which a person is treated both lovingly and in discontinuity with his or her past.[1] If a person is treated in continuity with the past, the treatment will not be gracious even if it is beneficial. A laborer who is paid for the work she has done at the agreed upon rate is not a recipient of grace because she deserves her pay based upon her *past* performance. If, however, a person is in need and receives needed aid without doing anything in the past that merits that aid (at least according to the moral and legal standards of his society), he has received grace. He has been treated both lovingly and in discontinuity with his past. "Everything old has passed away (...) everything has become new."

---

1. This is not the only way to understand grace. For example, St. Thomas Aquinas (1225–1275) says, "Grace perfects nature." This means that there is continuity (not discontinuity) between grace and nature. It indicates that nature can take us only so far, but the infusion of God's grace allows us to continue on the road to perfection begun by nature. When Paul says, "So if anyone is in Christ, there is a new creation," (2 Cor 5:17) he expresses the discontinuity between grace and nature. St. Thomas expresses the continuity between grace and nature.

Principalities and powers rely on everything being essentially the same. They no longer rule when everything is new, where grace happens, and where freedom is always possible.

Fyodor Dostoevsky's literary world is a world where grace, so conceived, is possible, but grace is never inevitable. Principalities resist grace. Principalities and Powers along with the necessities they create cannot mediate grace because they only take the present and extrapolate the present (as they conceive it) into the future. In other words, the only thing that Principalities and Powers promise us is more of the same. The Grand Inquisitor, for example, promised the people more food to fill their bellies. Our modern capitalist economic system promises more money in the future to people who, by working at the jobs all politicians promise, do what is necessary to "merit" their riches. Our technological necessities promise that more and better technology will meet all our needs. The benefits derived from necessities are all based upon past performance. They can only promise more and more of what we already have. Nothing is new. Necessities cannot grant anything that is discontinuous with the world they represent. They do not surprise us in life-giving ways. They cannot mediate grace. They do not survive when all things are new.

Franz Kafka (1883–1924) creates literary worlds in which grace is impossible and where, by extension, the rule of the Principalities is absolute. The protagonists in both *The Trial* and *The Castle* are in life and death quests to find gracious outcomes to their plights. In *The Trial*, the hero, K., is accused of a serious crime. He is not told what the crime is. He is not even informed of the location of his trial. He is merely told that if he is convicted of this unknown crime, there will be serious, possibly fatal consequences. The rest of the novel depicts K's futile efforts to find some-*body* who can either defend him in court, explain to him the nature of his crime or at least tell him where his trial is to take place. K. realizes that if this *body* is not found, he will be punished. K's search is a futile search for a gracious outcome.

Kafka's *The Castle* is also a futile search for a gracious outcome, but, perhaps, under a different necessity. Here a surveyor comes to town. He is told that he has a job to do. He is told that the consequences will be quite serious if he fails to perform his task, but he is not told what his job is. As is the case in *The Trial*, the rest of the book is a series of attempts on the part of the protagonist to find some-*body* who can tell him what he must do to fulfill his assignment. Unless this body is found, grace will not be possible.

In the tradition of Kafka, Joseph Heller's (1923–1999) popular book *Catch 22* demonstrates the relationship between grace and bodily presence more explicitly. His protagonist, Yossarian, wants to get out of military service. He figures the best way for him to do so is through an insanity plea. The camp psychiatrist tells him that, although he might very well be insane, his plea will be rejected because regulations say that a soldier who *requests* to be discharged because of insanity cannot possibly be insane. This is because trying to remove oneself from an insane situation is, in fact, a very sane thing to do. Yossarian thinks this logic makes sense until he asks about a pilot who is clearly insane. The doctor tells Yossarian that this man, though clearly insane, cannot be discharged because another regulation states that military personnel must formally *request* an insanity discharge.

Only now does Yossarian understand Catch 22. He is powerless. If he continues to be treated "by the book" (or in continuity with his past), he knows he has no hope. He knows he will not receive grace. So, like Kafka's characters, Yossarian looks for some-*body* with the power to dispense with regulations and treat him graciously. Furthermore, Joseph Heller profoundly conveys this relationship between bodies and grace by naming each chapter after some-*body* who Yossarian mistakenly hopes might have the power to bestow grace, refrain from treating him "by the book," and help him with his plight.[2]

Kafka describes a world where grace is impossible. His characters are thoroughly in bondage to and determined by legal and bureaucratic necessities. The actions of his characters indicate that grace is impossible precisely because they cannot find *a body* capable of bestowing grace. Nonetheless, in these futile quests for grace, Kafka reveals something very important. He discovers that if grace is an event in which a person is treated both lovingly and in discontinuity with the past, *grace must take an embodied form*. Grace (as well as love) does not happen through policy, It can only happen when a person encounters a body with the power to dispense with regulations and refuse to treat others "by the book." While Kafka does not believe that grace is possible in his world completely determined by social and political necessities, he does reveal the conditions under which grace might be possible. The right body must be encountered! Grace remains out of reach as long as those in need of

---

2. Gustafson, "Scandal of Particularity," 26–27.

grace do not encounter such a body.³ By the way, all sacramental acts require some form of bodily presence.

On Grace and Dialogue

In contrast to Kafka, all Dostoevsky's characters *can* encounter some*body* with the power to treat them both lovingly and in discontinuity with their past. Moreover, all Dostoevsky's characters have the potential to be surprised by grace, and all his characters *can* be agents of grace. This is because all of Dostoevsky's characters em*body* one idea or another. All their encounters can be loving and gracious despite the ugliness of the context in which the encounter occurs. "This is an open and honest surplus, dialogically revealed to the other person, a surplus expressed by the addressed and not by the secondhand word."⁴ To be clear, every encounter will not be gracious, but grace and love are always possible in any encounter—as the "onion" encounter between Alyosha and Grushenka demonstrates. Since dialogue between characters that embody ideas is always possible, Dostoevsky's dialogical method creates a world in which there is *a surplus of grace*. On the other hand, grace is impossible in Kafka's literary world even though his characters diligently search for it.

---

3. In the early days of my parish ministry, I would receive a telephone call from a woman every couple of months. L.N. would ask me for one of three things: food, heat or rent. At the time each cost about $125 a month. L.N. was very pathetic in every way. She had dire emotional problems. She was not very smart. Her physical health was terrible. Moreover, the religious necessities under which she lived prevented her from divorce (she thought she would be damned to hell if she got a divorce). Consequently, welfare agents told her that she could not receive aid from the state because her estranged husband already received it for both of them. (This may or may not have been the case I do not know. I do know she thought it was). Despite her pathetic state, she taught me more about the relationship between grace and embodiment than the theologian who introduced me to this concept, Robert W. Jenson—who taught me a great deal. It was through my relationship with L.N., I began to grasp the existential need of Kafka's characters as well as ourselves to find some-*body* who could treat them graciously. The way L. N. survived, you see, was by going to the Yellow Pages (if you are born after 1990, you may have to use Wikipedia to find out what the Yellow Pages are) and calling the area clergy in alphabetical order until she received the food, rent, and heat that she needed to make it through the month! Despite her obvious physical, emotional, and mental difficulties, she knew that she could not live unless she found some-*body* who would treat her lovingly (give her what she needed) and in discontinuity with her past. While she may not have been able to articulate it, L.N. was far more aware of the fact that she lived by grace than anyone I have ever met.

4. Bakhtin, *Toward a Reworking*, 261.

A Concluding Literary and Biblical Postscript

Mikhail Bakhtin is often credited with discovering and articulating Dostoevsky's dialogical style. To describe this literary style, Bakhtin contrasted it with the more common *monological* style of writing. The most universal characteristic of monological writing is monological authors always possess *a surplus of knowledge*—a truth, fact, or disposition that is known only to the author. When a monological author reveals his or her surplus knowledge, the author helps the reader make sense of the novel's heretofore unrelated content. Bakhtin chose Leo Tolstoy's short story *Three Deaths* to illustrate monological writing.[5] This story narrates the deaths of a rich noblewoman, a coachman, and a tree (Tolstoy was hardly bereft of imagination), each of whom dies at the same place and time. Tolstoy uses these three deaths as the optimal point from which he, through his surplus knowledge as a monological author, evaluates each life. Since death closes all conversations between the dead and the living, and since nothing new can be said by the departed ones, there are no more surprises that can be gleaned directly from Tolstoy's characters. Only Tolstoy's surplus knowledge can supply us with knowledge about the noblewoman, the coachman, and the plant.

Bakhtin selected this story because it is a premiere example of monological writing. In this story dialogue never happens *between* the dead individuals, and even when they were alive, they never communicated.

> The lives and deaths of all three characters, together with their words, lie side by side in a unified, objective world and are even externally contiguous, but they know nothing about one another and are not reflected in one another. They are self-enclosed and deaf; they do not hear and do not answer one another. There are not and cannot be any dialogic relationships among them. They neither argue nor agree.[6]

The author provides all knowledge of whatever relationship there may be between the self-enclosed worlds of the characters in *Three Deaths*. Tolstoy enjoys an enormous amount of "surplus knowledge." He alone knows everything about the three formerly living beings. Tolstoy, not his characters, evaluates all three lives and all three deaths. This lack of

---

5. Many critics of Bakhtin say that this contrast is not fair to Tolstoy because Tolstoy was much more artistic than this one story suggests. I totally agree, but this particular story is an extreme example of a monological style where Tolstoy holds a monopoly on the surplus knowledge making *Three Deaths* an extreme example of what Bakhtin means by monological writing.

6. Bakhtin, *Dostoevsky's Poetics*, 69–70.

dialogue between the characters themselves and between the characters and the author makes Tolstoy the lone source of wisdom, knowledge, and power. In this story we only hear the author's voice.

Most monological stories do not go to this extreme. Characters do engage in dialogue with each other. They do influence each other, and they are known to influence the author by forcing the author to adjust the storyline. Characters often surprise both monological and dialogical authors just as human creatures in the Bible surprise the Biblical God and can change the story line.[7] But when characters surprise a monological author, the author still reserves the right to use surplus knowledge to reject the character's ability to surprise.

Indeed, most readers *expect* the author to use surplus knowledge to complete an "unfinished" story. Readers often think a work of fiction is incomplete if its ending does not, to the reader's satisfaction, tie all the diverse elements of the novel into a neat package that resolves all the novel's unanswered questions. This "finalizing" activity means that, to a large degree, authors of monological fiction must cast a "mantel of objectivity over every point of view they do not share" with any character or idea expressed in the novel. Monological authors will say the last word about the characters, events, and ideas with which the author has an issue.[8] In saying the last word, monological authors often silence their characters. Silence means the character is finalized. Silence means the characters have nothing more to say. Silence means that dialogue is no longer possible. Silence means that, for all practical purposes, the character is now dead.

This is precisely what Dostoevsky, at his best, refuses to do. His dialogical style forces him to express his views through the way he organizes the dialogue and his fictional world rather than using a monological author's surplus knowledge to "sneak up and ambush" his characters and his readers.[9] There is no surplus knowledge; for, the dialogical method means that all knowledge is present in the novel's characters. The author only knows what all the characters know and no more. The author possesses no surplus knowledge. His knowledge never exceeds the knowledge that his characters have already expressed in the story.

The Brothers Karamazov is Dostoevsky's best expression of dialogical writing, and Ivan Karamazov is the best expression of Dostoevsky's

---

7. Fretheim, *The Suffering of God*, 45–54.
8. Bakhtin, *Dostoevsky's Poetics*, 68.
9. Emerson, "Prefatory Comments," 245.

ability to refrain from the use of surplus knowledge. Ivan has received a great deal of credit from modern philosophers and theologians who discuss the theodicy issue. He is so persuasive that great minds like Friedrich Nietzsche (1844–1900), Albert Camus (1913–1960) and perhaps Elie Wiesel (1928–2016) believed that nothing more need be said about the theodicy question after Ivan's *tour de force*.[10] Yet, the power of Ivan's argument conceals the undeniable fact that Ivan Karamazov is not and has never been a living, breathing human being. Ivan was born as a literary character that emerged from Dostoevsky's creative mind. He was brought to life on the written page, but Ivan leapt out of the pages of *The Brothers Karamazov* and now has a life of his own.

Ivan's emancipation from his author testifies to the effectiveness of Dostoevsky's dialogical methodology; for, Fyodor Dostoevsky himself *opposed* nearly everything Ivan said! Dostoevsky fervently rejected Ivan's atheism. He opposed Ivan's reliance on reason as the only way truth can be expressed, and he did not think that Ivan had said the last word about evil in God's world. In fact, he wrote *The Brothers Karamazov* to refute his character Ivan Karamazov as well as Ivan's "impeccable" argument. He emphasized that he was not Ivan. Instead, Ivan is a character in his novel. "This is *his* language, *his* style, *his* pathos not mine."[11]

Dostoevsky leaves nothing of consequence outside of the consciousness of his major characters. His heroes always embody one idea or another, and they are always offered dialogue. This being so, Kafka's contention that grace, conceived as being treated lovingly and in discontinuity with one's past, depends on finding some-*body* capable dispensing grace is quite valid even though non-existent in Kafka's work. Like love, grace requires embodiment. In Kafka, we find no such *body*. In Dostoevsky there is a surplus of such *bodies*. There is a surplus of grace.[12] Dostoevsky, in his attempt to refute Ivan, offers the practice of ministry as the way to address the world's evil, and, in contrast to Kafka, his dialogical style creates a fictional world where grace, love and ministry are possible and perhaps our only source of hope. Ministers, we have said, use their imaginations to discover what can be said or done in the name of Jesus that opens the future rather than close the future. "Successful" ministers demonstrate that grace and love are possible no matter how great our

---

10. Bauckham, "Theodicy," 83–97.
11. Frank, *Dostoevsky*, 791.
12. Most Christians believe we encounter Jesus' embodied presence in the sacraments which are thought to be sources of grace and love.

bondage to necessities and to death. They also demonstrate that grace and love require a body.

An Important Reminder about Grace

If grace means being treated both lovingly and in discontinuity with one's past, an act of grace requires encountering a body with the power to dispense with regulations and grant us what we need rather than what necessities declare we have or have not earned.

The Bible: An Example of Dialogical Writing?

Bakhtin discovered, to the satisfaction of the many literary critics in his debt, that all the ideas present in Dostoevsky's fiction are *embodied* in his characters. Since the particular idea a character embodies is inseparable from the character's very being, these characters are *embodied ideas*. These embodied ideas govern the action of the fiction Dostoevsky writes, and they extend the ideas they embody into Dostoevsky's fictional world.[13] If a character changes or repents, they do so after *listening* to another character(s) in dialogue. As Rowan Williams aptly notes in his comments on Bakhtin, Dostoevsky never presents the "Last Word."

> So for Dostoevsky, in Bakhtin's reading, narrative is argument and argument is narrative. The only way in which we are to move toward a sustainable truth, a truth that is more than either a private ideology or a neutral description, is by being immersed in the interaction of personal agents and speakers. We as readers are being engaged by the open-ended narrative of persons in dialogue, invited to continue the dialogue when we have stopped reading, because we are like the characters we have been listening to, we are agents who are formed by the exchange of words.[14]

Most readers, however, do not expect or even want the novels they read to have open futures. We expect authors to write in a *monological* style. We expect our authors to have surplus knowledge. We expect them to be like an all-knowing, omniscient God who knows every detail of past, present, and future.

13. Bakhtin, *Dostoevsky's Poetics*, 79.
14. R. Williams, *Dostoevsky*, 113.

Our preference for a monological author may reflect our preference for the omniscient God that we, I think mistakenly, assume is the biblical God. The assumption of the biblical God's omniscience is an often unnoticed and perhaps unwarranted theological assumption. Without consulting biblical evidence to the contrary, most people think that the biblical God is more like the all-knowing monological author who speaks the last word and is never surprised by his creatures. This, however, may just be another instance of our preconceived ideology preventing us from seeing the biblical facts.

There is ample biblical evidence that the biblical God is often surprised by human beings (usually because they have sinned in unanticipated ways), and that the biblical God allows human opposition. In his book *The Suffering of God: An Old Testament Perspective* Terrence Fretheim suggests that on many occasions God admits divine knowledge is incomplete. For instance, in Jeremiah 3:7 God admits mistakes about Israel's future actions. "*And I thought,* 'After she had done all this she would return to me'; but she did not return." God often uses the word "perhaps" (*ûlay*) to indicate God's uncertainty about the future. "The word of the Lord came to me, 'Son of Man (. . .) prepare for yourself an exile's baggage, and go into exile by day in their sight (. . .) *Perhaps* (*ûlay*) they will understand, though they are a rebellious house." (Ez 12:1–3).

Fretheim also recognizes that divine speech often includes the conditional word "if" (*'im*) which also displays God's uncertainty about the future. "*If* (*'im*) you obey this word, then there shall enter in the gates of this house kings who shall sit on the throne of David (. . .) but *if* you do not heed these words (. . .) this house shall become a desolation." (Jer 22:4–5). The use of the word "if" implies that God *does not know* how this will turn out. The outcome depends on the people to whom God grants the autonomy to do what they decide to do.[15] As Dostoevsky's dialogical method does not overwhelm or annihilate his characters, the biblical God respects the autonomy and integrity of human beings and all creation.

An overlooked component of the creation story in Genesis 1 is the implication that human beings were created for a conversation with God. According to the story, God speaks *about* all creation, blesses all creation, and declares all creation good. God does the same with humanity. God creates human beings. God blesses us, but then God does something

---

15. Fretheim, *The Suffering of God*, 45–54.

different and often overlooked. "God blessed them and *God said to them*," (Gen. 1:28). God speaks about all creation, but God speaks *about and to* humanity! Apparently, God expects a response different from the rest of creation; for, God has created a being capable of conversation. We are created for dialogue with the creator God. This is our purpose, and since prayer is a conversation with God, we are created to be praying beings.

Such conversation requires that the partners in dialogue—both God and human beings—be autonomous. It requires that the partners in dialogue *listen* to one another, and listening requires that the partners in dialogue make an adjustment because of what was said. The Bible's surprise is that sometimes God listens. Sometimes God even repents! Sometimes God changes because of what God heard in dialogue (prayer) with human beings. In short, God makes adjustments because of human prayers. (Sometimes human beings do so as well).

No event in Hebrew Scripture illustrates the length to which God goes to make the sort of adjustment listening requires than Moses' prayer on Mt Sinai. Moses has been on the mountaintop for a long time. The recently emancipated slaves below grow impatient. They demand that Aaron (Moses' second in command) *make* them a god to lead them. Aaron complies and quickly fashions a golden bull—Wall Street has a similar statue outside the New York Stock Exchange. God sees this and becomes enraged. The following dialogue between Moses and the biblical God ensues.

> And the Lord said to Moses, "Go down; for *your* people whom *you* brought up out of the land of Egypt have corrupted themselves; they have turned aside quickly out of the way which I commanded them; they have made for themselves a molten calf, and have worshiped it and sacrificed to it, and said, 'These are your gods, O Israel, who brought you up out of the land of Egypt!'" And the Lord said to Moses, "I have seen this people, and behold, it is a stiff-necked people; now therefore let me alone, that my wrath may burn hot against them and I may consume them; but of you I will make a great nation."
>
> But Moses besought the Lord his God, and said, "O Lord, why does thy wrath burn hot against thy people, whom *thou* hast brought forth out of the land of Egypt with great power and with a mighty hand? Why should the Egyptians say, 'With evil intent did He bring them forth, to slay them in the mountains, and to consume them from the face of the earth?' Turn from thy fierce wrath and *repent of this evil* against *thy* people. Remember

Abraham, Isaac and Israel, thy servants, to whom thou didst swear by thine own self, and didst say to them 'I will multiply your descendants as stars of heaven, and all this land that I have promised I will give to your descendants, and they shall inherit it forever.'" *And the Lord repented of the evil* which he thought to do to his people.—(Ex. 32:7–14, RSV, emphases mine)

According to Brevard Childs, we often overlook the key phrase in this text where God demands, "Now, therefore, *let me alone* that my wrath may burn hot against them." Apparently, God has already made the decision to destroy Israel. All God needs is for Moses to give God some space so that this decision can be implemented. Moses, however, refuses to obey God. He does not leave God alone so that God's wrath may burn hot against Israel. Instead, Moses enters a conversation with God. Moses prays.

Childs notes that Moses makes three points in his prayer. First, Moses suggest that the newly emancipated slaves God now wishes to obliterate are relatively new at being God's chosen people, and they should be cut some slack. "O Lord, why does thy wrath burn hot against thy people, whom thou (just now?) brought forth out of the land of Egypt?" Second, Moses argues that God's proposed act against these people would be terrible for public relations. "Why should the Egyptians say, 'With evil intent did He bring them forth to slay them in the mountains and consume them from the face of the earth." (Clearly, the recruitment of another group of "chosen people" would be quite difficult if this story were widely circulated!) Finally, Moses reminds God of God's own promises to Abraham, Isaac, and Jacob.[16]

Moses convinces the God of Israel *to repent of the evil he was about to do to Israel.* The new relationship between God and Israel was being formed. It was to be a dialogical relationship—a relationship Moses insisted upon when he intervened on Israel's behalf. This new relationship demanded that both God and Israel had to listen to each other. Both had to make adjustments to what the other said, and, in this instance, God adjusted by *repenting of the evil* God presumably would have done if Moses had not intervened. But Moses prayed. He insisted that the dialogue with Israel continue. He refused to believe that God had spoken the final word about Israel.

At his best, Dostoevsky's dialogical method mimics the dialog between Moses and God. If conversation becomes impossible it is only

---

16. Childs, *Exodus*, 567–69.

because the character commits suicide, or, like Ivan Karamazov, the character thinks the last word has been spoken. As Rowan Williams often and aptly notes, there is no "Last Word" in Dostoevsky. The same refusal to say the last word runs rampant throughout the biblical narrative. In both the biblical world and Dostoevsky's fiction grace is always possible. They are both worlds where even dry dead bones revive (Ez. 37), and where Jesus rises from the grave.

If Grace Is Possible What is Reality?

Non-Self-Sufficiency

The dialogical method encountered in Dostoevsky's fiction and the Bible itself has profound philosophical and theological implications that cut against the grain of modern thought. For example, if partners in dialogue are different after dialogue occurs, if they, like the biblical God, *repent of the evil* they are about to do, if, like Alyosha, Dmitri and Grushenka, their adjustments make them different persons, it follows that dialogue plays a fundamental role in the creation of the self. It is through dialogue that we discover who we are—as even God did in dialogue with Moses. Dialogue's fundamental status in the creation of the self, therefore, compels us to reconsider some commonly held assumptions about the self, self-consciousness, self-awareness, and self-sufficiency.

If dialogue is essential to the self's creation, René Descartes (1596–1650) and the rest of the Enlightenment are wrong when they say that the self is an autonomous decision making "substance." This is because a substance is defined as "that which is capable of independent existence." If dialogue is essential to self-creation, the self is not "capable of independent existence." If dialogue with another creates the self then the self cannot be essentially alone, single, and isolated. We can pretend we are independent, but this pretense leads to insanity like it did to Ivan.

In a world where grace is possible, a healthy self can emerge and flourish through dialogue with other selves. We receive our names from others. We are taught by others. Our identities emerge in conversation with others. It is through dialogue that we influence one another, and we discover who we are—as even the biblical God did in his dialogue with Moses. No self can stand alone. The self requires a community of other selves to exist. This led Bakhtin to coin the term *Non-Self- Sufficiency* to describe the fact that the individual human self requires another, external self or selves in order to exist.

Non-Self-Sufficiency does not reject the existence of the self. It rejects the Enlightenment's (and Aristotelian) version of a self that presumes the self to be single, isolated, and non-communal.

> I am conscious of myself and become myself only while revealing myself for another, through another, and with the help of another. The most important acts constituting self-consciousness are determined by a relationship toward another consciousness (toward a *thou*). Separation, dissociation, and enclosure within the self is the main reason for the loss of one's self. Not that which takes place within, but that which takes place on the *boundary* between one's own and someone else's consciousness, on the *threshold* (between one human being and another). And everything internal gravitates not (inward) toward itself but is turned to the outside and dialogized, every internal experience ends up on the boundary, encounters another, and in this tension-filled encounter lies (a self's) entire essence (...) Thus does Dostoevsky confront all decadent and idealistic (individualist) culture, the culture of essential and inescapable solitude. He asserts the impossibility of solitude, the illusory nature of solitude. The very being of (human beings) is the *deepest communion. To be* means *to communicate*(...) It means to be for another, and through the other, for oneself.[17]

Since the self cannot even exist apart from dialogue, human selves are not self-sufficient. Moreover, when we try to be self-sufficient, we risk insanity. This understanding of a dialogical self is diametrically opposed to modern capitalism (and many other philosophical schemes as well) because capitalism presumes that human beings are the lonely, isolated, individual selves that both Bakhtin and Dostoevsky reject.

In contrast, Non-Self-Sufficiency describes the human self, self-consciousness, and self-awareness as originating in dialogue with others. Indeed, a human who rejects conversation, dialogue and community is hardly human. This is true of Ivan Karamazov, and it was true of other characters like The Underground Man who Dostoevsky created years before Ivan. Both were isolated. Both tried to be self-sufficient. Both believed they had said "the last word," and because of their isolation both characters lived in despair, and both lost their minds.

---

17. Bakhtin, "Toward a Reworking," 250.

Dostoevsky's literary methodology is not anti-individualistic. It merely denies the radical individualism of the modern world. Instead, Dostoevsky's dialogical method—along with what I believe to be the dialogical method implicit in the Bible—teaches that the essence of humanity is found in communion or dialogue with others. Furthermore, the dialogical method reveals that the isolation implicit in the radical individualistic philosophy that undergirds modern capitalism and other modern worldviews is a form of premature death. For, death is the same as being unheard, unrecognized, unremembered, alone, and completely isolated.

Surplus of Grace

Grace is always possible in both the world the biblical God creates and Dostoyevsky's fictional world. A monological author, or an omniscient God always possess surplus of *knowledge*, but in worlds of dialogue, there is always surplus of grace. In these dialogical worlds, love, grace, and ministry, while never inevitable, are always possible.

Sometimes grace is offered, but it is not accepted. It is resisted. When grace is resisted, little changes, and we continue to be subject to the necessities that "determine" us and the Principalities that rule us. In The Apostle Paul's words, we "submit again to the yoke of slavery." Sometimes, however, dialogue helps the interlocutors recognize that a word of grace has been spoken, and they have experienced a word of life. Often this new situation is quickly forgotten, and they return to normalcy. But sometimes one or both partners in dialogue repent and change their lives (as happened in the "onion" conversation between Alyosha and Grushenka). When someone changes or repents, that person changes because an external word has been spoken by another at the right moment.

Jesus notes similar phenomena when he explains The Parable of the Sower to his disciples.

> "The Sower sows the word. These are the ones on the path where the word is sown: when they hear, Satan immediately comes and takes away the word that is sown in them. And these are the ones sown on rocky ground: when they hear the word, they immediately receive it with joy. But they have no root and endure only for a while; then when trouble or persecution arises on account of the word, immediately they fall away. And others are those sown among the thorns: these are the ones who hear the word, but the cares of the world, and the lure of wealth, and the

A Concluding Literary and Biblical Postscript

desire for other things come in and choke the word, and it yields nothing. And these are the ones sown on the good soil: they hear the word and accept it and bear fruit, thirty and sixty and a hundredfold." (Mark 4: 14–20)

Worlds in which there is a surplus of grace understand time differently than it is understood in worlds where grace is thought impossible. The difference between two Greek words for time helps us understand this difference. One the one hand, there is the sort of time characterized by the Greek word *Chronos*. It is from this word that we get our word chronology. *Chronos* time is sequential time where one moment follows another moment *ad infinitum*. Since no one moment is more important than another in *Chronos* time, time is often interpreted as one meaningless moment after another with nothing of any real note or importance ever happening. If *Chronos* time is the only time there is, grace is impossible.

Both the Bible and Dostoyevsky's novels are often concerned with *Kairos* time. *Kairos* time is the right time. It is the moment we have been waiting for. It is the moment that is pregnant with possibilities. The Gospel writers Matthew, Mark and Luke all begin Jesus' public ministry with Jesus' proclamation, "The time is fulfilled (*Kairos*), and the kingdom of God has come near, repent and believe in the Gospel." (Mark 1:15). In other words, the Gospels here describe *Kairos* time where the incarnate Word of God (the embodied Word of God) penetrates the ordinary sequence of *Chronos* moments and infuses the moments of *Chronos* time with new possibilities.

When these new possibilities are grasped, they enable repentance and change. *Kairos* time literally makes a new world possible by transforming or impregnating *Chronos* time with truth and meaning. *Kairos* time takes the moments of *Chronos* time and turns them into grace-filled events that can shape the future. The moments of *Chronos* time do not change. These moments may appear to most as one meaningless moment after the next, but their meaning explodes with new possibilities when transformed to *Kairos* time. Grace and love are events of *Kairos* time.

Kairos time is always possible but never inevitable. The possibilities for grace in *Kairos* time are limitless, but these possibilities depend on seeing moments in *Chronos* time as ways to experience the love and grace implicit in *Kairos* time. Furthermore, the more we are on the lookout for *Kairos*/Grace time, the more likely we are to find it; for Kairos time is present in many *Chronos* moments if we look. Listening, other acts of active love and repentance are the way we look for *Kairos* time, but such watchfulness would lead nowhere if *Kairos* time did not reveal itself within *Chronos* time—the seemingly mundane sequence of one meaningless event after another.

Ministry Can Happen Only in a World Where Grace is Possible

Both Dostoevsky and the Gospels speak of encounters that create *Kairos* time through *Chronos* time, and ministry can happen when these encounters happen, Additionally, ministry transforms lives in unforeseen, gracious, and loving ways, and these transformations are not always a one-way street! As the biblical God was changed by dialogue with Moses, Jesus' self-understanding and His mission may have been changed by a conversation with a Gentile woman.

> Jesus left that place and went away to the district of Tyre and Sidon. Just then a Canaanite woman from that region came out and started shouting, "Have mercy on me, Lord, Son of David; my daughter is tormented by a demon." *But he did not answer her at all.* And his disciples came and urged him saying, "Send her away, for she keeps shouting after us." He answered, "I was sent *only* to the lost sheep of the house of Israel." But she came and knelt before him, saying, "Lord help me." He answered, "It is not fair to take the children's food and throw it to the dogs." She said, "Yes, Lord, yet even the dogs eat the crumbs that fall from their masters' table." Then Jesus answered her, "Woman, great is your faith! Let it be done for you as you wish." And her daughter was healed instantly. (Matt 15:21–28, emphasis mine)

A preconceived notion that God or even The Son of God cannot change might prevent us from seeing that Jesus may have changed His worldview and mission when He encountered this desperate, brave, intelligent, and loving mother. Before this encounter, Jesus appears to believe that His mission was "*only* to the lost sheep of the house of Israel." He changed his mind after this encounter. He listened to this magnificent woman, and she helped Him redefine his ministry.

Jesus listened. He repented, and His repentance changed his mission. The episode demonstrates that listening is not simply the ability to repeat what was said. It is not simply being present in a room when someone addresses you. Listening is one way practitioners of the art of ministry can recognize a *Kairos* event within *Chronos* time. What makes listening, listening is that the *one who listens makes an adjustment in his or her life because of what the partner in dialogue said.* It might not be the adjustment that the partner had in mind, but one who listens always makes an adjustment. If listening does not happen, adjustments are not made. When adjustments are not made, the speaker is treated as if she does not matter, or, to put it more bluntly, the one who fails to listen treats the speaker as if she were dead. Like love and grace, listening opens a future that had once seemed closed and ruled by the forces of death.

When Jesus encounters the Canaanite woman, He appears not to listen. But her pleas, her creativity, her tenacity, and her wit *make* Him listen. Because He listens, Jesus makes an adjustment. He redefines his ministry. He changes his agenda because he heard the woman. He may have wanted to take the woman's plea as a moment of *Chronos* time—a moment that would pass by unnoticed like all *Chronos* moments. Instead, He listened. In doing so a *Chronos* moment became a grace-filled *Kairos* event. Moreover, it became a grace-filled event for both Jesus and the woman because the lives of Jesus, the woman and her daughter were transformed. Where death may once have reigned supreme, life with all its possibilities emerged.

Jesus' encounter with the Canaanite woman is similar in structure to encounters between many of Dostoevsky's characters. In both Dostoevsky and the Bible, dialogue is always possible, and dialogue creates a possible *Kairos* event. *Kairos* events are impossible in Kafka's fictional world, and *Kairos* events are perceived to be impossible in our own world when we think we live without God.[18] Dostoevsky thought that his own nineteenth century Russia was far along in the process of rejecting its Russian Orthodox roots and denying God's existence. In his view, this would be disastrous because Russia would then lose its transcendental source of truth that each *Kairos* event (or iconic experience) reveals. His novels remind his readers that grace and love can still emerge from the ashes if people are aware that grace and freedom are always possible because all *Chronos* time contains *Kairos* events.

Grace, freedom and love depend on the world being like the one the biblical God creates or the fictional world created by Dostoevsky's dialogical method. Such a world gives us opportunities to encounter some*body* who can speak a penetrating gracious word into moments where grace and love may not even be deemed a possibility. This happens when

---

18. This our current plight.

a person listens and thereby discerns what is needed. A loving act follows whereby a person offers what was needed. The offer can be rejected or accepted. If accepted, the person's life is different. This difference might just be momentary, or it can be life-long. In case you haven't noticed, such events are synonymous with the practice of ministry. Both Dostoevsky's fiction and the Bible create worlds in which such ministry is possible.

Can Ministry Relieve the World of Its Evil?

The Elder Zosima had two guidelines for practitioners of the art of ministry: small acts of active love and remembering that we are responsible to all people, for all people and for everyone. A similar guideline has also been used in this book, namely, a person who practices the art of ministry must ask the question, "What can we now say or do in the name of Jesus that opens the future rather than closes the future." These admonitions require our immediate attention to the present. They require dialogue and listening. They require bodily presence; therefore, these acts of love and grace are concrete acts. There is no abstract version of love or of "love in general." Love (and grace) are always small, concrete, embodied, and local. This compels the question, "Can these small acts of grace and love adequately address the evil, sin, and suffering that appears to be global in scope?"

Small acts of embodied love and dialogue appear to be so miniscule when faced with terrorism, the depletion of the world's resources, climate change, pollution, modern war, genocide, suffering, antisemitism, racism, poverty, sexism, *et cetera*. Our actions, it seems, must be "bigger" or more global if we are to fight such evil. Our actions must, we believe, be institutional if they are going to have global impact. Zosima's second guideline—we are responsible to all people, for all people and for everyone—has the potential to extend our struggle against human evil to a global level, but addressing the evils of antisemitism, racism, institutional poverty, and sexism still requires small, individual acts of repentance. Even Jesus, when he faced The Grand Inquisitor, responded with a kiss on "his cold dead lips." This was clearly a small, embodied, loving response, but what effect did it have on this mass murderer?

To Dostoevsky's credit he neither disregards the obstacles nor abandons the small acts of love that he proposes as the only way the Principalities and Powers can be opposed and human evil fought. *The Brothers*

Karamazov demonstrates the power of ministry within a family that is so dysfunctional that the murder of the father of these Karamazov brothers appears reasonable and intelligible even if it was criminal. Furthermore, it is from within this dysfunctional family (a family perhaps less dysfunctional than the family of Abraham, Isaac, and Jacob) that Alyosha Karamazov, becomes a master of the art of ministry. He became a master of the art of ministry by focusing on the small things—his conversation with Grushenka, gathering a group of young boys, helping a destitute, impoverished family, supporting those who grieved the loss of Ilyusha, eating pancakes, and remembering the blessedness of the events surrounding these experiences. He confronted evil, sin and suffering where he found it in the "little ones" and "little things" that he encountered in his everyday life.

The Bible has much the same focus. The biblical God choses a rather insignificant group of people to be the chosen people of God. Rarely are they ideal partners. Nonetheless, God listens to them. God adjusts to their sin. God remains in dialogue with them to this day. Sometimes they listen, and sometimes they do not, but God is not a disembodied presence. God speaks to them through burning bushes, whirling winds storms, prophets, and many outsiders. And, of equal importance, they continue to speak to God.

In the Christian New Testament, Jesus becomes the incarnate (embodied) Word of God who is proclaimed to be present in the beginning and who will be present in the end. In such a world, grace will always be possible because Jesus, the embodied presence of God, will always be present. Jesus does not promise to be everywhere, but He does promise to be present in certain domains that we sometimes call sacraments. In Holy Communion He literally promises to be embodied in the bread and wine of the Passover Meal saying, "This is my body," and "This is my blood." But there are more such promises—though they are often overlooked. Jesus promises such presence wherever "two or three are gathered in my name, I am there among them." (Matt 18:20). He promises to be present among the least of these saying, "Truly I tell you, just as you did to one of the least of these who are members of my family, you did to me." (Matt 25:40). He even promises to be present in another strange, overlooked place when he tells his disciples, "Whoever welcomes one such child in my name welcomes me; and whoever welcomes me welcomes not me but the one who sent me." (Mark 9:37). Each place where Jesus promises to be present is small. Each might appear insignificant, but remembering these promises can lead to discovering His presence in these sacramental events, and this can be transformative.

For example, as a pastor I sometimes suggested that people who are mildly depressed (not clinically depressed, but consistently bummed out) volunteer to work among the poor. On all occasions those who took this advice reported that they had had a wonderful experience. Moreover, it was often a surprise to them that, although they had come to minister to the people who were in need (the least of these), they found that they were the ones who received ministry. They often felt less depressed and sad. They were less self-absorbed because the people they encountered and the tasks they performed took them out of their inner, isolated selves and made them focus on others. In some sense they felt freed and liberated.

On a more personal note, I had a great deal of difficulty when I became a father. I often felt that my children were interrupting me from doing the things that I wanted to do. While I was not completely miserable, something happened a few months after my second child, Gregory, was born that completely changed my attitude toward parenting. One night it was my turn to get up with Greg. I was exhausted that night, and he refused to go back to sleep when I put him back to bed. Actually, he *would* go back to sleep, but he would wake no more than ten minutes later and after I had, for a brief moment, fallen asleep. This went on all night. It was like sleep deprivation torture. I was getting quite angry at an innocent child, and it was becoming a little dangerous for the boy. But fortunately for me and for Greg an event happened that I attribute to the Holy Spirit. I "remembered" that I would be preaching on Mark 9:33–37 the next week. This passage had the phrase, "Whoever welcomes one such child in my name, welcomes me, and whoever welcomes me welcomes not me but the one who sent me." While there was, to my knowledge, no formula that told me how to welcome my child in Jesus' name, I made one up that night. It was at that point that I received both Gregory and his brother Matthew in Jesus' name, and it was at this point that I became a new person or at least a new father. I was transformed both as a father and as a person through this sacramental event; for, I always remembered this event, and from then on, I received children—particularly my own children and grandchildren—in Jesus' name. My priorities changed, and my life was transformed.

Encountering Jesus in the places He has promised to be present is often transforming. These encounters can be "the beginning of the beginning and the foundation of the foundation" as it was for me with respect to fatherhood. These events are *Kairos* events moments that could easily be missed in mundane *Chronos* time. They are, in fact, miraculous, but they are still *small* acts of active love. They will always be small acts because love and grace always assume an embodied form. There is no way that those who practice the art of ministry can possibly move beyond these small acts, and this is a disappointment to many.

Ivan Karamazov was also disappointed when he heard of the suffering of innocent children. Like many of us, he blamed God for refusing to intervene and stop such senseless evil. He refused his ticket to paradise because he thought God's Kingdom is being built on the suffering of innocent children. Like many, Ivan thought that God should use the omnipotent power at God's disposal to remedy the world's evil. Like most of us, Ivan's ultimate belief was that big actions on the national or global scale are the only remedy possible for global systemic problems like evil. So, since God did not seem particularly interested in intervening to stop evil, Ivan could not see how anything he did could matter, so he did not help. He became paralyzed. At the end of the book, Ivan was mentally damaged and his testimony about Dmitri's innocence was thought by the jury to be the testimony of a mad man.

Our reaction to evil is much like Ivan's. We "know" that there is nothing we can do, so we do not even try. The collapse of the earth's environment, the evils of racism, the acts of terror, antisemitism, sexism, and poverty are so overwhelming that, like Ivan, we believe we are impotent. While I am not optimistic about our chances of individual acts of love and repentance overcoming the world's evil, *I do think that we, along with Ivan, overestimate the power of the world's evil and underestimate the power of these small acts of love.*

In fact, it is almost impossible for our governments, corporations, universities, and religious institutions to successfully address the global evils like racism, soil erosion, sexism, ecological destruction, and war. In the first place, these human evils—evils that derive their seemingly autonomous death-dealing power from unacknowledged and unconfessed sin—themselves have their origin in *individual* human acts. They are global evils precisely because so many of us refuse to confess our responsibility for these individual sins. Moreover, our governments, religious institutions, corporations, and universities do not help because they benefit from these unconfessed sins.

> The religion and environmentalism of the highly industrialized countries are at bottom a sham because they make it their business to fight against something that they do not really wish to destroy. We all live by robbing nature, but our standard of living demands that the robbery shall continue. (...) The great obstacle is simply this: the conviction that we cannot change because we are dependent on what is wrong. But this is an addicts excuse, and we know that it will not do.[19]

Asking these large institutions to fight these evils not only supports the power of unconfessed sins, but falsely promotes the idea that only large, top-down solutions can answer the problems that plague our communities, nations, institutions, and planet. Without overwhelming hope, but with certainty nonetheless, it appears that only individual acts of love and repentance can address the evils that appear to be in control.

Consider what has been said about the world's necessities. In their quest to be universal and global, necessities present themselves as the way everything must be. In their efforts to become universal, necessities define what is "reasonable" and thereby limit what is possible. They enforce the notion that it is impossible to change the way things are. Political necessity *must* employ the power of death, and nations justify the use of this power with the belief in redemptive violence that asserts that war is the gateway to peace.[20] The myth of redemptive violence obscures the fact that the power of death—the permission and ability to "legally" kill—is essential to the power of any nation. A nation only rules because it can kill. Any nation trying to expand its power is resisted by another nation with the same goal and the same power to kill. This means that "if necessary" a nation stands ready to kill innocent ones in its quest for universality. Even though nations may try to avoid war, political necessity often gives our nations "no choice" but war. Nations must ultimately kill if they are to survive as a nation. If a nation refuses to kill when it is "necessary" to kill, its adversaries will use lethal force to destroy that nation. It is really that simple.

This means our political institutions cannot solve the problem of evil in the world. Through diplomacy they might temporarily avoid conflict, but "if pushed to its limits" history clearly demonstrates that a nation will have "no alternative" but war. Nations will fight the death-dealing power of other nations with the only power they have, the same evil,

---

19. Berry, "Word and Fresh," 754–55.
20. Wink, *Engaging the Powers*, 13–33.

death-dealing power. Nations will try to match force with even more force, but, even if they "win," it is very likely they will kill more innocent men, woman, and children than would have died if their defeated enemy had quickly "won" the war. Instead of creating peace, the peace that the myth of redemptive violence promises, we create more carnage. It is the political necessities established by the Principalities that dictate that the nations of the world take part in the insanity of war if they are to survive.

If we remain subject to political necessities, there is no alternative to the carnage of war. The nations of the world can do nothing about evil but give us more evil. Since they are all in bondage to political necessity, nations will return evil for evil, life for life, innocent ones for innocent ones. When diplomacy fails as it often does, nations can do nothing other than increase the evil they are trying to destroy. (As the United States' response to the terrorist attacks surrounding September 11, 2001, and Israel's response to Hamas' terrorist attacks on October 7, 2023, indicate, nations *must* kill innocent men women and children on a larger scale when attacked. They can do nothing else).

Hope only resides in the free acts of those who have entered the realm of political necessity and have the courage and wisdom to refrain from succumbing to political necessities. Like all people who practice the art of ministry, their task is to find a way where there appears to be no way. This is the role of a true diplomat—a person who voluntarily enters the realm of political necessity with the hope and skill to somehow stop his or her nation from succumbing to political necessity at least for a brief period. Diplomats cannot eliminate war. Probably only the elimination of nations and the Principalities behind them can eliminate war, however, the small acts of love and repentance can prevent some wars from erupting.

To use the words of Wendell Berry once again, "Only love can bring intelligence out of the institutions and organizations, where it aggrandizes itself into the presence of the work that must be done. Love is never abstract. It does not adhere to the universe or the planet or the nation or the institution or the profession, but to the singular sparrows in the street, the lilies of the field, 'the least of these my brethren.' Love is not, by its own desire, heroic. It is heroic only when compelled to be. It exists by its willingness to be anonymous, humble, and unrewarded."[21] Acts of love are embodied acts directed at individual or beloved communities.

---

21. Berry, "Word and Flesh," 754.

The art of ministry asks that we exercise our freedom in the context of other necessities as well. Those who enter economic necessities, for example, might take a difficult, terrible, and demeaning job to feed their families, or create a business to support a community. In these cases, people subject themselves to economic necessity for the sake of others. The death and resurrection of Jesus gives us the freedom to choose life even in the midst of necessities. This is just like Alyosha's ministry. Zosima sent him into the dysfunction of the Karamazov family to help them discover new possibilities to the ways they were living, and, against great odds, Alyosha managed to do so. It was there that Alyosha fought the evil long perpetuated by his family. He did so through small acts of active love, repentance and recognizing his responsibility to all people, for all people and for everyone amid circumstances that can only be described as difficult and dire.

No one person can do everything, but as Catholic Bishop Ken Untener prayed in a prayer for Oscar Romero, "We cannot do everything, and there is a sense of liberation in realizing that. This enables us to do something and do it very well."[22] Small acts of active love give us focus and direction, but they require our attention. Dostoevsky's characters—particularly Zosima and Alyosha—are examples of the sort of focus and attention the art of ministry asks of us as we use our freedom to enter all the necessities that the Principalities and Powers have created. Here we try to answer the question, "What can we say or do in this unique context that is life-giving rather than death-dealing?" This can lead to acts of Christian freedom where we select among all that is lawful, the one or two things that express our God-given freedom to choose life in a world were only death-dealing necessities only appear to prevail.

---

22. Humphreys, "Can Money Serve," 25.

Acknowledgments

MY MOTHER AND FATHER, Charlotte and Emil Gustafson, were my first mentors in the art of ministry. This happened as much through the places to which their ministries took us as it did through their example. Baltimore was one such place. It was there, in high school, at a time of great racial strife, that Teddy Smith and I would sometimes cut school, walk the streets of Baltimore, and discuss race relations. A few weeks before graduation, and a few weeks after the assassination of Martin Luther King Jr., he angrily summarized his teachings on white privilege (he did not call it that) telling me that even if I failed in life, I probably would be "better off" than he would be if he succeeded simply because I am white and he is black. I could not deny this truth. It was then and there that I reluctantly began my still incomplete repentance for my own racism and my responsibility for my country's racism.

Just two years later, the death of my seven-year-old brother Todd Emil Gustafson was another "affliction" that changed my life. Until his death, the one thing I did not want to be was a pastor like my father, but Todd's death changed this. I began to understand that death is the enemy, but I also discovered that remembering the fact of death, remembering you are mortal, allows you to prioritize things in life. It keeps you from wasting time doing worthless things. Todd's death pushed me to a deeper understanding of Christianity as well, and, influenced by Teddy's words, I chose James Cone's *Black Theology and Black Power* as one of the first books on theology I ever read. This book has always guided my theological reflections.

In seminary I fell under the influence of many people who greatly influenced my understanding of ministry. Robert W. Jenson's question,

"What can we say or do in Jesus' name that opens the future?" became, for me, a question I always have asked in my attempts to engage in ministry. Iver Haugen was both my supervisor when I was a chaplain at St. Elizabeths Hospital and my supervisor during my internship. He conveyed to me much spoken and unspoken knowledge on the "nuts and bolts" of ministry. He was to me like Zosima was to Alyosha.

While I had heard about "embodied words" in classes on sacramental theology, Leana Norris, a person to whom I mistakenly thought *I* was ministering, demonstrated the concrete, everyday way that grace and love takes an embodied, incarnate form. Ruth Powell taught me that ministry, marriage, and life are not a competition, but loving acts made possible by the "entanglements" that don't just compose life but are life.

Charles Courtney introduced me to Dostoevsky and Ivan Karamazov's repudiation of all previous efforts by Christians to make rational sense of the fact of sin, evil and suffering in a world created by a loving, benevolent God. Thinking about Ivan led to me teaching a very popular course titled "Sin, Evil and Suffering" during my years teaching theology at The Lutheran Theological Seminary at Gettysburg. In many and various ways, the students who took that class helped me come to a much better understanding of the issues involved in theodicy, and, of even more importance, how sin, evil and suffering can be the starting point for ministry itself.

Some very good friends have accompanied me throughout life's journey and have helped me with this book. Bill Doran has always engaged me in theological discussion. I have always been blessed by his willingness to talk with me even when our discussions take some very strange paths. Bill read this manuscript and made some good suggestions. As is usually the case, I used some of his recommendations, and others I did not. Don Wilcox has been another sojourner in ministry. He too encouraged me in my writing. At first, he was reluctant to read the manuscript because he "did not know enough about Dostoevsky." He agreed to do so because I told him that the reason I wanted him to read it was to see if his lack of "Dostoevsky knowledge" prevented him from understanding the book. It did not. In fact, he told me it was terrific. I am thankful for his encouragement.

As usual, my wife, Brenda Lange–Gustafson, read my manuscript in its many and varied renditions. She always prevents me from making serious errors in format and content, and she makes sure that my writing is somewhat intelligible. That being said, her significance far exceeds her obvious abilities as an editor. Her love, compassion, kindness, empathy, faithfulness, and resolve are virtues that have enriched my life in innumerable ways.

Finally, my grandchildren–Charlotte Wong Gustafson, Scotti Louise Gustafson, Luke Wong Gustafson, and Emelia Dorothy Gustafson–have taught me much about the art of ministry, and since the oldest of this group is now just five years old, I suspect that they did so without knowing it. I hope this day never comes, but someday, if they ever wonder about the significance and importance of their lives, I would like to somehow "get word to them" that before they could speak, they not only saved my life at a time of physical crisis, but they blessed me in other profound ways. If I ever unknowingly did for my grandparents what they have done for me, there is no way that I would ever think I had accomplished little because it simply could not be so. Their many gifts to me demonstrate that we can minster without even "knowing" it. All I can say to them is "Thank you."

Bibliography

Alexander, Michelle. *The New Jim Crow: Mass Incarceration in the Age of Colorblindness.* New York: The New Press, 2011.
Andelman, David A. *A Shattered Peace: Versailles 1919 and the Price We Pay Today.* New York: Wiley, 2014.
Arendt, Hannah. *Eichmann In Jerusalem: A Report on the Banality of Evil.* New York: Penguin, 1963.
Augustine, Arelius. *The Confessions of St. Augustine. Select Library of Nicene and Post-Nicene Fathers.* Vol. 1. Series 1. Grand Rapids, MI: Eerdmans, 1987.
Bakhtin, Mikhail. *Problems of Dostoevsky's Poetics.* Translated by Caryl Emerson. Minneapolis: University of Minnesota Press, 1984.
———. "Toward a Reworking of the Dostoevsky Book." In *Critical Essays on Dostoevsky,* edited by Robin Feuer Miller, 247–64. Boston: C.K. Hall, 1986.
Baptist, Edward, E. *The Half Has Never Been Told: Slavery and the Making of American Capitalism.* New York: Basic, 1999.
Bauckham, Richard. "Theodicy from Ivan Karamazov to Moltman." *Modern Theology* (4) (1988) 83–97.
Beckert, Sven. *Empire of Cotton: A Global History.* New York: Vintage, 2015.
Berry, Wendell. "Word and Flesh." In *Wendell Berry Essays 1969–1990,* edited by Jack Shoemacher, 751–56. New York: Library of America, 2019.
Bonhoeffer, Dietrich. *Ethics.* Translated by Nevil Horton Smith. New York: Touchstone, 1995.
Browning, Christopher R. *Faithful Months: Essays on the Emergence of the Final Solution.* New York: Holmes and Meier, 1985.
Butler, Judith. *Precarious Life: The Powers of Mourning and Violence.* London: Verso, 2004.
Cairns, Scott. *The End of Suffering: Finding Purpose in Pain.* Brewster, MA: Paraclete, 2018.
Childs, Brevard. *The Book of Exodus: Old Testament Library.* Philadelphia: Westminster, 1974.
Cone, James. *Black Theology and Black Power.* New York: Seabury Press, 1969.
Contino, Paul, J. *Dostoevsky's Incarnational Realism: Finding Christ among the Karamazovs.* Eugene, OR: Cascade, 2020.

Diangelo, Robin. *White Fragility: Why It's So Hard for White People to Talk about Racism*. Boston: Beacon, 2018.

Dostoevsky, Fyodor. *The Brothers Karamazov*. Edited and translated by Susan McReynolds. Second Norton Critical Edition. New York: W. W. Norton, 2011.

———. *The House of the Dead and Poor Folk*. Translated by Constance Garnett. New York: Barnes and Nobel, 2004.

———. *Notes From Underground*. Edited and translated by Michael R. Katz. Second Norton Critical Edition. New York: W. W. Norton, 2001.

———. *A Writer's Diary*. Edited by Gary Saul Morson. Evanston, IL: Northwestern University Press, 2009.

Douglas, James W. *The Nonviolent Coming of God*. Maryknoll, NY: Orbis, 1991.

Ellul, Jacques. *The Ethics of Freedom*. Edited and translated by Geoffrey W. Bromiley. Grand Rapids, MI: Eerdmans, 1976.

———. *The Technological Society*. Translated by John Wilkenson. New York: Vintage, 1964.

Emerson, Carly. "Prefatory Comments on 'Toward a Reworking of the Dostoevsky Book.'" In *Critical Essays on Dostoevsky*. Edited by Robin Feuer Miller, 243–46. Boston: C.K. Hall, 1986.

Eze, Emmanuel Chuckwudi, ed. *Race and the Enlightenment: A Reader*. Oxford: Blackwell, 1997.

Fasching, Darrell. *The Ethical Challenge of Auschwitz and Hiroshima: Apocalypse or Utopia*. Albany, NY: State University of New York Press, 1993.

Fitzgerald, Matt. "What Should We Pray For?" *The Christian Century*. November 4, 2020, 32–35.

Flender, Harold. *Rescue in Denmark*. New York: MacFadden, 1964.

Frank, Joseph. *Dostoevsky: A Writer in His Time*. Princeton: Princeton University Press, 2010.

Frederickson, George M. *Racism: A Short History*. Princeton: Princeton University Press, 2002.

———. "Slaves and Race: A Southern Dilemma." In *American Negro Slavery: A Modern Reader*, 34–58. New York: Oxford University Press, 1979.

Fretheim, Terrence E. *The Suffering of God: An Old Testament Perspective*. Philadelphia: Fortress, 1984.

Fulton, Alice. "Cascade Experiment." In *Powers of Congress*. 1–2. Louisville: Saraband, 2010.

Galbraith, John Kenneth. *The Affluent Society*. Boston: Houghton Mifflin, 1958.

Goldstein, David, J. *Dostoevsky and the Jews*. Austin, TX: University of Texas Press, 1981.

Gossett, Thomas F. *Race: The History of an Idea in America*. New York: Oxford University Press, 1997.

Graeber, David. *Debt: The First 5000 Years*. Brooklyn: Melville House, 2011.

Gritsch, Eric W. *Martin Luther's Anti-Semitism: Against His Better Judgment*. Grand Rapids, MI: Eerdmans, 2011.

Gustafson, Scott W. *At the Altar of Wall Street: The Rituals, Myths, Theologies and Mission of the Religion Known as the Modern Global Economy*. Grand Rapids, MI: Eerdmans, 2015.

———. *Behind Good and Evil: How to Overcome the Death-Dealing Character of Morality*. West Conshohocken, PA: Infinity, 2009.

———. *Biblical Amnesia: A Forgotten Story of Redemption, Resistance and Renewal.* West Conshohocken, PA: Infinity, 2004.

———. "From Theodicy to Discipleship: Dostoevsky's Contribution to the Pastoral Task in The Brothers Karamazov." *Scottish Journal of Theology* (45) (1992) 209–22.

———. *Ministry with the Power of Jesus.* Lawrenceville, VA: Brunswick, 1991.

———. "The Scandal of Particularity and the Universality of Grace." *Religious Traditions and the Limits of Tolerance.* Edited by Louis J. Hammon and Harry M. Buck, 24–29. Chambersburg, PA: Anima, 1988.

Heller, Joseph. *Catch 22.* New York: Simon and Schuster, 1961.

Hick, John. *Evil and the God of Love.* San Francisco: Harper & Row, 1978.

Hillberg, Raul. *The Destruction of European Jews: Student Edition.* New York: Holmes and Meier, 1985.

Humphreys, José, II. "Can Money Serve as a Gift in God's Economy of Generosity rather than a Commodity That Leads to Inequality?" *Sojourners* (52) no. 9, 20–25.

Irenaeus. *Against Heresies. Ante-Nicene Fathers.* Vol. 1. Grand Rapids, MI: Eerdmans, 1983.

Jackson, Robert Louis, editor. *Dostoevsky: New Perspectives.* Englewood Cliffs: Prentice Hall, 1972.

Journet, Charles. *The Meaning of Evil.* New York. P.J. Kennedy and Sons, 1963.

Juergensmeyer, Mark. *Terror in the Mind of God: The Global Rise of Religious Violence.* Berkley: The University of California Press, 2000.

Kafka, Franz. *The Castle.* New York: Knopf, 1968.

———. *The Trial.* New York: Knopf, 1968.

Kaufman, Andrew, D. *The Gambler Wife: The True Story of Love, Risk, and the Woman Who Saved Dostoevsky.* New York: Riverhead, 2021.

Keller, Catherine. *Cloud of the Impossible: Negative Theology and Planetary Entanglement.* New York: Columbia University Press, 2015.

Klein, Naomi. *The Shock Doctrine: The Rise of Disaster Capitalism.* New York: Picador, 2007.

Long, Charles, H. *Significations: Signs, Symbols and Images in the Interpretation of Religion.* Aurora, CO: Davies Group, 1995.

Miller, Robin Feuer, ed. *Critical Essays on Dostoevsky.* Boston: C.K. Hall, 1986.

———. *Dostoevsky's Unfinished Journey.* New Haven: Yale University Press, 2007.

Milton, John. *Paradise Lost.* Middletown, DE: www.digireeds.com, 2016.

Mintz, Sidney W. *Sweetness and Power: The Place of Sugar in Modern History.* New York: Penguin, 1985.

Morson, Gary Saul. "The God of Onions." Reprinted in *The Brothers Karamazov.* Second Norton Critical Edition, 785–800. New York: W. W. Norton, 2011.

———. "Verbal Pollution in the Brothers Karamazov." *Critical Essays on Dostoevsky.* Edited by Robin Feuer Miller, 234–42. Boston: G.K. Hall, 1986.

———. *Wonder Confronts Certainty: Russian Writers on the Timeless Questions of Why Their Answers Matter.* Cambridge, MA: Belknap, 2023.

Nouwen, Herni J.M. *In the Name of Jesus: Reflections on Christian Leadership.* New York: Crossroad, 1991.

Peck, M. Scott. *People of the Lie: The Hope for Healing Human Evil.* New York: Simon and Schuster, 1983.

Polanyi, Michael. "Faith and Reason." *Journal of Religion* (41) 237–47.

———. *Personal Knowledge: Towards a Post-Critical Philosophy*. New York: Harper & Row, 1964.

Polanyi, Michael, and Harry Prosch. *Meaning*. Chicago: University of Chicago Press, 1975.

Saiving, Valerie. "The Human Situation: A Feminist View." In *Womanspirit Rising*, edited by Carol B. Christ and Judith Plaskow, 25–42. San Francisco: Harper, 1979.

Smith, Adam. *Wealth of Nations*. New York: Bantam, 2003.

Sorkin, Andrew Ross. "How Mandela Shifted Views on Freedom of Markets." *New York Times*. December 9, 2013. Http://dealbook.nytimes.com/2013/12/09/how-mandela-shifted-views-on-freedom-of markets/?.

Summers, Lawrence. "The Bank Memo." The Whirled Bank Group. 1991. www.whirldbank.org.

Thurston, Bonnie Bowman. *The Widows: A Women's Ministry in the Early Church*. Minneapolis: Fortress, 1989.

Tiger, Lionel. *The Manufacture of Evil: Ethics, Evolution and the Industrial System*. New York: Harper & Row, 1987.

Tilley, Terrence, W. *Evils of Theodicy*. Eugene, OR: Wipf and Stock, 2000.

Tolstoy, Leo. "Shakespeare and the Drama." In *Last Steps: The Late Writings of Leo Tolstoy*, edited by Jay Parini, 207–68. New York: Penguin, 2009.

Tunimanov, T.A. "The Narrator in The Devils." *Dostoevsky: New Perspectives*. Edited by Robert Louis Jackson, 145–75. Englewood Cliffs, NJ: Prentice Hall, 1972.

Tutu, Desmond. *No future Without Forgiveness*. New York: Doubleday, 1999.

Verghese, Abraham. *Cutting for Stone*. New York: Vintage, 2009.

Weil, Simone. *Gravity and Grace*. New York: Routledge, 2002.

———. *Waiting for God*. New York: HarperCollins, 1973.

Westermann, Claus. *Creation*. Translated by John J. Scullion. Philadelphia: Fortress, 1974.

Wilkerson, Isabel. *Caste: The Origins of Our Discontents*. New York: Random House, 2020.

Williams, Delores S. *Sisters in the Wilderness: The Challenge of Womanist God-Talk*. 20th Anniversary Edition. New York: Orbis, 2013.

Williams, Rowan. *Dostoevsky: Language, Faith and Fiction*. Waco, TX: Baylor University Press, 2011.

Wink, Walter. *Engaging the Powers: Discernment and Resistance in a World of Domination*. Minneapolis: Fortress, 1992.

———. *Naming the Powers: The Language for Power in the New Testament*. Minneapolis: Fortress, 1984.

———. *Unmasking the Powers: The Invisible Forces that Determine Human Existence*. Minneapolis: Fortress, 1986.

Index

Aaron, 184
Abraham, 112, 117–18n3, 137, 193
absolute religious beliefs, 53, 53n10
absolutist ideology, 140–41
abstractly, defining evil, 14–15
accepting gifts, 74
accomplishments, 36, 43, 154
acknowledgement of sins, 134–36
action plot structure in *The Brothers Karamazov*, xiii–xiv, 9, 29, 84–85
active love
    "all things are lawful," 48, 114
    Alyosha's afflictions, 81
    Alyosha's conversion to the ministry of active love, 93–95
    Alyosha's growth in the art of ministry, 79–80
    The Church of Active Love, 116–31
    Dmitri's conversion to the ministry of active love, 95–99
    Dostoevsky's antisemitism, 159
    faith, 74–76
    Kairos time, 190
    Kolya Krasokin, 122–23
    leap of faith, 28
    listening, 69–71
    the one thing a person needs, 65–66
    small acts of, xv, 132, 167, 192–98
    transgressions, 110
    Zosima's ministry, xvii–xviii, 48, 64–65, 132–33, 192–98
acts of love. *See* active love; embodied acts of love

Adam and Eve, 133
adjustments, 13, 68–71, 125, 156, 159, 163, 184–85, 186, 191
afflictions, 81–84, 100–101, 105
African Americans, 141–48, 150, 154–56
African American Womanist theology, 155–56
African National Congress (ANC), 144–45
Agrafena Alexandrova Svetlova. *See* Grushenka
Alexander, Michelle, 143n12
allegory, 88–93
"all things are lawful," xvii, 45–48, 62–63, 73, 109–11, 112–14
Alyosha Karamazov, xiii–xix
    afflictions, 81–84
    "all things are lawful," 113–14
    antisemitism, 161–62
    art of ministry, 78–80, 193, 198
    The Church of Active Love, 116–31
    commissioning of, 76
    conversion to the ministry of active love, 93–95
    dialogical method, 186
    evil(s), 8
    foundational dialogue with Ivan, 27
    freedom *versus* happiness, 39
    The Grand Inquisitor, 30
    Grushenka and Alyosha convert each other, 84–88
    Ilyusha's Funeral, 128–31
    Ivan's argument, 15–16

Alyosha Karamazov (*cont.*)
    Kolya Krasokin, 123–28
    mentor/apprentice relationship, xii, 77–78
    the one thing a person needs, 66
    "onion" encounter, 130, 178, 188
    parables and preaching, 89
    prayer and confession as acts of Christian freedom, 99–102
    schoolboys, 118–23, 127
    transgressions, 105–15
ambiguity, 108, 115
American Civil War, 143–44
American life, 158–59
American slavery, 159
amnesia, 63–64, 135–36, 137, 141, 161–62
ANC (African National Congress), 144–45
Andrey, 97–98
annihilation, xv, 14–15, 150, 153
antisemitism, 158–74
    deliberate amnesia, 135–36, 141, 161–62
    Dostoevsky's, xix–xxi, 162–74
    global evils, 133
    and Luther, 167n12
    parables, 91–93
    repentance and confession, 153, 156–57
    small acts of love, 167, 192, 195
    unconfessed sins, 135, 148–53, 158
apartheid, 144
    Apostle Paul, xv, xvii, 17, 22, 42, 46, 109, 154, 188
    Apostolic Commission, 70n8
appetites, 40
Arendt, Hannah, 150
Arina Petrovna, 120, 122–23
Aristotle, 52
Armor of Christ, 20
art and the human imagination, 51–53
artistic knowledge, 49, 77, 136
art of freedom, xviii–xix
art of ministry, ix–x
    accepting gifts, 74
    Alyosha's conversion to the ministry of active love, 93–95

    Alyosha's mastery of, 78–80, 116, 123–27
    book's outline, xiii–xix
    choosing life, xii–xiii
    Christian freedom, 40–61
    Dmitri's conversion to the ministry of active love, 95–99
    Dostoevsky's antisemitism, 158–59
    evil(s), 7–8, 15–16
    freedom, 37
    grace and dialogue, 181–82
    imagination set upon ministry, 62–63
    listening, 68–71
    mentor/apprentice relationship, 77–78
    parables and preaching, 88–93
    pastoral authority, 71–72
    prayer and confession as acts of Christian freedom, 99–104
    racism, 141–48
    responsibility of all Christians, x–xii
    responsibility to all people, 132–33, 135, 158–59, 168, 192, 198
    sacraments, 67
    self-justifications, 163–65
    thanksgiving, 73–74, 74n11
    transgressing doctrine, 72–73
    transgressions, 105–15
    unconfessed sins, xx
    in a world where grace is possible, 190–92
    Zosima's adages for ministry, 63–65, 132–33, 192–98
    Zosima's mastery of the, 62–76
arts and unspoken knowledge, 48–51
Atwater, Lee, 146, 146n16
Augustine, Arelius, 2–3, 2–3n2
Augustinian theodicies, 2–3, 5, 6–8
authority, 49–50, 71–72
autonomous death-dealing power, 133–35, 141, 143
autonomy, xii–xiii, 9, 39, 56, 66, 183
axioms, 25–26

Bakhtin, Mikhail, 179, 179n5, 182, 186–87
Baptist, Edward E., 143n12
Barbara Nikolaevna, 120–21, 122

Index

Beckert, Sven, 143n12
beneficial things, 45–48
Berry, Wendell, 197
Bible, 111–12, 133, 173, 182–88, 189, 190–92, 193
biblical God, 2, 39, 174, 183–85, 188, 190–92, 193
biological necessities, 42
black liberation theology, 154–55
black women, 155–56
bodily presence, 176–78
bondage, xii–xiii, xvii, 36–37, 39, 41, 43–44, 56, 62, 69, 73, 88, 89, 111, 127, 129, 132, 177, 182, 197
The Bondage of the Will (Luther), 40–41
boundaries, 110–12
bracketing, 28–29
breathing, 29
bring socially diverse people together, 125, 128, 132
The Brothers Karamazov (Dostoevsky)
    action plot of, xiii–xiv, 9, 29, 84–85
    Alyosha's afflictions, 81–84
    Alyosha's conversion to the ministry of active love, 93–95
    antisemitism, 160–61
    book's outline, xiii–xix
    The Church of Active Love, 116–31
    dialogical method, 180–81
    Dmitri's proposed escape, 112–15
    freedom *versus* happiness, 39
    Grushenka and Alyosha convert each other, 84–88
    Ilyusha's Funeral, 128–31
    Katerina Ivanovna Verhovtseva, 116–17
    Kolya Krasokin, 122–30
    limits of reason, 8–10
    mentor/apprentice relationship, 77–78
    ministry plot, xiii–xiv, 29, 85–86
    movement from the fact of evil to ministry, 15–16
    parables and preaching, 89
    prayer and confession as acts of Christian freedom, 99–104
    "The Rebellion" episode, ix–x, 5–8, 24, 26–27, 29, 30
    the schoolboys, 118–23, 127
    small acts of love, 192–93
    struggle against evil, 20
    Trinity in, 27
bureaucratic processes, 150–53
Butler, Judith, 128

Caesar, 56
Cairns, Scott, 81, 84
Calhoun, John C., 142–43
Camus, Albert, 181
Canaanite woman, encounter with, 190–92
capitalism, 58–59, 140n7, 165–66
Captain Snegiryov, 119–22, 123, 127, 128
The Castle (Kafka), 176
Catch 22 (Heller), 177
Catholicism, 148–49
certainty in religious beliefs, 53, 53n10
change, 188–89
characters, 21
characters and dialogical writing, 180, 182–83
Childs, Brevard, 185
choosing life, xvii, xviii–xix, 39, 46, 96, 99
chosen people of God, 185, 193
The Christian Century, 148
Christian ethics, xii, 62
Christian freedom, xii–xiii, xvi–xvii, 39, 40–61, 62–63, 99–104, 110–12, 114–15, 198
Christianity, 5, 34, 64, 80, 81, 89–93, 158
Christian life, xvii, xix, 42
Christian New Testament, 193
Christians, 1–2, 148–49
Chronos time, 189–90, 191, 195
church and excommunication, 69–70
The Church of Active Love, 116–31
cleansing of the temple, 28–29
communal life, xix
community, 50, 186–87
Cone, James, 154–55
confession, 72–73, 74–76, 99–104, 124–27, 134–36, 143–44, 146–47, 153–57
consciousness of mortality, 63–65

Index

Contino, Paul, 66, 72–74
continuity, 175, 175n1
conversation with God, 183–86
Corinthian church, xvii
Cosmic Powers, 17, 21–25, 32
cosmological poem, 78–79
Courtney, Charles, 1
covenant, 90, 92
creation, 3–5, 14, 29, 183–84
creation of the self, 186
Crime and Punishment (Dostoevsky), 165–66
crucifixion and resurrection of Jesus, xii, xix, 16–17, 28, 37, 42–44, 45, 48, 56, 62, 112, 198

death, xvii–xix, 26, 42–43, 128–31
death-dealing
    American slavery, 159
    of antisemitism, xx–xxi, 167, 173, 174
    authority, 72
    autonomy, 39
    of capitalism, 166
    decision-making, xiii, xix, 62
    evil(s), 17–18, 21, 133–36
    forgiveness, 100
    global evils, 195–98
    imagination set upon ministry, 63
    isolation, 93
    last word, 12n11
    necessities, 36–37
    parables, 87
    racism, 142–48
    repentance and confession, 156
    theodicies, 10
    of unconfessed sins, 132–57, 161–62, 168
    as unilateral, 31–32
    utilitarianism, 58–60
decision-making process, 40, 58–59, 63–64, 80, 108
denying God's existence, 22, 29, 191
Descartes, René, 25, 186
detached, objective knowledge, 57–61
The Devil, xv, 21–25, 60
Dew, Thomas R., 142

dialogical method, 178–82, 182–86, 186–88, 190–92
dialogue, 21, 47, 108, 119, 178–82, 184, 186–88, 192–93
Diangelo, Robin, 143n12, 146n16
diplomacy, 196–97
discontinuity, 175–78, 178n3, 182
divine providence, 142
Dmitri Karamazov
    action plot, xiii–xiv
    conversion to the religion of active love, 95–99
    dialogical method, 186
    Grushenka, 84–85
    interrogation, 101–4
    Katerina Ivanovna Verhovtseva, 116–17
    limits of reason, 8–9
    prayer and confession as acts of Christian freedom, 99–104
    proposed escape, 112–15
    transgressions, 105–15
    trial, 21–25
dominant culture, 155–56, 165, 165n9
Dostoevsky (Williams), 12n11, 182
Douglas, James W., 111n7
dysfunction, 87, 117–18n3, 193, 198

eating meat sacrificed to idols, 47
economics, 58–60
    economic behavior, 139–40
    economic ideologies, 138
    economic inequality, 145
    economic necessities, 33, 36, 43, 198
    economic self-interest, 140–41
efficiencies, 34–36
Egypt, 174
embodiment, 177, 181–82
embodied acts of love, 192–97
embodied ideas, 21, 182
encountering a body, 177–78
Engaging the Powers (Wink), 17n8
England, 149
Enlightenment, 2n2, 186–87
eternal life, 130
Euclidian reasoning, 24, 25–26, 60
Europe, 158
everyday language, 17–19

Evil and the God of Love (Hick), 2–4
evil(s), xiv–xix, 14–39
    antisemitism, 148–52
    Cosmic Powers, 21–25
    ethical problem of, 102
    Euclidian reasoning, 25–26
    freedom *versus* happiness, 37–39
    global evils, xviii, 132–33, 195–98
    The Grand Inquisitor, 30–32
    leap of faith, 26–29
    necessities, Principalities rule through, 32–37
    opposing evil, 1–13
    Principalities and Powers, 16–21
    repentance and confession, 156–57
    Rich Man, 137–38
    small acts of love, 167, 192–98
    unconfessed sins, 132–57
The Evils of Theodicy (Tilley), 2n2
excess of nature, 82–83, 94
excommunication, 69–70, 70n8
explicit racist language, 145–46

faith, 26–29, 74–76, 94, 104
fatherhood, 194–95
Father Paissy, 93–94
feelings or thoughts, 107–9, 165
feminist theology, 155
fig tree story, 28
final arbitrator of truth, 2n2
First Corinthians, 44–47
Fitzgerald, Matt, 148, 148n18
forgiveness, 73, 88, 100
four propositions, 1–2
France, 149
Frank, Joseph, 101, 172
freedom, xii–xiii, xvi–xix, 9, 37, 37–39, 40–41, 43, 44–48, 62–63, 88, 108, 127, 130, 191–92
The Freedom of the Christian (Luther), 41
free will, 40–41
Fretheim, Terrence, 183
"From Theodicy to Discipleship" (Gustafson), x
frontier, 110–11
Fulton, Alice, 42n2
functionary, 151–53

Fyodor Karamazov, xiii, 8–9, 22, 65–66, 84, 95–96, 100, 102, 117, 123, 160

Galatians, xvii, 41, 62
GDP (Gross Domestic Product), 145
geometries, 25
Gerasene Demoniac, 31
Germany, 148–52
gifts, 74
global evils, xviii, 132–33, 195–98
God, xiv, 1–2
    "all things are lawful," 113
    autonomy, 39
    Bible as example of dialogical writing, 182–86
    Christian freedom, 45–46
    evil(s), xv, 3–5, 14–15
    grace of, 97–98
    Ivan meets a Cosmic Power, 21–25
    Ivan's rebellion, 7
    leap of faith, 27–29
    limits of reason, 8–10
    plight of the poor, 138–39
    prayer and confession as acts of Christian freedom, 99–104
    Principalities and Powers, 16–20, 32
    transgressions, 110
God's chosen people, 185, 193
Goldstein, David, 161
good and evil, 14–15, 34, 36, 133
Gospel of John, xi, 54, 78, 93
Gospels, 54, 104, 114, 136
Gossett, Thomas F., 141n9, 143n12
grace, 175–78, 178n3
    and dialogue, 178–82
    of God, 97–99, 105, 175n1
    Grushenka and Alyosha convert each other, 87–88
    Kolya Krasokin, 127
    ministry in a world where grace is possible, 190–92
    nature, 175n1
    Non-Self-Sufficiency, 186–88
    sacraments, 181n12
    small acts of love, 192–95
    surplus of, 188–90
Graham, Richard, 79

The Grand Inquisitor, xv, 27, 30–32, 35, 37–39, 42, 44, 53, 56–57, 72, 127, 129, 137–38, 176, 192
greatest good, 58–59
Grigory, 22, 95–96, 100
Gritsch, Eric W., 167n12
Gross Domestic Product (GDP), 145
Grushenka, 84–88, 89, 95–98, 99–104, 106, 111, 114–15, 117, 127, 178, 186, 188, 193
guilt, 72–73, 159

happiness, 37–39, 44, 57, 62, 127
Hebrews, 112
Heller, Joseph, 177
Herodians, 56
hero's story, 108
Hick, John, 2–4, 2n2, 5
hierarchical design, 70
high moral ground, 163–65
Hillberg, Raul, 150
Hinduism, 93
Hitler, Adolph, 149
Holocaust, xx, 7–8, 91, 148–53, 161, 166–67, 174
Holy Fool, 22
Holy Spirit, 41, 127
hope, 181, 197
The House of the Dead (Dostoevsky), 159–60, 170–71
human element, 57–61
humanity, 183–84, 188
human reason, xv, 8, 10, 24, 26, 40
"The Human Situation" (Saiving), 153–54
human soul, 40
human will, 40–41
humility, 26

"I Am" metaphors, 54–55
ideology, 138–41
Ilyusha, 120–21, 122–25, 128–31, 193
imagination(s), 37, 43–44, 47–48, 51–53, 56, 62–63
individual human acts, 132, 195–96
individualistic understanding of freedom, 46

institutional poverty, 133, 135, 136–41, 141–42, 153, 156–57, 159, 168, 192, 195
intellect, 33–34, 40
"The Invisible Hand" theory, 139–41, 140n7
Irenaeus, 2–3n2, 2–5, 7
Isaac, 185, 193
Isay Fomich Bumstein, 159–60
Islam, 93
isolated individualism, 46, 113, 126
isolation, 92–93, 152, 187–88
Israel, 90, 92, 183–85
Ivan Karamazov, xiii–xv, 1
    "all things are lawful," 45–46, 110, 113–14
    Cosmic Powers, 21–25
    dialogical method, 180–81, 186
    Dmitri's proposed escape, 106, 113–15
    Euclidian reasoning, 25–26
    freedom *versus* happiness, 39
    The Grand Inquisitor, 30
    leap of faith, 26–29
    Non-Self-Sufficiency, 187
    prayer and confession as acts of Christian freedom, 102
    Principalities and Powers, 20
    "The Rebellion" episode, ix–x, 5–8, 24, 26–27, 29, 30
    small acts of love, 195
    theodicies, 15–16

Jacob, 185, 193
James, 131
Jefferson, Thomas, 142
Jenson, Robert W., 43n3, 178n3
Jesus
    choosing life, xii–xiii, xix
    Christian freedom, 41–45, 62
    cleansing of the Temple, 28–29
    crucifixion and resurrection of, xii, xix, 16–17, 28, 37, 42–44, 45, 48, 56, 62, 112, 198
    encountering, 181n12, 194–95
    encounter with the Canaanite woman, 190–92
    Euclidian reasoning, 26

Index

faith, 76
fig tree story, 28
freedom *versus* happiness, 37–39
The Grand Inquisitor, 30–32
Kairos time, 189
last word, 54–57
necessities, 32–37
the one thing a person needs, 65
Parable of the Sower, 188–89
Paul's statement to the Galatians, xvii
Peter's future ministry, x–xi
Satan's second temptation of Christ, 83–84
self-emptying love, 154
small acts of love, 192–98
"The Wedding at Cana of Galilee," 93–95
Jewish stereotypes, 159–60
Jews, 90–93, 149–53, 159–61, 162–67, 168, 173–74
Jim Crow, 111, 143
Job, 11–13, 14, 25, 53
John, 131
John the Baptist, 78–79
Journet, Charles, 14–15
Judaism, 91–93, 166, 172–73
judgment, 47, 56, 110
Juergensmeyer, Mark, 53n10
Just, Willy, 151
justice, 100

Kafka, Franz, 176–77, 178, 178n3, 181, 191
Kairos events/time, 189–90, 191, 195
Katerina Ivanovna Svetlova, 95
Katerina Ivanovna Verhovtseva, 116–17, 119–24, 127
Keller, Catherine, 26n13
Kierkegaard, Søren, 26
knowledge, surplus of, 179–81, 179n5, 182, 188
knowledge and human reason, 26
Kolya Krasokin, 122–30

"A Lady of Little Faith," 75–76
laity, x–xii
language, 17–19
last word, 12n11, 53–57, 70, 87, 97–98, 110, 125, 180–81, 182–83, 186, 187
Law and the Prophets, 137
Lazarus, 136–39, 162
leap of faith, 9–10, 26–29, 49–50, 112
liberalization, 60
life-giving
  beneficial, 47
  choosing life, xii–xiii
  decision-making, 62
  Dmitri's proposed escape, 115
  forgiveness, 100
  imagination set upon ministry, 63
  leaps of faith, 29
  necessities, 36–37
  parables, 87–88, 93
  self-emptying love, 155
limits of Euclidian reasoning, 25–26
listening, 13, 15, 68–71, 106, 126, 156, 163, 168–69, 182, 184, 189–90, 190–92
living human beings, 16–17, 31
Liza Khokhlakova, 161
Lizaveta, 22
Long, Charles H., 165n9
love, xv, 27–29, 100–101, 103–4, 130, 154–56, 159, 178, 181–82, 181n12, 188–90, 191–92, 192–98
Luke, 189
Luther, Martin, x, 40–41, 73, 167n12
Lutzenburger, José, 60–61
lying, 107–10

Madame Khokhlakova, 74–76
malheur (affliction), 81–84
Mandela, Nelson, 144–45
Marey, 170
marginalization, xviii, 18–19, 154–56
Mark, 189
Markel, 64, 168
Martin Luther's Antisemitism (Gritsch), 167n12
materialistic socialism, xx, 166
Matthew, 69–70, 70n8, 189
McDuffie, George, 142
meaning, 189
memories, 130

mentor/apprentice relationship, xii, xvi, 49–51, 77–78, 79–80
metanoia, 104
metaphors, 54–55
metaphysical freedom, 40–41
Miller, Robin Feuer, 86–87
ministry plot structure in *The Brothers Karamazov*, xiii–xiv, 29, 85–86
modern capitalism, 187–88
moments, 188–90, 191, 195
money, 33
monological writing, 179–80, 179n5, 182–83, 188
morality, 33–34, 112, 133
    moral code, 151–52
    moral evil, xv, 16
    moral ground, 163–65
    moral questions, 56
Morson, Gary Saul, 26–27, 26n13, 166
mortality, 63–65
Moses, xix, 137, 184–85, 186, 190
mourning, 67, 128–29

Naming the Powers (Wink), 17n8
Nastasya, 68–71, 128
nations, 196–97
natural necessities, 32–33
nature, 16, 175n1
Nazis, 149–53, 157, 166–67
necessities, 32–37, 39, 42–48, 110–12, 127, 130–31, 138, 176–78, 196–98
"The New Jim Crow," 143
New Testament, 173
Newton, Isaac, 51–52
Nietzsche, Friedrich, 181
nihilism, 102, 166
Nikita, 68
Nikolay Parfenovich, 101
Nikolay Perforovich, 103
Nina Nikolaevna, 120–30
non-Jews, 150
Non-Self-Sufficiency, 186–87
nonviolent resistance, 111n7
Notes from the Underground (Dostoevsky), 165
Nuremburg trial, 144

Old Testament, 173–74
omniscient God, 182–83, 188
the one thing a person needs, xvii, 65–67, 69, 71–72, 73

"The Parable of the Onion," 86–88
Parable of the Sower, 188–89
Parable of the Tenants, 89–93
parables, 86–93
Parks, Rosa, 111, 111n7
partners in dialogue, 186
past, 178, 178n3
pastoral authority, 71–72
pastoral counseling, 89
pastoral encounters, 76
patience, 13, 15
Paul, 41–42, 44–48, 62, 175n1
Pavel Fyodorovich Smerdyakov, xiii, 22–25, 45, 95, 102, 107, 110, 123–24
peasants, 74–76, 157, 159, 169–74
Peck, Scott, 133, 134, 167
people of Israel, 112
The People of the Lie (Peck), 134
personal knowledge, 57, 60
Peter, xi, 131
Philip, 55
Philippians, 154
Polanyi, Michael, 50, 57, 61
political necessities, 33, 36, 177, 196–97
The Possessed (Dostoevsky), 165
possibilities, 43–44, 87–88, 189–90
prayers, 98, 99–104, 184–85
presence, 13, 15
"priesthood of all believers," x
Principalities and Powers, xv–xvi, 16–21
    Christian freedom amid necessities, 45
    death-dealing power, 42
    dominion of, 30–32
    evil(s), 133, 137–38
    freedom *versus* happiness, 38–39
    grace, 176
    hierarchical design, 70
    imagination set upon ministry, 63
    jobs, 38n28
    necessities, Principalities rule through, 32–37

racism, 142, 143, 147–48
   repentance and confession, 153
   small acts of love, 192–98
   surplus of grace, 188
   unconfessed sins, 135, 147–48, 157, 168
   and Wink, 17n8
propositional form, 15
Protestantism, 149
The Protocols of the Elders of Zion, 166–67
Ptolemy, 52
public policy, 58–60
pursuit of one's economic self-interest, 140–41

race, 141n9
Race (Gossett), 141n9
racism, 133, 135, 141–48, 143n12, 153, 155–57, 159, 162, 166, 168, 192, 195
radical capitalism, 46, 165–66
radical individualism, 188
radical utilitarianism, 60
Ratikin, 82–84, 82n8, 85, 95
rational answers, 12–13
rationalism, 166
rational theodicy, 10
reason, 2n2, 8–10, 11–13, 14, 25–26, 27–28, 29, 181
reasoning process, 91–92, 142, 164
"The Rebellion" episode, ix–x, 5–8, 24, 26–27, 29, 30
redemptive violence, 196–97
reinterpretations, 89, 127
religion, 33–34
religion and politics, 56
religious necessities, 33–34, 37, 43, 99–100
repentance, 17–20, 68–71, 142, 143n12, 147, 153–57, 159, 173, 184–85, 188–90, 192, 195–98
responsibility, 134–36, 141–42, 148–49, 168
responsibility to all people, 132–33, 135, 158–59, 168, 192, 198
restraints, xvi–xvii, 46
Rich Man, 136–39, 153, 162

righteousness, 99–100
Rockefeller, John D., 139
Roman Legions, 31
Romero, Oscar, 198
Russia, 191
   Russian Christianity, 166
   Russian culture and society, 157, 159, 160–61, 168–74
   Russian intelligentsia, xx, 64, 110, 165–66, 171–72
   Russian Orthodoxy, 166, 172–73

sacraments, 67, 181n12, 193–94
Saiving, Valerie, 153–55
salvation, 54–55, 73
Sampson, Anthony, 145
Sarah, 117–18n3
Satan, 32–34, 37–38, 83–84
schoolboys, 118–23, 127
sciences, 50–51
scientific knowledge, 52, 57
self, 186–88
   self-awareness, 186–87
   self-consciousness, 186–87
   self-creation, 186
   self-emptying love, 154–56
   self-expression, 172
   self-giving, 154
   self-interested pursuit of profit, 140–41
   self-justifications, 163–65
   self-lacerations, 121–22
   self-sufficiency, 186–87
sexism, 133, 135, 141, 153, 156–57, 159, 168, 192, 195
sexist language, 18–19, 21
Shakespeare, William, 48
Significations (Long), 165n9
silencing of characters, 180
sins, xviii, 2–4, 6–8, 10, 11–12, 25, 41, 133–36, 147–48, 153–57, 162, 173, 192–93
slavery, 142–43, 154–55, 159
Smith, Adam, 139, 140n7
Smurov, 118, 120, 123, 129
Social Darwinism, 138–40
social functions of the church, 125
social hierarchy, 66, 70, 72, 153

Socialist Petrashevsky Circle, 169
social necessities, 33, 36, 42, 177
social status, 70, 75, 135, 153–57, 165, 168
socio/economic necessities, 138
some-body, 177, 178, 178n3, 180–81
South Africa, 144–45
"The Southern Strategy," 146
Spencer, Herbert, 138–39
spirit of perverseness, 172
sticky little leaves, 27–29
suffering, ix, xiv–xv, 3–4, 5–8, 10, 11–13, 14–15, 18, 20, 25, 102, 105–6, 192–93
The Suffering of God (Fretheim), 183
suffering of innocent children, xiv, 5, 20, 83, 195
suicide, 96–100
Summers, Lawrence, 59–61
supernatural realm, 21–25, 26
surplus knowledge, 179–81, 179n5, 182, 188
surplus of grace, 188–90
survival, 155–56
synoptic Gospels, 56

taxes, 56, 146
teachers, 77–78
technological necessities, 34–36, 43, 176
Temple, 28–29
Terror (Juergensmyer), 53n10
thanksgiving, 73–74, 74n11
theodicies, xiv, xv–xvi, 1–3, 2n2, 5–10, 14–21, 27–28, 30, 181
theorems, 25–26
this side of the kingdom, 115
Thomas, 55
Thomas Aquinas, St., 175n1
Three Deaths (Tolstoy), 179, 179n5
Thurston, Bonnie Bowman, 74n11
Tilley, Terrence W., 2n2, 15
time, 189–90
Tolstoy, Leo, 48, 179–80, 179n5
transgressing doctrine, 72–73
transgressions, 105–15
transmission of knowledge, 49, 77–78
Treaty of Versailles, 148–49

"The Tree of the Knowledge of Good and Evil," 133
The Trial (Kafka), 176
Trinity, 27
true confession, 103–4
truth, 8–9, 25–26, 53–55, 80, 181, 182, 191
Tutu, Desmond, 144

unacknowledged sins, 133, 134, 136, 153, 157, 161, 195
unconfessed sins, xviii
 antisemitism, xx–xxi, 148–53, 158
 death-dealing power of, 132–57, 161–62, 168
 evil(s), 132–57
 institutional poverty, 136–41
 racism, 141–48
 reasoning process, 164
 repentance and confession, 156–57
 small acts of love, 195–96
The Underground Man, 187
United States, 149–50
universality, 33–37, 42, 45, 127, 154, 196
Unmasking the Powers (Wink), 17n8
unspoken knowledge, xvi, xviii, 48–51, 53, 57, 67, 73–74, 77–78, 80, 135–36
Untener, Ken, 198
utilitarianism, xx, 58–60, 166
utopianism, 166, 172

victims, 153, 156, 161–62
violence, 42, 53n10, 119, 142, 147, 154, 165, 170, 196–97
war, 20, 195–97
"The War on Drugs," 143
The Wealth of Nations (Smith), 140n7
"The Wedding at Cana of Galilee," 93–95, 129
Weil, Simone, 81
"What Should We Pray For?" (Fitzgerald), 148n18
White Fragility (Diangelo), 146n16
white people, 143–48, 150, 154–56, 168
The Widows (Thurston), 74n11
Wiesel, Elie, 181
will, 40–41

Williams, Delores, xiii, 155–56
Williams, Rowan, 12n11, 182, 186
Wink, Walter, 17n8
women, 18–19
Word of God, 20, 54, 189, 193
World Bank, 59–60
worldviews, 17–18, 125, 188, 190
worst-case scenario, 71–72
A Writer's Diary (Dostoevsky), 162–63, 166
writing, act of, 78

'Yidism, xx, 164, 166–67
Yossarian, 177

Zosima, xv–xvi, xvii–xviii, 62–76
    active love, 28, 48, 64–65, 132–33, 192–98
    "all things are lawful," 114
    Alyosha's afflictions, 81–83
    Alyosha's conversion to the ministry of active love, 93–95
    Alyosha's growth in the art of ministry, 79
    art of ministry, 63–65, 132–33, 192–98
    commissioning of Alyosha, 76
    death of, 78, 81–82, 99, 101
    Dostoevsky's antisemitism, 167–68
    Ivan's rebellion, 7–8
    listening and repenting, 68–71
    Madame Khokhlakova, 74–76
    mentor/apprentice relationship, xii, 77–78
    the one thing a person needs, 65–67
    pastoral authority, 71–72
    responsibility to all people, 132–33, 135, 158–59
    thanksgiving, 73–74
    transgressing doctrine, 72–73

www.ingramcontent.com/pod-product-compliance
Lightning Source LLC
Chambersburg PA
CBHW060602230426
43670CB00011B/1927